East Coast Rivers

CRUISING COMPANION

Photographs © 2008 Janet Harber

Additional photography:
Page 3, 43, 127 ©Chris Neale; Page 13 (bottom), 18, 95, 102 (top), 118, 128, 133, 142, 160, 165, 169, 170 (bottom),
172 (bottom), 177, 179, 181, 185, 188, 193 ©Sealand Aerial Photography Ltd; Page 62 (bottom), 63 (left), 79, 115, 121 (centre)
©www.realessex.co.uk; Page 78 (bottom) ©Ipswich Borough Council; Page 89, 90 ©Cracknell/Moreno (Walton & Frinton
Yacht Club); Page 105 (bottom) ©Holly Ramsay; Page 123, 137, 152, 156, 157 (bottom), 170 (top) ©MARINAS.com; Page 126
(top), 140, 146 ©John Langrick; Page 130 ©Robert Edwards*; Page 135 ©John Perry (Hostellers Sailing Club); Page 143, 145
©Christina Bowers; Page 150 ©Danny Robinson*; Page 151 (bottom), 153 (bottom), 154 (bottom), 162 (top) ©Judy Jones;
Page 155, 158 (bottom) ©Christine Matthews*; Page 159, 171, 172 (top) ©Medway Council
* can be contacted through www.geograph.org.uk/http://creativecommons.org/licenses/by-sa/2.0/

For Wiley Nautical
Executive Editor: David Palmer
Project Editor: Brett Wells
Assistant Editor: Drew Kennerley

For Nautical Data
Cartography: Jamie Russell
Art Direction: Jamie Russell
Cruising Companion series editor: Lucinda Roch

ISBN-13: 978-0-470-99092-6

IMPORTANT NOTICE

Printed by SNP Leefung Printers Ltd, China

Contents

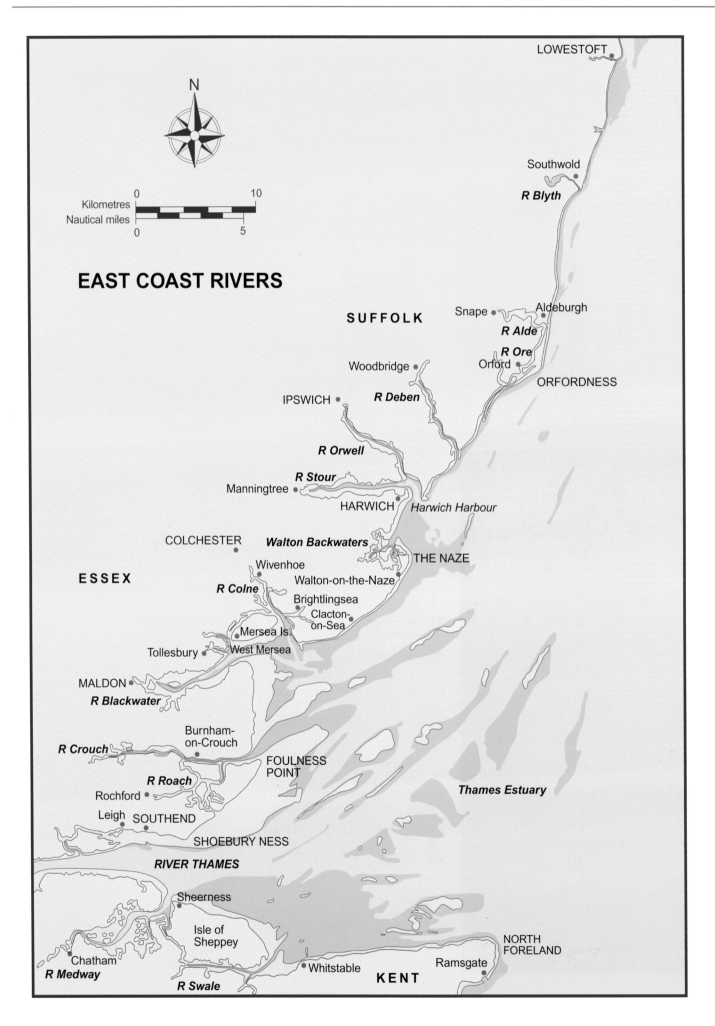

EAST COAST RIVERS

N

Kilometres
Nautical miles

0   10

0   5

SUFFOLK

Snape • ● Aldeburgh

R Alde

R Ore

Woodbridge • Orford •

ORFORDNESS

IPSWICH •

R Deben

R Orwell

R Stour

Manningtree •

HARWICH   *Harwich Harbour*

COLCHESTER •   *Walton Backwaters*

Wivenhoe •   THE NAZE

Walton-on-the-Naze •

ESSEX

R Colne

Brightlingsea •

Clacton-on-Sea •

Mersea Is.

Tollesbury •   West Mersea

MALDON •

R Blackwater

Burnham-on-Crouch

R Crouch

FOULNESS POINT

R Roach

Rochford •

Leigh •   SOUTHEND

Thames Estuary

SHOEBURY NESS

RIVER THAMES

Sheerness •

Isle of Sheppey

NORTH FORELAND

Chatham •   Whitstable •   Ramsgate •

R Medway

R Swale   **KENT**

LOWESTOFT

Southwold

R Blyth

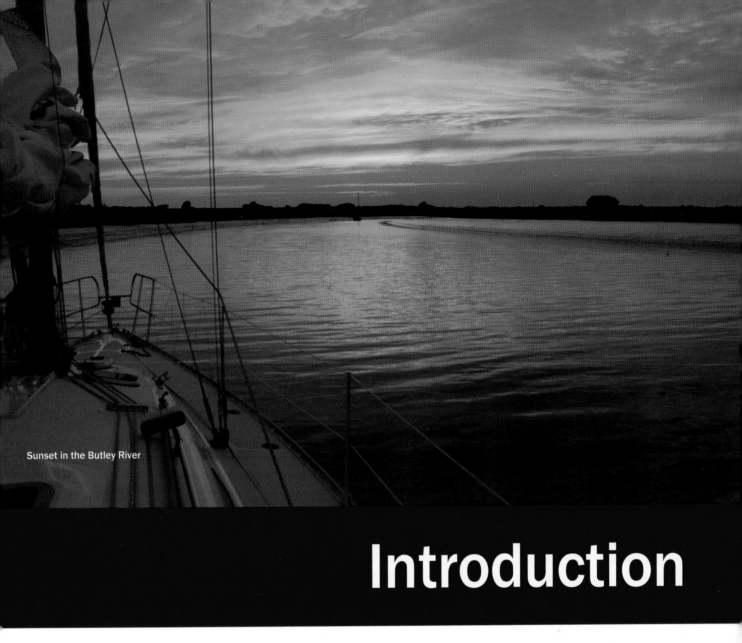

Sunset in the Butley River

Introduction

This 19th edition of *East Coast Rivers* has a new publisher, Wiley Nautical. The book is larger, returning to its former A4 format, and contains more pages than previous editions. Coverage has been extended to include Ramsgate, which strictly speaking is not on the East Coast. However, as it is a strategic port of call on a Thames Estuary crossing whether you are sailing to or from The Channel, France or Belgium, I hope it will be a useful additional chapter.

Also new this time is my potted history of the book *East Coast Rivers* and its connection with my family, from its beginnings in 1956. The archive photographs used to illustrate this section give a flavour of the way things were 50 years ago, before the days of glassfibre boats and marinas.

Text and charts in all other chapters have been thoroughly updated and numerous new photographs have been incorporated, including aerial views. The extra pages have allowed me to weave a thread of local maritime history into the text, drawn from tales of leisure yachting and trading under sail. I have dipped into old sailing books, now mostly out of print, to find relevant extracts and snippets from yachting and cruising writers such as the Wyllies, Archie White,

James Wentworth Day, Francis B Cooke, Hervey Benham, Maurice Griffiths, to name but a few.

On the East Coast the historic link with plough and sail is still much in evidence – hence my frequent references to barges, bawleys, smacks, sprits and sprats, and wharves at the top of creeks that are 'no more than enlarged drainage ditches', to quote Hervey Benham.

As ever, essential up-to-date information for the yachtsman is contained in these pages, and we have added detail and telephone numbers for pubs and restaurants, especially those popular ones where you may need to book a table. Shoreside walks and relevant OS maps, bird and nature reserves, museums or sites with maritime connections are also listed.

Since publication of the previous edition, at Brightlingsea a conspicuous new apartment development has been built on the site of the former James and Stone shipyard. On the quay at Mistley a large part of the old maltings buildings has been converted into luxury flats.

At Whitstable, the plans for regenerating the South Quay include a supermarket and holiday flats; at Faversham, Standard Quay continues to come under intense pressure from property speculators to close;

The Waterfront Café and Tide Mill at Woodbridge

there has been some development along the waterfront at Burnham-on-Crouch but at Woodbridge plans for the old Whisstocks yard are still being rejected. Sittingbourne YC is campaigning for an opening bridge across Milton Creek so that its clubhouse will not be cut off when a new by-pass is constructed.

It seems that developers are lurking round the corner of any disused wharf, failing boatyard or little chandlery which could have the potential to be turned into desirable waterside residences, art galleries or tea-rooms.

So we are still sailing in changing times on the East Coast, but with the aid of the Wiley Nautical website we will be able to update this cruising companion with relevant information much more frequently and easily than we have ever done before.

We will also have links with and publish updates on the website which bears our title, eastcoastrivers.com. This site was originally created as debenentrance.com by Chris Woods, following on from John White, harbour master at Felixstowe Ferry, and Terry Clarke, of Small Craft Delivery in Woodbridge, who for many years produced the printed Deben entrance sketch map. Eastcoastrivers.com now produces very useful laminated sketch plans of the Deben and Ore entrances on an annual basis.

ACKNOWLEDGEMENTS
In his preface to the first edition of *East Coast Rivers* (1956) Jack Coote wrote: 'any success the book may have will be largely due to the enthusiastic help that I have received from many kindred spirits who sail the rivers of the Thames Estuary.'

These words are just as true for the 19th edition (2008), although it is mostly a new generation of friends and fellow sailors who continue to keep us up-to-date just as enthusiastically.

For this edition I am indebted to Nick Ardley (once again for Smallgains, Canvey, Medway, Swale and other places); Christina Bowers (Leigh-on-Sea); Bernard Hetherington, Harbour Master (Brightlingsea); John Langrick of the Roach Sailing Association (Roach, Havengore, Thorpe Bay and Benfleet); The Ramsays, Mike, Sue and Holly (West Mersea, Tollesbury and the Blackwater); John Skellorn (River Thames); Dick Smith (Royal Temple Yacht Club Ramsgate); Mark Wakelin (Harbour Master Burnham-on-Crouch); Chris Woods and to all those who carry out the Deben and Ore entrance surveys.

Finally, I must thank Judy and Graham Jones (my sister and brother-in-law) for being unfailingly supportive.

Graham has been connected with *East Coast Rivers* and the Coote family ever since he met and married my sister Judy some 40 years ago. He has always been closely involved with information gathering, taking photographs and reading proof pages. When Jack started taking his own aerial photographs for the book, it was his son-in-law Graham who flew the aeroplane for him. After Jack died, Graham went on to fly similar photographic missions for me. We had a memorable flight on a glorious September day last year when I took the aerial shots of the Suffolk rivers that appear in this book. Many other photographs, including the front cover, have been taken from aboard Graham's boat *Sandack*, which he sailed up to the end of last season. Sadly he did not live to see these pictures published.

DEDICATION
This book is dedicated to the memory of Graham Jones, friend and fellow sailor.

Janet Harber
Sudbourne, September 2008

NOTES

CHART DATUMS

Lowest Astronomical Tide (LAT)

Although it has the effect of indicating that some creeks, swatchways and anchorages sometimes dry out, when many of us have never seen them without water, adoption of LAT as the datum for this book is necessary in order to be in accord with Admiralty charts. Horizontal datum of waypoints is WGS 84.

BEARINGS

The bearings given throughout the book are magnetic and the variation in the area of the Thames Estuary is approximately 2 degrees west, decreasing by about 8 minutes annually.

TIDES

Although there are times when tides, as Para Handy said, 'is chust a mystery', they do tend to follow patterns that are useful to know. Spring tides occur a day or so after both new and full moons – hence the term high water full and change (HWFC).

Neap tides occur midway between each spring tide. Remember there is always more water at low water neaps than at low water springs.

The time of high water at any given place is roughly 50 minutes later each day.

All tidal information is approximate, so allow a safety margin whenever possible. Watch the barometric pressure – a change of one inch in pressure can make a difference of a foot in the level of water.

The level of water does not rise and fall at a constant rate during the flood or ebb tide. The amount by which a tide will rise or fall in a given time from high water can be estimated approximately by the 'Twelfths' rule, which is simply indicated as follows:

Rise or fall during	1st hour	$^1/_{12}$	of range
Rise or fall during	2nd hour	$^2/_{12}$	of range
Rise or fall during	3rd hour	$^3/_{12}$	of range
Rise or fall during	4th hour	$^3/_{12}$	of range
Rise or fall during	5th hour	$^2/_{12}$	of range
Rise or fall during	6th hour	$^1/_{12}$	of range

NAVIGABLE DISTANCES

RIVER THAMES	M
Sea Reach No 1 Buoy to	
Southend Pier	6
Sheerness	5
Holehaven	11
Gravesend	19
Erith	25
Greenwich	35
London Bridge	41
Southend Pier to	
Sheerness	6
Havengore entrance	9½
Leigh (Bell Wharf)	3
Benfleet	6½

RIVER MEDWAY	
Sheerness (Garrison Pt) to	
Queenborough	1½
Gillingham	8
Upnor	10½
Rochester Bridge	12½

RIVER SWALE	
Queenborough to	
Kingsferry Bridge	2
Harty Ferry	9
Columbine Buoy	15

RAMSGATE	
Ramsgate Harbour Entrance to	
Whitstable	22
Sheerness	34
Harwich	40
Burnham-on-Crouch	44

RIVER CROUCH	
Whitaker Beacon to	
Foulness	7
Roach Entrance	9½
Burnham	12

Burnham to	M
Fambridge	5
Hullbridge	7
Battlesbridge	9
Foulness to	
Bench Head Buoy	
(via Ray Sand)	8
Bench Head Buoy (via Spitway)	18

RIVER ROACH	
Entrance to	
Paglesham	4
Havengore Bridge	5

RIVER BLACKWATER	
Bench Head Buoy to	
Sales Point	4
Nass Beacon (West Mersea)	5
Bradwell Quay	6
Osea Island	10
Heybridge Basin	13
Maldon (Hythe)	14½

RIVER COLNE	
Colne Bar Buoy to	
Brightlingsea	4½
Wivenhoe	8
Colchester (Hythe)	11

THE WALLET	
Knoll Lightbuoy to	
Clacton Pier	4
Walton-on-the-Naze (Pier)	9
Stone Banks Buoy	12½
Harwich Entrance	15

HARWICH	
Harbour Entrance to	
Burnham (via Wallet and Spitway)	30
West Mersea (via Wallet)	23
Brightlingsea (via Wallet)	22

	M
Woodbridge Haven	
(Deben Entrance)	6
Orford Haven (Ore Entrance)	10

RIVER STOUR	
Harwich Harbour Entrance to	
Wrabness	6½
Mistley	9½
Manningtree	11

RIVER ORWELL	
Harwich Harbour Entrance to	
Pin Mill	6½
Ipswich	11

RIVER DEBEN	
Felixstowe Ferry to	
Ramsholt	3
Waldringfield	5½
Woodbridge	9

RIVER ORE	
Shingle Street to	
Havergate Island	3
Orford Quay	5

RIVER ALDE	
Orford Quay to	
Slaughden Quay (Aldeburgh)	6
Iken Cliff	11
Snape Bridge	12½
Southwold to	
Orford Haven	20
Harwich Harbour	30

LOWESTOFT	
Harbour Entrance to	
Southwold	10
Orford Haven	30
Woodbridge Haven (Deben entrance)	33
Harwich	40

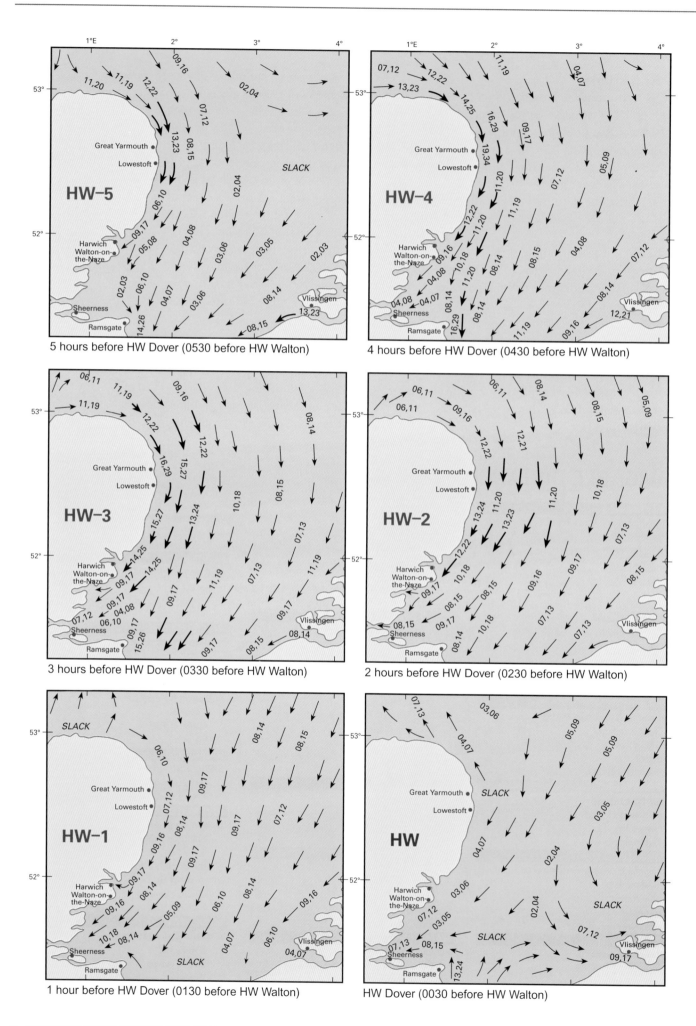

5 hours before HW Dover (0530 before HW Walton)

4 hours before HW Dover (0430 before HW Walton)

3 hours before HW Dover (0330 before HW Walton)

2 hours before HW Dover (0230 before HW Walton)

1 hour before HW Dover (0130 before HW Walton)

HW Dover (0030 before HW Walton)

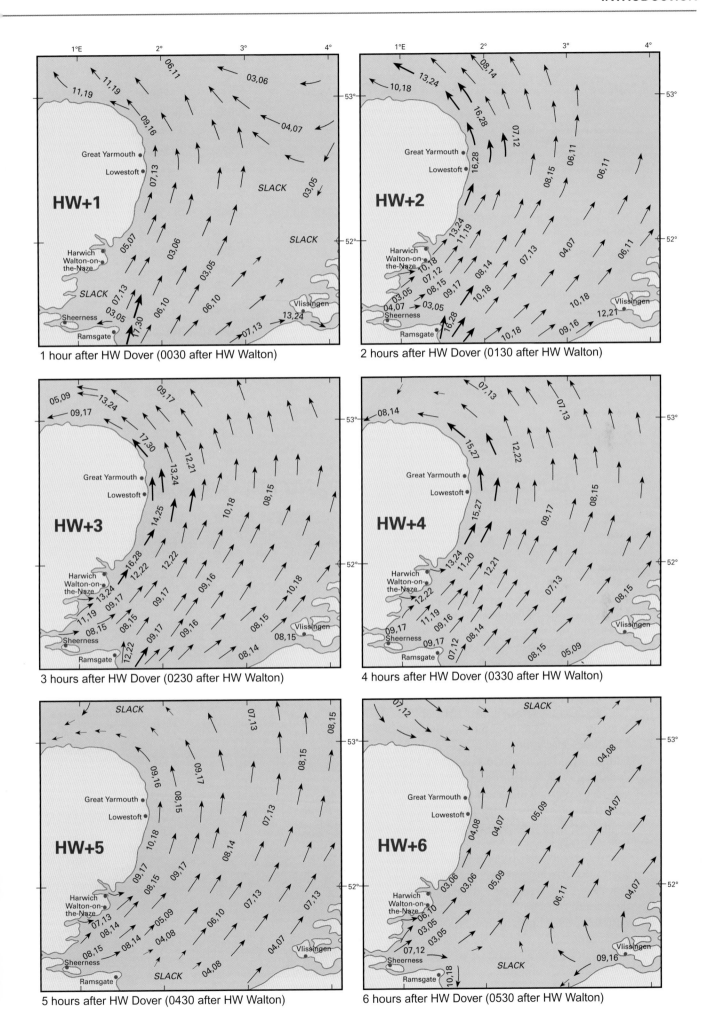

1 hour after HW Dover (0030 after HW Walton)

2 hours after HW Dover (0130 after HW Walton)

3 hours after HW Dover (0230 after HW Walton)

4 hours after HW Dover (0330 after HW Walton)

5 hours after HW Dover (0430 after HW Walton)

6 hours after HW Dover (0530 after HW Walton)

ABBREVIATIONS AND SYMBOLS

✈	Airport	⊖	Fishing harbour/quay	↻	Public telephone
⚓	Anchoring	▨	Fish farm	⇌	Railway station
⚓̸	Anchoring prohibited	FV(s)	Fishing vessel(s)	✕	Restaurant
Ⓑ	Bank	⛽	Fuel berth	SWM	Safe water mark
⬓	Boat hoist	⚓	Harbour master	⚡	Shore power
⚙	Boatyard	Ⓗ	Heliport		Showers
Ca	Cable(s)	⚓	Holding tank pump-out	◥	Slipway
Ⓟ	Car park	✚	Hospital	SCM	South cardinal mark
⚓	Chandlery	ⓘ	Information bureau	SHM	Starboard-hand mark
✚	Chemist	IDM	Isolated danger mark	🛒	Supermarket
✝	Church	▣	Launderette	SS	Traffic signals
H24	Continuous	Ldg	Leading	Ⓥ Ⓥ	Visitors' berth/buoy
⚙	Crane	✦	Lifeboat	WPT⊕	Waypoint
⊖	Customs office	⚓	Marina	WCM	West cardinal mark
⚓	Direction of buoyage	NCM	North cardinal mark	⛵	Yacht berthing facilities
ECM	East cardinal mark	PHM	Port-hand mark	⚑	Yacht club
⚓	Ferry terminal	PA	Position approx.		
◀●◀	Fishing boats	✉	Post office		

BUOY COLOURS, LIGHTS AND FREQUENCIES

R	Red
G	Green
Y	Yellow
B	Black
W	White
BY	Black over yellow (north-cardinal)
YB	Yellow over black (south-cardinal)
BYB	Black-yellow-black (east-cardinal)
YBY	Yellow-black-yellow (west-cardinal)
BRB	Black-red-black (isolated danger)
FR	Fixed red
FG	Fixed green
Fl	Flashing light, period of light shorter than darkness. If followed by a number, this indicates a group of flashes eg Fl (3). Colour white unless followed by another colour eg Fl (3) G. Timing of complete sequence is given in seconds eg Fl (3) 10s – group flash three every 10 seconds.
LFl	Long flash ie period of light not less than two seconds.
Oc	Occulting light, period of light longer than the period of darkness.
Iso	Isophase light, equal periods of light and darkness.
Q	Quick flashing light, up to 60 flashes per minute.
VQ	Very quick flashing light, up to 120 flashes per minute.

Lowestoft Lifeboat reverses into her berth in the Yacht Harbour

Chapter one
Lowestoft

Tides	HW Dover −1.33. Range: springs 1.9m; neaps 1.1m
Charts	Admiralty 1536, 1543, SC5614; Stanfords 3; Imray C28, 2000 series; OS maps 156/134
Waypoints	E Barnard 52°25'.14N 01°46'.38E
	Corton 52°31'.14N 01°51'.37E
	N Pierhead 52°28'.32N 01°45'.39E
Hazards	Shoals and drying areas, sands continually shift and buoyage moved. Tides set strongly across entrance

In *Coastwise Cruising* (1929) Francis B Cooke describes 'the element of pleasurable excitement about entering a strange port in one's own vessel, for one never knows quite what one will find inside the pierheads.'

He wrote this on his approach to Lowestoft from the south and, having passed Kessingland, home of the novelist Sir Rider Haggard, they looked through the glasses and saw '...smack after smack emerge from the pierheads, bound for the Dogger Bank in quest of the nation's breakfast.'

Once inside the harbour they found it to be '...a jolly nice place. The band is discoursing music for us on the pier, and pretty girls in white frocks gaze at us as we get tea ready in the well. We have not been berthed very long ere a boat comes alongside with a cordial invitation from the Royal Norfolk and Suffolk Yacht Club to make use of their club-house during our stay.'

The nation no longer eats herring for breakfast and the fishing fleet is not what it was, but visiting yachtsmen continue to appreciate the unique mixture of seaside resort and commercial port to be found at

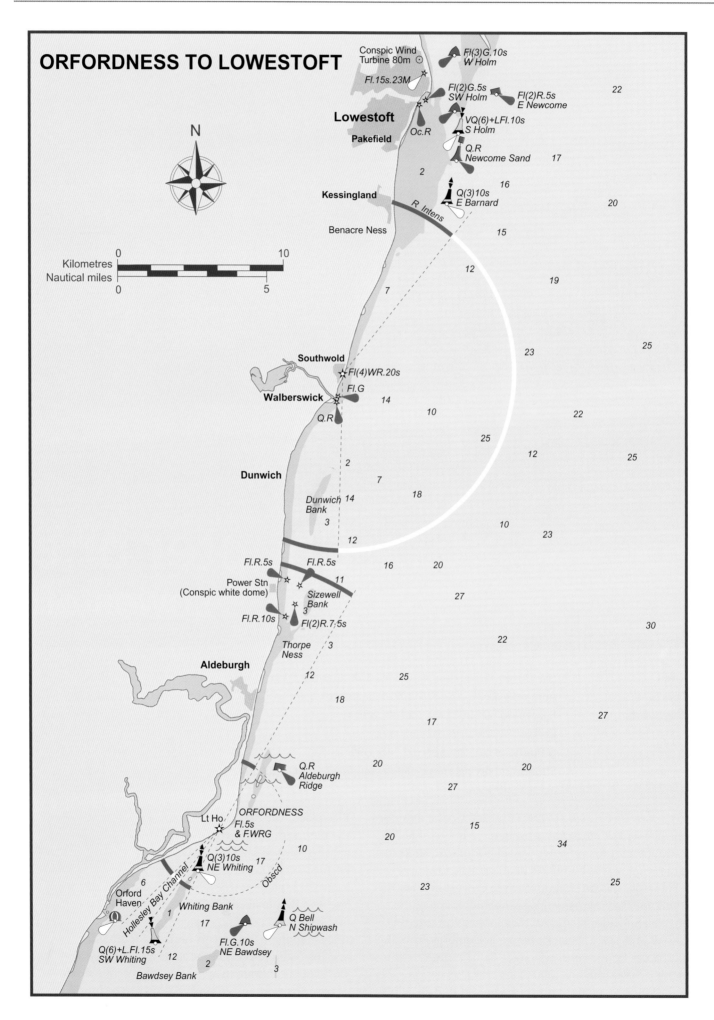

ORFORDNESS TO LOWESTOFT

N

Conspic Wind Turbine 80m ⊙

Fl.15s.23M

Fl(3)G.10s W Holm

Fl(2)G.5s SW Holm

Fl(2)R.5s E Newcome

22

Lowestoft

VQ(6)+LFl.10s S Holm

Oc.R

Pakefield

Q.R Newcome Sand

17

2

16

Kilometres

0   10

Nautical miles

0   5

Kessingland

Q(3)10s E Barnard

R Intens

20

Benacre Ness

15

12

7

19

23

25

Southwold

Fl(4)WR.20s

Fl.G

Walberswick

14

22

Q.R

10

25

12

25

Dunwich

2

7

Dunwich Bank

14

18

3

10

23

12

16

20

Fl.R.5s

Fl.R.5s

11

Power Stn (Conspic white dome)

Sizewell Bank

27

Fl.R.10s

3

Fl(2)R.7.5s

22

Thorpe Ness

3

Aldeburgh

12

25

18

17

27

20

20

Q.R Aldeburgh Ridge

27

Lt Ho

ORFORDNESS

15

Fl.5s & F.WRG

20

34

Q(3)10s NE Whiting

17

10

Obscd

6

23

25

Orford Haven

Whiting Bank

1

17

Q Bell N Shipwash

Q(6)+L.Fl.15s SW Whiting

12

Fl.G.10s NE Bawdsey

2

3

Bawdsey Bank

Lowestoft. The beaches north and south of Claremont Pier have Blue Flag awards.

The once-thriving fishing community, some of whom lived in upturned boats, in the 'Beach Village' which existed around Ness Point, were said to be the inspiration for David Copperfield. The original site was developed by Birds Eye and not much remains but there is a model of the Village in the Heritage Centre at Flint House, just off the High Street. Lowestoft's other literary connection is with Joseph Conrad, who arrived here from the Ukraine in 1878 and became a merchant seaman before turning to writing.

In the late 1990s the existing entrance to the yacht basin was closed off and another entrance was built at the end of the Inner South Pier. A new lifeboat station was constructed on the Heritage Pier, which bridges the filled-in gap of the old entrance. Since the opening of the improved Lowestoft Yacht Harbour marina and, further up Lake Lothing, the Haven Marina, many more yachtsmen are calling at Lowestoft. As the most easterly point in Britain, it serves as a useful departure or arrival point for Holland and the Continent, as well as being a gateway to the southern Broads.

APPROACHES

The strong appeal of Lowestoft to the visiting yachtsman is that the harbour can be entered at any state of tide, 24 hours a day, although conditions just outside the narrow entrance are sometimes extremely lively in wind-against-tide conditions. The fairway is dredged to a least depth of 4.7m but the sands shift and the buoys are moved accordingly.

The tide can set strongly across the entrance between the piers. About one mile east of the harbour entrance

The tide can set strongly across the entrance between the piers

the south-going stream begins at HW Dover –0600, and the north-going at HW Dover.

Lowestoft lighthouse (Fl 15s) is one mile north of the harbour entrance. Nearby on Ness Point is the conspicuous wind turbine 'Gulliver', said to be the tallest in the UK. The prominent white-painted light towers on the Outer Harbour piers are very easy to distinguish: the North Pier shows Oc G 5s and the South Pier Oc R 5s.

Equally prominent nowadays, adjacent to the North Outer Harbour Pier, are the conspicuous cranes of SLP Engineering. In fact the light tower on the North Pier is often dwarfed by huge rig structures or gas platforms being constructed on this site.

Approaching from the south or east, it is necessary to pick up the Newcome Sand and South Holm buoys, which mark the entrance to the Stanford Channel. This channel provides a safe, well-lit, deep water approach to the port between the two sandbanks. From the north

Lake Lothing (top left), the Yacht Harbour with Trawl Dock opposite (centre) and Haven Marina Hamilton Dock extension (bottom right)

Pontoon berths in the Lowestoft Yacht Harbour with the Royal Norfolk & Suffolk YC clubhouse beyond

(for example, coming from Great Yarmouth) it is normal to use the Corton Road channel, inside the Holm Sand, which is also lit.

In daylight and reasonable conditions, yachts approaching from the south are able to save time by using the unlit Pakefield Road channel, inside the Newcome Sand. Using this route, the Barnard shoal off Benacre Ness can be avoided by passing the Ness about a mile offshore, just inside the East Barnard east cardinal buoy.

Approaching the entrance, it is essential to observe the traffic signals on the south pier (green, white, green ENTER; red, red, red DO NOT ENTER). Some of the ships that use the harbour only just fit through the entrance so it would be disastrous to meet one coming the other way. A call to Lowestoft Harbour on VHF Ch 14 is always advisable.

THE HARBOUR

Once inside the entrance there is shelter from all quarters. Bear in mind that the outer harbour is fairly small so sails need to be dropped and stowed promptly before entering either the Royal Norfolk & Suffolk Yacht Club Yacht Harbour or the Hamilton Dock extension to the Haven Marina.

In the Trawl Dock there is a waiting pontoon for yachts bound through the harbour bridge for the Inner Harbour and Lake Lothing, where the Haven Marina and the Lowestoft Cruising Club are situated.

In the Outer Harbour, the entrances to the Waveney and Hamilton Docks and then to the Trawl Dock open up to starboard on the north side. The Yacht Harbour is in the south-west corner, with its entrance to port off the main channel leading to the lifting road bridge, the Inner Harbour and Lake Lothing. Beyond the road bridge on the north bank is a conspicuous silo.

Before entering the Yacht Harbour, you should contact the Royal Norfolk & Suffolk Yacht Club (on Marina Control Ch 80), which will give directions to a suitable

berth. There are traffic control signals on the eastern side of the Yacht Harbour entrance (only visible from inside) and, as it is relatively narrow and visibility is restricted, it is important to observe these signals on leaving – 3FR vertical no exit; GWG vertical proceed on instruction.

LOWESTOFT YACHT HARBOUR

The Royal Norfolk & Suffolk Yacht Club administers the Yacht Harbour and has excellent amenities available around the clock at its imposing, Grade II listed clubhouse – when the club was founded in 1857 it was

Lowestoft Port Guide – Local tel code 01502

Lowestoft Harbour and Bridge Control	Tel: 572286; VHF Ch 14.
Royal Norfolk & Suffolk Yacht Club, Lowestoft Yacht Harbour	Tel: 566726; Fax: 517981; VHF Ch 80.
Facilities	Toilets, showers, laundry, pump out.
Water and electricity	On pontoons.
Lowestoft Haven Marina	Tel: 580300; Fax: 581851; VHF Ch 80.
Fuel	Diesel at Yacht Harbour and Haven Marina, petrol from garages in town.
Stores	Supermarkets and shops across road bridge in town.
Repairs	Small crane at Yacht Harbour; 70 ton hoist at Haven Marina; Lowestoft Yacht Services (Lake Lothing) Tel: 585535; Mobile: 07887 616846; F Newson (Lake Lothing) Tel: 574902. Other yards and chandlery on Oulton Broad beyond Mutford Bridge.
Chandlery	Lowestoft Yacht Services, Tel: 585535.
Marine engineers	Small & Co, Commercial Road, Tel: 513538.
Marine electronics	Charity & Taylor, Battery Green Road, Tel: 581529.
Chart agents	Charity & Taylor.
Food and drink	Bar and restaurant at Royal Norfolk & Suffolk Yacht Club, restaurants, pubs nearby.
Transport	Railway station across road bridge; bus station town centre.

Opening times for Lowestoft Harbour Bridge (between Outer and Inner Harbours)
Subject to at least 20 minutes notice, yachts may be given a bridge opening at:
Mon-Fri 0300, 0500, 0700, 0945, 1115, 1430, 1600, 1900, 2100, 2400.
Sat/Sun/Bank Holidays 0300, 0500, 0700, 0945, 1115, 1430, 1730, 1600, 1800, 1900, 2100, 2400.

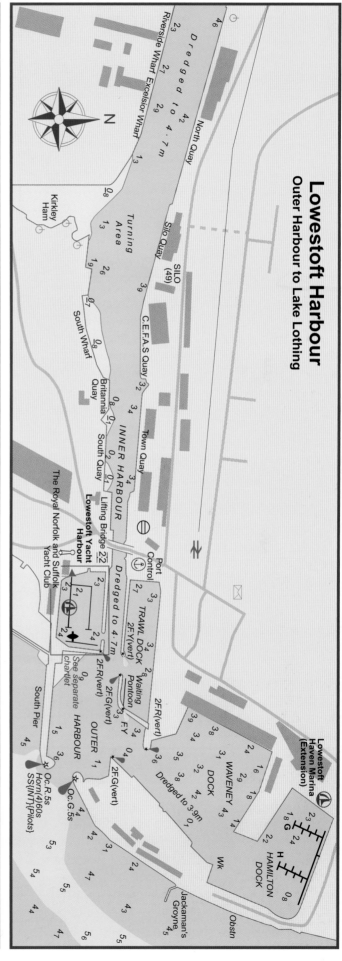

Lowestoft Harbour
Outer Harbour to Lake Lothing

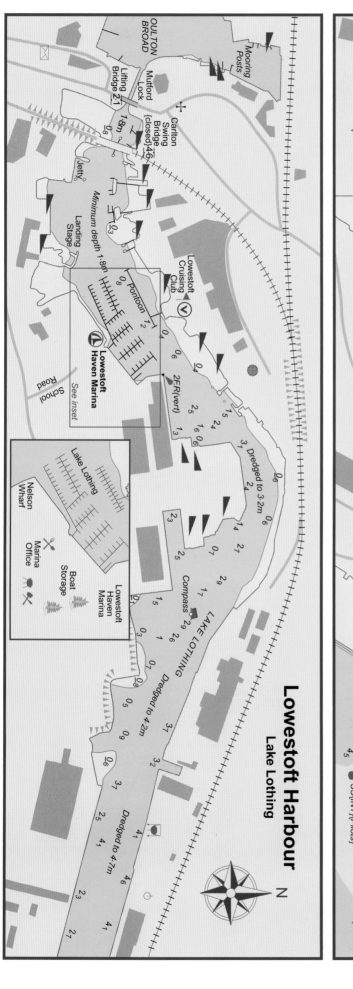

Lowestoft Harbour
Lake Lothing

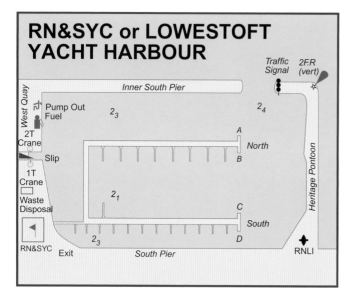

RN&SYC or LOWESTOFT YACHT HARBOUR

West Quay

Inner South Pier

Traffic Signal

2F.R (vert)

Pump Out
Fuel

2₃

2₄

2T Crane

A

North

B

Slip

1T Crane

Waste Disposal

2₁

Heritage Pontoon

C

South

D

RN&SYC

Exit

2₃

South Pier

RNLI

designed by Linton Hope for the Royal Norfolk & Suffolk Yacht Club in 1900. These elegant 24ft gaff-rig keelboats were originally varnished, which is why they became known as Brown Boats, although in recent years white glassfibre hulls have been built and the class has undergone a tremendous revival.

The beach at Lowestoft is a stone's throw from the club and supermarkets, shops and restaurants are not far away in the town centre, just across the road bridge.

Historic vessels, such as the Lowestoft sailing trawler *Excelsior* owned by the Cirdan Sailing Trust, are berthed on the Heritage Pontoon at the eastern end of the yacht harbour. The Lowestoft Lifeboat also berths here.

HAMILTON DOCK – HAVEN MARINA EXTENSION

In 2008 the Lowestoft Haven Marina opened an extension in the Hamilton Dock which provides 46 pontoon berths, including 20 for visiting yachts. All berths have water and electricity and there is a purpose-built toilet, shower and laundry block on site. A secure, coded gate gives access to the town via Hamilton Road. Visiting yachts can go straight through the Waveney Dock into the Hamilton Dock after calling the Haven Marina on VHF Ch 80 or telephoning for a berth allocation, Tel: 580300.

BRIDGE TO INNER HARBOUR

The road bridge to the Inner Harbour lifts at 10 appointed times a day during the week (slightly more often at weekends and bank holidays) and at other times when commercial ships are entering or leaving.

originally housed in an old railway carriage. Visiting yachtsmen are given a friendly welcome by manager David Schonhut and his staff. Among the facilities is an attractive sun lounge overlooking the marina, as well as a bar and restaurant. Bar meals are available from the sun lounge (fish and chips highly recommended) or there is an *à la carte* menu in the more formal dining room; breakfast is served daily, but needs to be booked in advance.

Various class championships are hosted by the club, the waters off Lowestoft being well suited to racing, and there are home fleets of Dragons, Squibs, Flying Fifteens, 707s and dinghies. During Lowestoft Sea Week regatta, usually in August, all the local classes are raced including the venerable Broads One-Designs,

Lowestoft Haven Marina is situated in Lake Lothing beyond the Inner Harbour

The road bridge lifted as a commercial vessel followed by two yachts pass through into the Inner Harbour

Lowestoft Harbour Control manages the bridge and requires 20 minutes notice. Craft waiting for the bridge to open should use the waiting pontoon at the east end of the Trawl Dock and monitor VHF Ch 14. While in the Trawl Lock call *Lowestoft Haven Marina* on VHF Ch 80 or 37 for berthing instructions.

LAKE LOTHING AND LOWESTOFT HAVEN MARINA

Lake Lothing is mainly commercial, particularly on the south side where there are docks and shipyards. The 140-berth Lowestoft Haven Marina is located on the south bank, 1¼ miles upriver from the harbour bridge, and is close to Mutford Lock at the entrance to Oulton Broad. Established by Associated British Ports, facilities at the marina include power and water to all pontoons (with 24-hour supervision), diesel, gas, 70-ton boat hoist, repair workshop, toilets, showers, laundry, bar and restaurant. Oulton Broad is nearby and Lowestoft town can be reached on foot via School Road or by train from Oulton Broad South.

Opposite Lowestoft Haven Marina, on the north side of Lake Lothing, is the Lowestoft Cruising Club, incorporating a small but attractive purpose-built clubhouse, hard standing and a secure car park. Members' yachts are berthed on either side of an extensive and secure pontoon along the bank in front of the club, which is less than a 10-minute walk from shops, restaurants, pubs and the railway station at Oulton Broad South. Visiting yachtsmen should contact the moorings officer, preferably in advance, to arrange a berth.

Next door to the club, Lowestoft Yacht Services has a modest shed, slip and crane, with a small chandlery situated alongside.

Various wrecks and hulks lying along the Lake Lothing shore give the place an air of dereliction, but at the International Boatbuilding Training College things look more hopeful and there are usually interesting

Lake Lothing Port Guide – Local tel code 01502

Lowestoft Haven Marina	Tel: 580300; Fax: 581851; VHF Ch 80.
Fuel	Diesel near boat hoist, Calor and Camping Gaz from office, petrol from garages in town.
Stores	Local shops at Oulton Broad, Asda and other shops can be found in Lowestoft.
Repairs	70 ton hoist at Haven Marina. Lowestoft Yacht Services, The Boatyard, Harbour Road, Oulton Broad. Tel: 585535; Mobile: 07887 616848. F Newson (Lake Lothing) Tel: 574902.
Chandlery	Lowestoft Yacht Services (Oulton Broad), Tel: 585535 – also do rigging. Jeckells, Bridge Road, Oulton Broad, Tel: 565007.
Marine engineers	JPC at Haven Marina Tel: 500712. Allerton Engineering, Harbour Road, Oulton Broad, Tel: 537870.
Marine electronics	KM Electronics, Brooke Business Park, Heath Road, Tel: 569079.
Food and drink	Waterfront Inn, bar (open daily 1100-2300) and restaurant at Haven Marina Tel: 583596. Pubs, hotels, restaurants, cafés and takeaways in Oulton Broad.
Transport	Railway station, Oulton Broad South, 10-minute walk. Connections to Lowestoft, Ipswich, Norwich and London.
Yacht clubs	Lowestoft Cruising Club, www.lowestoftcruisingclub.co.uk. Moorings officer Tel: 07913 391950.

wooden boats being built or undergoing restorations.

The yard near the railway bridge is F Newson, which has a slip for up to 80 tons and specialises in wooden boat restoration and mast making.

THE BROADS

To reach Oulton Broad from Lake Lothing, a rail bridge, a road bridge and then a lock must be negotiated. The openings are co-ordinated and available seven days a week during working hours by arrangement with the Mutford Bridge lock-keeper who will also advise you if your craft draws more than 1.7m.

Oulton Dyke links the western end of Oulton Broad with the River Waveney, which can be cruised upstream to just below Beccles. For craft with an air draught of less than 7.3m, the Yare can be reached from the Waveney by using New Cut to avoid the low A143 bridge at St Olaves. The Yare and the Waveney flow into Breydon Water to reach the sea at Yarmouth. The other tidal river, the Bure, also meets the sea at Yarmouth, but cruising on this river is restricted by fixed bridges which in addition prohibit access to the North Broads unless the mast can be lowered.

Licences are compulsory on The Broads – a temporary licence can be obtained from the Broads Authority in Norwich, www.tolls@broads-authority.gov.uk, or from Mutford Lock.

Oulton Broad Port Guide – Local tel code 01502

Mutford Bridge and Lock	Fee £8 (subject to review) – Operates in response to bookings 0800-1800 April to October, 0800-1100 November to March. Tel: 531778; VHF Ch 73 or 14 (occas).
Oulton Broad Yacht Station	Tel: 574946.
The Broads Authority, Norwich	Tel: 01603 610734; www.broads-authority.gov.uk.

Looking east, Oulton Broad in the foreground with the lock, road and rail bridges in the centre; Lake Lothing, the Inner and Outer Harbours of Lowestoft, top right.

The River Blyth, looking across from the Walberswick shore to the slipway and Harbour Marine Services at Blackshore

Chapter two
Southwold

Tides	HW Dover –1.05. Range: springs 1.9m; neaps 1.2m
Charts	Admiralty 1543, 2695 for entrance only; Stanfords 3; Imray C28, 2000 series, OS map 156
Waypoints	**Aldeburgh Ridge 52°06'.73N 01°36'.92E**
	Southwold N Pier 52°18'.80N 01°40'.53E
Hazards	Entrance. Not to be attempted in strong onshore winds. See www.eastcoastrivers.com for downloadable sketch plan of entrance

Rowland Parker, in his book *Men of Dunwich*, tells how – 'On the Night after New Year's Day' in 1286, 'through the Vehemence of the Winds and Violence of the Sea' the River Blyth found its way directly out to sea between Walberswick and Southwold rather than through the port of Dunwich.

The men of Dunwich did in fact manage to stop up the gap for a few years after, but on the afternoon of 14 January 1328, a north-easterly gale again coincided with the high tides of the month and the town of Dunwich was devastated; this time beyond any hope of recovery. From that time Southwold has been a port; at first for trading and fishing, but in recent years

simply as a pleasant haven for cruising yachts from both sides of the North Sea.

The River Blyth itself was once navigable beyond Blythburgh, as far into inland Suffolk as Halesworth where there was a wharf and a maltings. Later Halesworth was linked to Southwold by a single track railway line which fell into disuse in the early 1900s. The current footbridge linking the north and south shores of the harbour was built on the piers of the original railway bridge.

Southwold harbour is about as far north of Orfordness as Landguard Point is south of it – roughly 15 miles. There are several shoals lying a mile or so offshore between Orford Haven and Southwold. The largest of them, the Whiting Bank, is guarded at its northern end by the North East Whiting east cardinal buoy (Q (3) 10s) and at its southern end by the South West Whiting south cardinal buoy (Q (6) + L Fl 15s), while the Whiting Hook red can buoy (Fl R 10s) marks the western edge of the shoal.

A solitary red can buoy (QR) identifies the eastern side of the Aldeburgh Ridge, which lies about a mile offshore but has six to eight metres on its western side, very close to the shingle shore of the Ness itself.

The only snag when taking this inshore course round Orfordness is that overfalls occur on the ebb.

On the seaward side of the World Service radio masts on Lantern Marshes, just north of the Ness, it has been reported that instruments go haywire.

There is one other shallow patch, the Sizewell Bank, about a mile offshore opposite the conspicuous atomic power station, but this unmarked patch has some three metres over it at low water springs.

It should be noted that the direction of buoyage changes to the north of Orfordness; and north of Dunwich you leave the Thames Coastguard area and enter the Yarmouth Coastguard area.

A lighthouse – Fl (4) WR 20s – is situated in the town of Southwold about a mile to the north of the harbour.

Since entry to Southwold harbour should be made on the flood (the ebb runs out at anything up to six knots), it will often pay, when coming from the south, to use the north-going ebb and then wait off the harbour entrance for a while, either by heaving-to or lying to an anchor about a quarter of a mile south of the pierheads if the wind is light and offshore.

The South Pierhead at Southwold Harbour entrance, with Sizewell power station in the distance

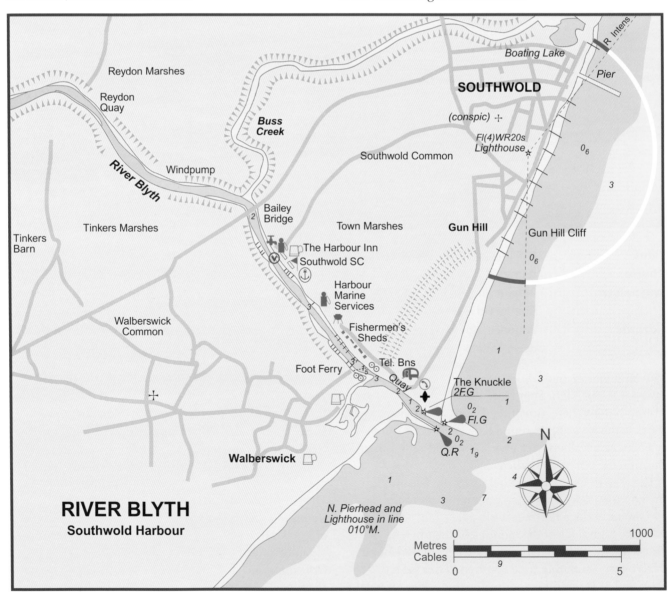

RIVER BLYTH

Southwold Harbour

The River Blyth looking east towards the harbour entrance and the North Sea beyond

The best time to go in is during the second half of the flood, as near high water as possible. Whenever there is a strong wind from any direction between the north-east and south-east, the entrance can be dangerous and certainly must not be attempted if two red flags or three vertical flashing red lights are shown on the north pier.

A flashing green light is shown from the north pier and a flashing red from the south pier.

A local fishing boat passing the Knuckle on her way out of the harbour; the lifeboat station can be seen on the right

The harbour entrance is constantly subject to change on account of the shifting off-lying sand and shingle shoals. For this reason it is imperative for both first-time visitors (and those who may have been into Southwold in previous years) to consult the harbour master, Steven Clouting (2008), beforehand to get the latest instructions. Steven can provide up-to-date information by telephone or fax on 01502 724712, and will give verbal pilotage via VHF Ch 9 after initial contact on VHF Ch 12.

In the height of the summer Southwold harbour can be very crowded and it is important to telephone before your visit to ascertain the availability of moorings. You should be prepared to raft up, and have plenty of rope ready for the necessary shorelines and springs. Bear in mind that the tidal flow up and down the narrow river is strong, up to six knots on a spring ebb.

Once inside the pierheads, steer for a pile structure at the inshore end of the north pier. This staging, known as the Knuckle, is marked by a beacon bearing

Looking across the River Blyth to Southwold Sailing Club near the red fishing boat and the Harbour Inn nearby

Along the north bank there are several stalls selling seafood

Southwold is a seaside resort with fine beaches and a pier

two vertical green lights. When abreast the Knuckle, cut tight around and follow the line of the dock wall. There is deep water for about 10m off the wall with room for two boats to pass, so it is as well to remember that collision regulations apply. At the end of the wall at the starboard-hand mark, alter course to port, heading towards the power cable warning sign until you are in mid-river. From here, continue upriver

midway between the stagings on either side.

There are permanent moorings on these wooden stagings, while the staging reserved for visiting yachtsmen is about a quarter of a mile beyond the ferry, on the north bank, just by the Harbour Inn.

Waveney District Council administers the harbour, and the harbour master's office is in the old Lifeboat shed near the visitors' staging.

John and Adele Buckley at Harbour Marine Services run a thriving boatyard and chandlery on the north bank at Blackshore, near the fishermen's sheds, where they specialise in work on traditional wooden boats. Near the slipway is the yard of G Brown & Son, shipwrights, boat builders and marine electricians, who also work on traditional craft. An annual rally of smacks and classic boats has become established in recent years (usually in June) at Southwold, the event being sponsored by Adnams, the local brewery.

Along the north bank, among the fishermen's sheds, are several stalls selling fresh fish, shellfish, smoked fish, fish and chips and the like.

The seaside resort of Southwold, with its good shops and hotels, is about one mile away. From the back of the Harbour Inn a footpath leads through the marshes and then across the golf course to the back of the town. Alternatively the Suffolk Coast and Heaths Path will take you to Southwold from near the ferry landing. This track runs behind the campsite and leads to one of several attractive greens at Gun Cliff where there are six eighteen-pounder Tudor guns said to have been captured by the Duke of Cumberland at Culloden. The Sailors' Reading Room is well worth a visit. Situated close to the lighthouse, it is home to a collection of maritime paintings, prints, photographs and models, including some of the local beach yawls, the lines of which were later used for pulling and sailing Norfolk and Suffolk class lifeboats. The church is one of Suffolk's finest, filled

Southwold Port Guide – Local tel code 01502

Harbour master	Steven Clouting Tel: 724712; VHF Ch 12 (also pilotage).
Water	Hose pipe on visitors' berth.
Stores	Basic requirements from chandlery at boatyard, otherwise from Southwold (approximately one mile).
Boatyards	Harbour Marine Services Tel: 724721; Fax: 722060; email: info@harbourmarine. uk.com; www.southwold harbour.co.uk. G Brown & Son Shipwrights and Boatbuilders Tel: 725050; Fax: 722731.
Repairs	Services, slip (up to 30 tons) and three hoists up to 30 tons, marine engineering.
Chandlery	At Harbour Marine (supplies Calor gas).
Transport	Railway stations at Darsham and Halesworth; bus service to Lowestoft.
Telephones	At chandlers, near north pier and at pub.
Yacht club	Southwold Sailing Club.
Food and drink	Harbour Inn (on quayside) Tel: 722381. Several fish stalls and eateries along the north shore. Many good hotels, pubs, restaurants, tea-rooms in town.

with good wood carving and a rare 15th century, brightly painted pulpit.

Southwold overlooks Sole Bay where, in 1672, the townspeople watched from the cliff tops as the British and Dutch fleets fought a bloody naval battle in which both sides suffered heavy losses. The British were eventually deemed to have won a narrow victory.

At the north end of the town is Southwold Pier. Originally constructed in 1900 but later swept away by storms, it was completely rebuilt in 2001. The new pier extends to 623ft and boasts a bar restaurant, family amusements and a landing stage for visiting ships such as PS *Waverley* and MV *Balmoral*.

WALBERSWICK

Although most yachtsmen land on the north side of the harbour and visit Southwold, Walberswick too is a charming little place that has attracted artists ever since the days of Charles Keene and Wilson Steer at the end of the last century.

Walberswick has also long been the holiday haunt of theatrical folk, and the Scottish architect, designer and water-colourist, Charles Rennie Mackintosh, lived here for a time.

There are two pubs – the 600-year old Bell near the ferry, and The Anchor, in The Street – both serve meals. In the village is a craft centre and teashop, plus an art gallery, and close by is an attractive little beach with good walks southward across the marshes to Dunwich or westward to the heathlands of the Suffolk Sandlings.

Walberswick hosts the annual British Open Crabbing Championship. Open to children of all ages, this keenly contested event is usually held in August.

The village can be reached by crossing the Bailey bridge upstream of the Harbour Inn and then taking the pleasant walk back down the south bank of the River Blyth. Alternatively, you can cross to the Walberswick side by getting the ferryman to row you over from near the fishermen's sheds.

Walberswick Port Guide
Local tel code 01502

Food and drink	The Bell, Ferry Lane, Tel: 723109. The Anchor, The Street, Tel: 722112.
Ferry	Daily June to September; weekends only during winter.

There are walks across the marshes to Dunwich from the Walberswick shore

There are moorings on wooden stagings on either side of the River Blyth; those for visitors are on the north bank near the Harbour Inn

Kylix, designed and originally owned by legendary East Coast sailor Maurice Griffiths, taking the flood up the River Ore

Chapter three
Orford River

Tides	At entrance – HW Dover +0.15. Range: springs 2.0m; neaps 1.7m
Charts	Admiralty 2052, 2695, SC5607; Stanfords Chart Pack 6; Imray C28, 2000 series; OS map 169
Waypoints	**Orford Haven Buoy** (liable to be moved) 52°01'.60N 01°27'.98E.
	For latest position contact Thames Coastguard – Frinton-on-Sea, Tel: 01255 675518
Hazards	Shoals and strong tides in entrance (seek up-to-date information from
	www.eastcoastrivers.com or from Aldeburgh Yacht Club)

In the opening chapter of his book *The Alde Estuary* (1973), WG Arnott describes how, like Hilaire Belloc before him, he 'prayed to the boat itself (since nothing else could hear me)…' as he entered the Ore one summer during a south-westerly gale. 'Two hearty gybes, a great swirling of many waters and we were in, being carried at terrific speed over the young flood past the shingle banks. How peaceful it all seemed of a sudden after the welter and bustle outside… Jack went below and put on the kettle for a well-earned cup of tea whilst we slid past Havergate Island…'

Arnott's words hold just as good today as they did 35 years ago, the tide still carries yachts in at a terrific

speed and countless crews must have drunk a well-earned cup of tea in the relative calm of the river once inside North Weir Point.

Orford Haven lies at the southern end of Hollesley Bay, some four or five miles north of the entrance to the Deben, but it is not easy to locate the actual entrance.

The only helpful landmarks are a Martello Tower about a mile south-west of the entrance proper and a few houses in two small rows just north of the tower.

The offing buoy ('Orford Haven' Sph RWVS Bell L Fl 10s) is in about 6m of water at low water springs and situated just under a mile east of the cottages at Shingle Street. The port and starboard-hand buoys, Oxley and

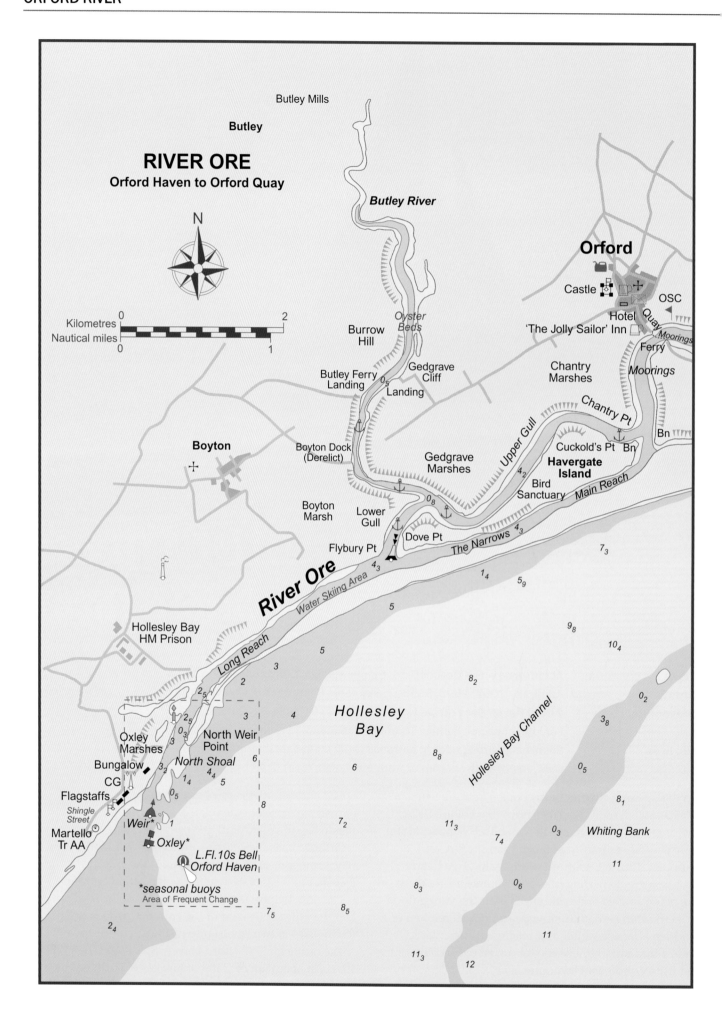

Butley Mills

Butley

RIVER ORE
Orford Haven to Orford Quay

N

Kilometres
Nautical miles

0   2
0   1

Butley River

Orford

Castle

OSC

Hotel
'The Jolly Sailor' Inn

Ferry

Moorings

Oyster Beds

Burrow Hill

Gedgrave Cliff

Chantry Marshes

Butley Ferry Landing

Landing

Chantry Pt

Boyton

Boyton Dock (Derelict)

Gedgrave Marshes

Upper Gull

Cuckold's Pt   Bn

Bn

Havergate Island

Boyton Marsh

Lower Gull

Bird Sanctuary

Main Reach

4₂

0₈

Dove Pt

4₃

Flybury Pt

The Narrows

7₃

River Ore

Water Skiing Area

4₃

1₄

5₉

5

Hollesley Bay HM Prison

Long Reach

5

5

9₈

10₄

3

2

8₂

0₂

2₅

3

4

Hollesley Bay

3₈

Oxley Marshes

2₅

North Weir Point

8₈

Bungalow

0₃

3

North Shoal

6

6

0₅

CG

3₂

4₄

5

Flagstaffs

0₅

1₄

8

8₁

Shingle Street

8₈

11₃

Hollesley Bay Channel

Martello Tr AA

*Weir**

1

0₃

Whiting Bank

*Oxley**

7₂

7₄

0₆

11

L.Fl.10s Bell
Orford Haven

8₃

seasonal buoys
Area of Frequent Change

8₅

7₅

11

2₄

11₃

12

The River Ore entrance at low water. Weir green conical (bottom left); Shingle Street and the bungalow (left);
North Shoal (right) and North Weir Point (top right)

Weir, are laid during the season to indicate the passage into the river between the shingle islet and the shingle bank extending south of North Weir Point.

As with the River Deben, the Ore reaches the sea through a narrow shingle banked outlet and as a result there is a shingle bar and several drying and shifting shingle banks or 'knolls' in the entrance. The bar and the knolls, and the fact that the tides run in and out of the river very strongly indeed, combine to make Orford Haven rather more difficult to enter than the Deben, together with the fact that there is no pilot on hand.

A beacon (orange and white post with orange diamond-shaped topmark) was erected by Trinity House in 1975 on the mainland shore just inside North Weir Point and has not been moved since. However, it is no longer possible to follow a direct course between the offing buoy and the beacon.

As the directions change from year to year, yachtsmen are fortunate that a survey of the entrance is carried out at the beginning of each season by Trinity House. The findings are incorporated onto the website www. eastcoastrivers.com (formerly debenentrance.com) which features downloadable up-to-date information, sketch maps and aerial photographs of both the Ore and the Deben river entrances. Sponsored by local marinas, chandleries and related companies, the sketch maps and photos are published annually in a laminated form available at local marinas and chandleries. The

Alde and Ore Association also publish its *Information and Guidelines* leaflet annually and this can be obtained from Aldeburgh Yacht Club.

Although given the dual names, the Ore and the Alde are merely different parts of a single river; the Ore being that part between the entrance (Orford Haven) and Randalls Point (between Orford and Slaughden Quay,

The offing buoy, Orford Haven, needs to be located before entering the River Ore

The buildings at Shingle Street seen from between Oxley and Weir buoys

while the Alde is the river thereon up to its navigable limit at Snape Bridge, a distance of about 16 miles.

THE RIVER ORE

Within the entrance the tidal streams run very strongly indeed; probably up to four knots on the flood and as much as five knots during the latter half of a spring ebb. Because of this, entry against the ebb is virtually impossible, while departure on the ebb is certainly not advisable.

While waiting for the flood a safe anchorage may be found inshore just south of the Martello Tower at Shingle Street, provided the wind is somewhere between south-west and north.

Probably the time to enter or leave the river is from

The barge *Mirosa* entering the river under sail has left Oxley close to port and is heading for the green conical Weir

about one hour after low water, depending on draught, when there should be sufficient water over the bar and the worst of the shingle banks will still be uncovered.

Given sufficient power (not less than five knots), it is safest to leave the river on the early flood when the tide outside will assist any boat bound south.

It is important to be aware that both the flood stream and the ebb continue to run into and out of the river for an hour after the change in Hollesley Bay.

THE ENTRANCE

When entering on the flood, a boat will tend to be carried into the river on the tidal stream. At the narrows at North Weir Point the streams are strongest and there is considerable turbulence caused by the streams from and to seaward around North Weir Point meeting the main north/south streams in the river.

In recent years shoal patches have been reported in mid-river between Oxley Marshes and North Weir Point, so caution should be exercised in this area.

LONG REACH

From the entrance to Dove Point, two miles to the north-east, the river is little more than 100m wide and runs between a featureless steep-to shingle bank to the south-east and a somewhat shallow shingle and mud shore backed by a sea wall to the north-west. This part of the Ore is known as Long Reach and there is an average of 6m all along it, although because the tides are so fierce and the holding in shingly mud is not very good, it is not advisable, except on a temporary basis or in an emergency, to bring up below Dove Point. There is a water-ski area in the upper part of Long Reach, below Flybury Point.

At Dove Point the river divides around Havergate Island, one part running along the south and the other along the north side of this narrow island. There is a fairly extensive mud spit extending from Dove Point, which is marked by a black and yellow buoy bearing a south cardinal topmark.

The barge *Mirosa* almost inside the river; Weir green conical to starboard and the bungalow on the shore at Shingle Street (left)

HAVERGATE ISLAND

Havergate is an important RSPB bird reserve, famous for its breeding avocets and terns in spring and large numbers of migrating waders and wildfowl in autumn. Landing is prohibited but the island is open on certain weekends and Thursdays during the summer and can be visited by booking places on the RSPB boat from Orford Quay. Reservations need to be made beforehand via the RSPB Minsmere reserve visitor centre on Tel: 01728 648281.

MAIN REACH

The most direct route up river to Orford Quay is Main Reach, which passes between the east side of Havergate Island and the attenuated shingle bank that stretches from Orfordness down to North Weir Point. The southern half of Main Reach is known as The Narrows. Here the river is hardly more than half a cable wide and the tides, particularly the ebb, still run very strongly. In The Narrows there are sometimes lobster pots which are not necessarily very well marked, so a good look out should be kept. At the top of Main Reach the river turns northerly towards Orford, about a mile away, and it is then possible to find good holding ground out of the main tidal stream.

A red spherical buoy is sometimes located in Main Reach at the point where the other arm of the river emerges from the west side of Havergate Island.

The River Ore looking north from above the entrance, Orfordness is in the top right

LOWER AND UPPER GULL

This other arm first of all turns northerly round Flybury Point, and for about half a mile the reach is known as the Lower Gull: one of the best anchorages for a boat waiting to leave the river. The tides still run strongly in Lower Gull, but the holding is better than anywhere in Long Reach. Another good anchorage is in Abraham's Bosom, off the north side of Havergate Island abreast its narrowest part.

At the top of Lower Gull a fairly large creek known as the Butley River branches off in a north-westerly direction. The main stream at this point turns south-easterly for about half a mile and then again turns to the north-east into Upper Gull. A good lookout should be kept around here for lobster pots. At the northern end of the Upper Gull the channel turns easterly once more and continues for nearly a mile before uniting with Main Reach between Chantry and Cuckold Points.

On average there is a greater depth of water through Lower Gull and Upper Gull than through Main Reach.

THE BUTLEY RIVER

This river or large creek leaves Lower Gull and at first follows a westerly direction for a quarter of a mile before turning north past Boyton Dock and Butley Ferry. The entrance to the creek is marked by a starboard-hand withy, and there is good anchorage just inside with about 2m at low water springs. Shallow draught boats can sometimes lie afloat as far up as Gedgrave Cliff amid pleasant surroundings.

The Butley Oysterage is active in the upper reaches of the river near the Cliff. The beds or trays may not be marked by withies, but there are courteous notice-boards indicating the extent of the layings (beds), so visiting yachtsmen should respond by taking care not to anchor above Gedgrave.

Landing is possible at most states of the tide, either at the semi-derelict Boyton Dock or at the Ferry landings, half a mile further north. The Butley ferry service between the Boyton and Orford shores, linking to the Suffolk Coast Path, runs at weekends and occasionally during the week in the summer. A pulling dinghy, sponsored by the Alde and Ore Association, is manned by volunteers; it carries foot passengers and bikes (but not tandems) and can be pre-booked on Tel: 07913 672499.

From Gedgrave beach on the east bank there is a pleasant walk of about two miles to Orford – the nearest source of supplies. Since the closing of The Bell pub at Boyton, there is not so much reason to land on the west bank although there is a shop, garage and pub at Hollesley, about three miles away. A walk of just over two miles northwards on the Suffolk Coast Path will bring you to Butley Mills, now converted to holiday apartments, at the head of the Butley River.

ORFORD QUAY

Above Chantry Point the river widens and deepens a little, having between 8 and 10m of water up to Orford Quay. Extending from the east bank just below the

Leaving the Butley River, the derelict building at Boyton Dock can be seen on the left

The keep of Orford Castle is a conspicuous landmark from anywhere in the river south of Orford

moorings at Orford there is a mud bank that diverts the channel towards the opposite shore for a short distance. The drying edge of the mud is marked by a perch.

The keep of Orford Castle (90ft) is a conspicuous landmark from anywhere in the river south of Orford, and will have been clearly visible from Lower Gull or Main Reach.

In 1165 Henry II decided to build a castle at Orford, which was when the original quays were constructed for unloading the building materials. The castle was completed in 1173, just in time to be used in Henry's conflict with his barons. Orford became a flourishing port, sending wool to the Continent at first and later handling coastal trade in coal and grain until 1939.

The view from the top of the keep (nowadays kept by English Heritage) well repays the climb, as does the equally impressive panorama from the tower of St Bartholomew's church, which was built around the same time as the castle and where there are some excellent brasses and a rare and beautiful font.

Moorings are laid on both sides of the channel for half a mile above and below Orford Quay. A few moorings

are made available by the New Orford Town Trust for visitors and these can usually be found halfway along the trot of moorings below the Quay on the Orfordness shore. For payment of mooring fees or to enquire about

St Bartholomew's church in Orford was built at about the same time as the castle

The Orford Sailing Club pontoon can be accessed until around half tide

The Watch House on the quay at Orford

temporary use of a mooring, contact the Quay Warden. In common with other popular destinations in the area, in the summer holiday period the demand for visitors' moorings often exceeds the supply. The Town Trust Quay Warden's office is on the quay and a workboat operates on the river between Orford and the entrance.

Landing at the quay itself, or at the slipway and shingly beach north of it, is possible at all states of the tide. The MFV *Lady Florence*, a familiar sight on the river, operates mini cruises from the quay all the year round. The RSPB ferry runs from the quay to the society's reserve on Havergate Island; the National Trust launch operates between the quay and the Ness; and local fishing boats also come alongside to land their catch.

The slipway is used for launching and recovering visiting speedboats and trailer-sailers and occasionally used by a National Trust landing-craft vehicle ferry coming and going to the Ness. So both the quay and slipway can get pretty busy during summer holidays and fine weekends.

Upstream of the quay, on the seawall, is the Orford Sailing Club clubhouse; the club has its own launching ramp and pontoon and welcomes visiting yachtsmen. A fresh water hose pipe and a tide gauge are situated on the end of the pontoon, which dries at low water. There is water for most boats until around half tide and a visiting yacht can lie alongside the pontoon for up to an hour, but must be attended.

The Black Beacon on Orfordness was built in 1928 to house an experimental 'rotating loop' navigation beacon

Quay Street in Orford

Orford Port Guide – Local tel code 01394

New Orford Town Trust	Town Hall Tel: 459172.
NOTT Quay Warden	Philip Attwood NOTT Office on the Quay, Tel: 459950; Mob: 07528 092635; VHF Ch 08/16.
Water	Stand-pipe on the quay, hose pipe on Orford Sailing Club pontoon.
Stores	General store (off-licence and post office) off square. Butcher, fish shop and smokehouse near square.
Fuel	Petrol, diesel and paraffin from Friends Garage in town (¾ mile, cans).
Scrubbing	Near the quay.
Transport	Buses from market square to Ipswich and Woodbridge (infrequent).
Yacht club	Orford Sailing Club: clubhouse Tel: 450997; Honorary Secretary Tel: 450090.
Telephone	In car park.
Post office	In general store.
Food and drink	Butley Orford Oysterage restaurant, Tel: 450277; Crown & Castle hotel Tel: 450205; Jolly Sailor Tel: 450243; King's Head Tel: 450271; Fish & Chip van by the Castle Wednesday evenings from 1630-1930; Waterside Café near the quay.

Landing on the opposite shore, that is on the Orfordness side, is prohibited by the National Trust, which owns Orfordness. A secret military site from 1913 to the mid-80s, the Ness is the largest vegetated shingle spit in Europe and is well worth a visit for its fascinating natural, local and military history. The National Trust ferry runs from the quay in July, August and September between 1000 and 1400 (Tuesday to Saturday); from Easter to the end of June and in October visits are on Saturdays only. Buy your tickets and an informative guidebook from the National Trust office on the Quay.

Orford's market square boasts the Butley-Orford Oysterage seafood restaurant and shop, plus The Kings Head pub, the Crown and Castle hotel with its Trinity Restaurant and, down Bakers Lane beside the Town Hall, Richardson's Smokehouse (follow your nose to the source of the enticing oak smoke). There is a well stocked village shop with off licence, and a butchers just off the square.

Nearest the quay, a little way up Quay Street opposite the car park, is the Jolly Sailor, an ancient inn steeped in local history. Legend has it that the body of the infamous 18th century smuggler, Will Laud, was brought here after he had been shot by the Preventative Men on the beach near Orfordness.

Orford is steeped in maritime history

The little Thames barge *Cygnet* alongside the Maltings quay with Snape bridge beyond

Chapter four
The River Alde

Tides	HW Slaughden Quay approximately 1hr 15mins after high water at entrance.
	HW Snape Bridge approximately 1hr after HW Slaughden.
	Range: Slaughden Quay springs 2.5m; neaps 1.1m
Charts	Admiralty 2695, SC5607; Stanfords Chart Pack 6; Imray C28, 2000 series; OS map 156
Hazards	Because of winding gutway, make passage between Slaughden and Snape only on rising tide

Above Orford the river turns easterly for a short way and then, abreast Raydon Point, the direction becomes north-easterly along Pigpail Reach. At Raydon Point a water pipe crosses the river to connect with the lighthouse at Orfordness, and the position of the pipe is marked by notice boards.

About 1¼ miles above Orford, the river becomes the Alde and turns more northerly with deeper water towards the west bank, although all through Blackstakes Reach and Home Reach up to Slaughden Quay the best water will be found roughly midway between the banks. Several racing marks (spar buoys) are located in midstream along these upper reaches of the Alde; fleets of Dragons, Squibs, Loch Longs

and other keelboats and the local Lapwing clinker-built dinghies are raced from Aldeburgh Yacht Club. Between Orford and Slaughden the depths vary between 5 and 7m at low water, and the width of the low water channel remains about 200m.

SLAUGHDEN QUAY

Abreast the conspicuous Martello Tower, about a quarter of a mile below Slaughden, the river narrows and shallows for a short distance before deepening again and changing direction abruptly off the quay itself. At this point, the River Alde is separated from the sea only by the sea wall and shingle beach – not much more than 100m in all.

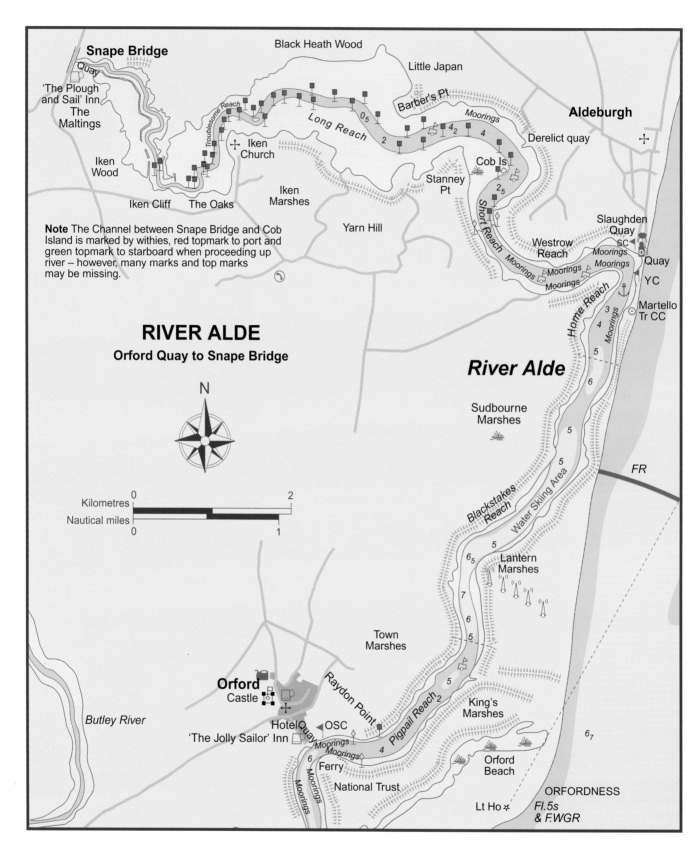

Snape Bridge
Quay
'The Plough and Sail' Inn
The Maltings
Iken Wood
Iken Cliff
The Oaks
Black Heath Wood
Little Japan
Troublesome Reach
Iken Church
Long Reach
Barber's Pt
Moorings
Aldeburgh
Derelict quay
Cob Is
Iken Marshes
Yarn Hill
Stanney Pt
Westrow Reach
Slaughden Quay
SC
Moorings
Moorings
Moorings
Moorings
D
Quay
YC
Short Reach
Home Reach
Martello Tr CC

Note The Channel between Snape Bridge and Cob Island is marked by withies, red topmark to port and green topmark to starboard when proceeding up river – however, many marks and top marks may be missing.

RIVER ALDE
Orford Quay to Snape Bridge

N

| Kilometres | 0 | | 2 |
| Nautical miles | 0 | | 1 |

River Alde
Sudbourne Marshes
FR
Blackstakes Reach
Water Skiing Area
Lantern Marshes
Town Marshes
Butley River
Orford
Castle
Raydon Point
Pigpail Reach
King's Marshes
Hotel Quay
OSC
'The Jolly Sailor' Inn
Moorings
Moorings
Ferry
National Trust
Orford Beach
ORFORDNESS
Fl.5s & F.WGR
Lt Ho

In the 16th century Slaughden Quay was the port area of Aldeburgh – busy with fishing, shipbuilding and coastal trade in salt, fish and coal. Nowadays trade is in pleasure craft – boatyards, two sailing clubs and many moorings. The moorings are administered by the Aldeburgh Yacht Club and are laid athwart the stream on both sides of the channel above Slaughden Quay – boats are moored fore and aft and are closely packed.

If you require a mooring, consult the yacht club or Brian Upson at Upson's Boatyard.

There are three visitors' moorings on which it is possible to raft up on the east side of the river, more or less abeam of the Martello Tower. This particular tower, known as 'CC', was the northernmost of the chain that stretched round from the South Coast and it is completely different from all the others, being

The River Alde makes a huge change of direction at Ferry Point; Slaughden Quay and Aldeburgh Yacht Club can be seen (centre), with the Martello Tower 'CC' (right)

The visitors' moorings at Aldeburgh are abeam of the Martello Tower

Upson's boatyard at Slaughden Quay

quadrafoil in shape. It is currently owned by the Landmark Trust and let out for holidays. There is room to anchor, on the east side, between the visitors' moorings and the Aldeburgh Yacht Club starting hut. On the west side of Home Reach, opposite the Martello tower, there are several rows of keelboat moorings.

When you have either anchored or moored, there is clean landing at the quay near Upson's, on the shingle next to it, or at the pontoons in front of Aldeburgh Yacht Club, which welcomes visiting yachtsmen. Peter Wilson's Aldeburgh Boatyard, about a quarter of a mile towards Aldeburgh from the quay, offers laying-up facilities and chandlery, and specialises in restoring and building classic wooden yachts. Among the boats restored, and in some cases rebuilt, here are Dragons, Six Metres, Loch Longs, a 50 Square Metre windfall yacht, a Mylne yawl, and a replica of the famous Folkboat *Jester*. The distinctive red hulls and tall rigs of two Eight Metres, the restored *If*, originally built in the 1930s, and *Ganymede*, built by Peter in 2007, can often be seen on the Alde if they are not away racing at international regattas.

The major boatyard, with slipway and boathoist, is at Slaughden Quay, where RF Upson & Co builds wooden and glassfibre fishing and work boats as well as offering repair facilities.

ALDEBURGH

Aldeburgh has long been held in high regard by visiting yachtsmen. Frank Cowper wrote in his *Sailing Tours* that it was '...a capital place for boating;' he went ashore to try out an Aldeburgh bathing machine and declared

There is room to anchor between the visitors' moorings and the yacht club starting hut

Aldeburgh Yacht Club

Slaughden Quay, Aldeburgh Port Guide
Local tel code 01728

Moorings	Aldeburgh Yacht Club Tel: 452562 or Brian Upson Tel: 453047.
Water	At yacht club or stand-pipe on quay.
Stores	Shops in Aldeburgh (1 mile). Co-op Foodstore 0830-2000 Monday to Saturday; 1000-1600 Sundays. Early closing on Wednesdays.
Fuel	Diesel from Upson's. Petrol in town (cans).
Gas	From chandlery.
Repairs	Upson's Boatyard slipway and hoists, Tel: 453047.
Chandlery	At Aldeburgh Boatyard nearby, Tel: 452019.
Transport	Buses from Aldeburgh to Saxmundham (eight miles). Trains from Saxmundham to Ipswich and London.
Yacht clubs	Aldeburgh Yacht Club Tel: 452562. Slaughden Sailing Club.
Food and drink	Many hotels, pubs and restaurants in town. Bar and catering at Aldeburgh Yacht Club on weekends and Wednesday evenings.

Aldeburgh High Street is a good place to eat and drink ashore

his dip to be '...very salt and pick-me-uppish.' The fine town, with its Tudor moot hall, has many cultural connections starting with George Crabbe, the 19th century poet, who was born in The Borough. His poem *Peter Grimes* became the inspiration for Benjamin Britten to write the opera of that name. Britten, who lived in Crabbe Street, founded the now world famous Aldeburgh Festival in 1948. The controversial scallop sculpture memorial to Britten is located on the shingle beach towards the north end of the town.

The High Street is a good place to provision – there is a Co-op and several shops offering fresh seafood and other local produce. For eating ashore there is a huge selection of hotels, pubs, restaurants, bistros, cafés, bars, and the justly popular Aldeburgh Fish and Chip Shop.

Many of the attractive cottages in Aldebugh are holiday homes

ABOVE SLAUGHDEN

Above Slaughden the river changes direction and turns inland in a general westerly direction for the five or six miles to Snape Bridge. The character of the river now begins to change and, while the banks become further apart, the low water channel becomes narrower.

Hazelwood Marshes and the Inner Alde Mudflats are Suffolk Wildlife Reserves. A footpath, known as the Sailors' Path, runs slightly inland on the north bank from near Aldeburgh golf club to Snape – it offers an alternative route on foot to Snape (at any state of the tide). This route is thought to have been used in the past by local men who worked at the Maltings in winter and fished from Slaughden and Aldeburgh during the summer months.

From Westrow Reach, the river is frequently marked by withies (some of which have been replaced by posts), with red can topmarks to port and green or with twiggy branches to starboard. These marks are necessarily very numerous – Aldeburgh Yacht Club moorings committee members do their best to maintain them – and local and visiting yachtsmen owe them thanks for undertaking this formidable task. In the days when barges and colliers were trading here there were up to 40 beacons which were used and probably named by the pilots. The 'Lovely Anne' beacon in Church Reach recorded the misdeeds of a schooner of that name which always managed to get ashore at that spot.

These days some of the marks can be in a poor state having lost or broken topmarks and occasionally some are missing altogether. Recent silting has caused changes, particularly in the Little Japan area of Long Reach and around Iken church. For this reason a small boat able to take the ground safely, a lifting-keeler or a dinghy is perhaps the best bet for exploring the upper reaches. *The Ore and Alde Association Guidelines* (published annually) contains a sketch chart showing the marks, but this is no guarantee of their position or their existence. The OS Explorer Map 212 Woodbridge and Saxmundham is also useful as, although it does not show the marks, it does indicate the approximate direction of the gutway in the upper reaches.

The marks are not very conspicuous in certain conditions of light, so a very careful lookout must be kept to see that none is missed. It is advisable to commence a trip to Iken Cliff or Snape Bridge early on the tide so that the tortuous channel can be seen and the marks more easily understood.

Through Westrow Reach and Short Reach there is about 4m in the channel at low water, and a starboard-hand beacon marks the edge of mud extending from the north bank. In Short Reach a power cable crosses the river and is pinpointed by the usual triangular topped beacons. At the top of Short Reach the channel turns north-easterly past two starboard-hand beacons and a port-hand beacon to Stanny Point. A racing buoy

The upper reaches of the Alde, Iken Cliff (bottom left) and Snape Maltings (top left)

is usually located off Stanny Point, but in any case a metal beacon (topped by a swan emblem) marking the remains of the now eroded Cob Island will serve to identify this point in the river.

A derelict brickworks quay and some moorings will be seen over on the east shore and here the channel turns back to the north-west, round a series of three port-hand beacons. Next, three beacons to starboard and three beacons to port mark the channel round Barber's Point and into Long Reach. By this time, the low water channel is but a cable wide, with depths of about 1.5m.

Past Barber's Point, the river widens towards high water to nearly a mile between its banks and, while marshland lies to the south, Black Heath Woods reach down to a sandy beach on the north shore at a spot known locally as 'Little Japan'. At the western end of Long Reach a series of four port-hand beacons follow the course of the channel to where it turns sharply to the south towards Sandy Point. Then the channel turns north-westerly into Short Reach and south-westerly again into Church Reach – the ancient thatched church of St Botolph's stands on a wooded promontory less than a quarter of a mile away on the Iken shore. After this the channel turns westerly into Lower Troublesome Reach and south again into Upper Troublesome Reach.

Beyond the two Troublesome Reaches, the channel closely approaches the shore near a sandy beach, above which a group of oak trees grows. This spot, known as

'The Oaks', is very pleasant and offers good landing near high water. Then comes Cliff Reach, leading up to Iken Cliff itself, where the low water channel again comes to within 20 yards of the shore.

IKEN CLIFF

There is only a metre or so of water at best in the channel abreast Iken Cliff, but the bottom is mud and the spot provides one of the most attractive anchorages on the Alde. There are one or two small boat moorings here and a few dinghies on the foreshore. The 45ft barge *Dinah* (built in Rochester as a yacht in 1887) is kept here and can often be seen moored fore-and-aft just to port of the channel.

A port-hand mark shows the channel past the ancient thatched church of St Botolph on the Iken shore

The Thames yacht barge *Dinah* on her mooring at Iken Cliff, looking downriver towards the church

SNAPE BRIDGE

It is just over a mile from Iken Cliff to Snape Bridge, and the channel, which becomes little more than a gutway, winds between mudbanks and reedbeds, and virtually dries out at low water. However, it is possible for craft drawing up to 2m to reach the quay alongside the Maltings at Snape Bridge, where they must take the mud if staying for more than about an hour. The last tortuous mile or so is marked by a series of port-hand cans and starboard perches.

The virginia creeper-clad maltings were built in the mid-19th century by Newson Garrett, father of the pioneering woman doctor, Elizabeth Garrett Anderson. The malt was taken to London in two steam barges which brought back barley. The maltings closed in 1965 and soon afterwards the concert hall was built as a centre for the Aldeburgh Festival in June, but now it is used throughout the year for many other performances, as well as the Snape Proms in August. The annual Snape Proms programme includes dates when the tides suit those wishing to come by boat.

The original maltings buildings were developed into the Snape Riverside Centre comprising craft shops, exhibitions, galleries and restaurant. Recent ongoing development includes new rehearsal rooms and residential housing. The Maltings is a popular tourist attraction, so the quayside can be crowded on bank holidays and fine summer days.

There is a nominal charge for overnight mooring alongside at The Maltings, where some extra ladders have been added along the quayside to make getting ashore from a yacht easier. The little, tiller-steered Thames barge *Cygnet* (built on the Medway in 1881) sails from here and her topsail is a familiar sight as she twists

Snape Bridge Port Guide – Local tel code 01728	
Maltings Quay Office	Tel: 688303.
Water	On quayside.
Stores	Shop with post office in Snape village (open mornings).
Food and drink	Plough and Sail Tel: 688413; The Crown Tel: 688324; Golden Key Tel: 688510; Concert Hall restaurant, teashop at Maltings.
Snape Maltings Concert Hall	Box Office Tel: 453543.

and turns through the reedbeds near the top of a tide.

The Plough and Sail, the Concert Hall restaurant and the Granary Tea Shop offer a variety of meals. There is water on the quayside, but the nearest supplies, along with two more pubs, the Crown and the Golden Key, are at Snape village, about half a mile away over the bridge.

Approaching the Maltings at Snape, early on the tide

Alongside at Snape Maltings

A Leigh bawley, a vintage motor cruiser and a modern lifting keel Parker yacht alongside at Woodbridge Tide Mill

Chapter five
The River Deben

Tides	At entrance – HW Dover +0.25. Range: springs 3.2m; neaps 1.9m (HW Woodbridge approximately 45mins after high water in entrance)
Charts	Admiralty 2693, SC5607; Stanfords Chart Pack 6; Imray Y16, 2000 series; OS Map No 169
Waypoints	Woodbridge Haven Buoy 51°58'.20N 01°23'.85E (liable to be moved – for latest position contact Thames Coastguard Frinton-on-Sea Tel: 01255 675518)
Hazards	Strong tide and shoals in entrance (seek up-to-date information from Felixstowe Ferry harbour master or www.eastcoastrivers.com). Shoal near west bank between Felixstowe Ferry Sailing Club and Bawdsey Manor. 'Horse' shoal just upstream of Felixstowe Ferry

Inviting a friend to stay with him aboard his schooner *Scandal*, Edward FitzGerald, translator of *The Rubaiyat of Omar Khahyyam*, wrote: 'I think you would like this Bawdsey, only about a dozen Fishermen's Houses, built where our River runs into the Sea over a foaming Bar, on one side of which is a goodsand to Felixstowe and on the other an orange coloured crag Cliff towards Orford Haven; not a single respectable House or Inhabitants or Lodger; no white Cravats, an Inn with scarce a table and

chair and only Bread and Cheese to eat, I often lie here with my Boat: I wish you would come and do so.'

That was a 150 years or so ago, but the Ferry Boat Inn remains, although you may now have more than bread and cheese to eat should you wish.

For today's yachtsman who keeps his boat in the Medway, the Crouch or the Blackwater, a visit to the Deben will usually be made during the summer holiday cruise. The Woodbridge River, as the Deben

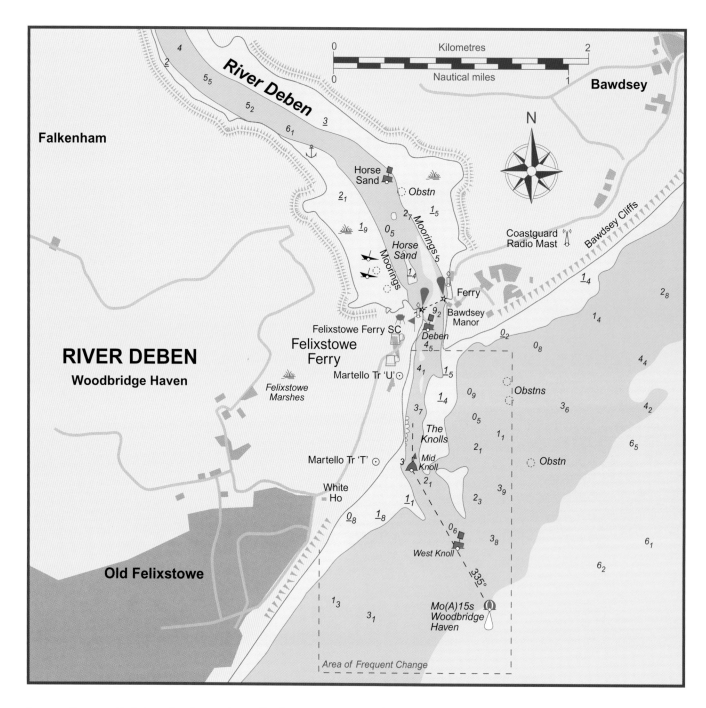

Falkenham

River Deben

Bawdsey

Horse Sand

Obstn

Horse Sand

Moorings

Moorings

Coastguard
Radio Mast

Bawdsey Cliffs

Ferry

Bawdsey
Manor

Felixstowe Ferry SC

Deben

RIVER DEBEN

Woodbridge Haven

Felixstowe
Ferry

Martello Tr 'U'

Felixstowe
Marshes

Obstns

The
Knolls

Obstn

Martello Tr 'T'

Mid
Knoll

White
Ho

West Knoll

335°

Old Felixstowe

Mo(A)15s
Woodbridge
Haven

Area of Frequent Change

is sometimes called, is only about nine miles long, but it is very attractive and nowadays, apart from Deben Cruises' MV *Jahan* which does river trips from Waldringfield, is entirely free from commercial traffic.

Perhaps the thing that comes first to the East Coast yachtsman's mind when he thinks of the Deben is that there is a shifting shingle bar at the entrance to Woodbridge Haven. This bar ought not to worry anyone unduly because there is a pilot on hand at almost all times during the summer months.

Many more yachts enter and leave the river than ever before and since most of them hail from Woodbridge, Waldringfield, Ramsholt or Felixstowe Ferry, their skippers usually have the benefit of local knowledge and so can often act as guide for the newcomer.

Entering the Deben – the West Knoll buoy and Martello Tower 'T'

Nevertheless, when there are no other yachts about and particularly for the first time 'over the bar', it is still a sound idea to consult the harbour master, John White, who will usually hear a call on VHF Ch 8, or come off by prior arrangement. His telephone number is Felixstowe (01394) 270106; mobile 0780 3476621. John White,

Entering the Deben – the Mid Knoll buoy and Martello Tower 'U'

who has been the Felixstowe Ferry harbour master for many years, was also, until recently, the ferryman. It was John who, with Terry Clark of Small Craft Deliveries, produced the indispensable Deben entrance sketch map and printed and distributed it annually until 2007.

Before visiting the Deben you are strongly advised to obtain the sketch chart which is now produced by assistant harbour master, Stephen Read, together with Trinity House and the website www.eastcoastrivers. com. This sketch chart is downloadable; it is also available in a handy laminated form from local marinas, yacht clubs and chandleries.

Stephen Read is the local Trinity House representative and is responsible for laying and maintaining the buoyage in the entrances to both the Deben and the Ore rivers. Stephen can also assist with pilotage into the river.

APPROACHES

Most yachts will approach Woodbridge Haven from the south – often from Harwich harbour, which is only six or seven miles away. A good time to enter the river is about two hours after low water, when there will be a least depth of about 2m over the bar. At low water springs in 2008 there was 0.6m on the bar. With so little water to spare, an entrance should never be attempted when there is a bad sea running. But the appearance of the surrounding shoal water would presumably be enough to scare anyone away on such occasions. A spring ebb can run out of the entrance at six knots and any attempt to enter at such times is certainly not recommended.

When the approach is from Harwich or from the Wallet, a course should be shaped to pass about half a

The Deben entrance at low water showing the Knolls, Felixstowe Ferry and the moorings beyond

Fishing boat ashore at Felixstowe Ferry

Felixstowe Ferry Port Guide
Local tel code 01394

Harbour master	John White Tel: 270106; Mob: 07803 476621; or call *Odd Times* on VHF Ch 08.
Assistant harbour master	Stephen Read Tel: 212512; Mob: 07860 191768.
Water	At yard.
Stores	Limited supplies from café. Fish stall near sailing club.
Chandlery	At boatyard or Seamark Nunn (Trimley St Martin) Tel: 451000.
Repairs	Felixstowe Ferry Boatyard Tel: 282173.
Fuel	Diesel from fuel berth near ferry jetty, petrol from garage in Felixstowe approximately three miles.
Transport	Infrequent bus service to Felixstowe (three miles).
Water taxi	Bawdsey ferry by arrangement Tel: 07709 411511.
Telephone	Box near Ferry Boat Inn.
Yacht clubs	Felixstowe Ferry Sailing Club Tel: 283705. Bawdsey Haven Yacht Club Tel: 410258 (Secretary).
Food and drink	Ferry Boat Inn Tel: 284203 and the Victoria Inn Tel: 271636; Ferry Café Tel: 276305 – fish and chips and all-day breakfasts.

mile off Felixstowe Pier. When approaching the Deben entrance, most of the details along the low-lying shore will be distinguishable – in particular the two Martello towers (Tower 'T' and Tower 'U'); the conspicuous and historic radar pylon just to the north of the entrance to Woodbridge Haven has been replaced by a new Coastguard Radio Mast.

Woodbridge Haven (lit Mo (A) 15s) buoy is maintained by Trinity House and is spherical with red and white vertical stripes.

In recent years the shoal from the Felixstowe shore has extended in a south-easterly direction while the shoal from the Bawdsey shore has advanced to the south. The entrance channel between The Knolls is marked by two

Felixstowe Ferry with the Horse Shoal (left) and the Bawdsey shore beyond; the barge motoring in is the *Victor*

It is possible to land from a dinghy at all states of the tide on the shingle beach by the fishermen's huts at Felixstowe Ferry

buoys named West Knoll and Mid Knoll respectively.

In 2008 the course to steer from the Haven Buoy was approximately 335°T to take you through this passage. Leave the West Knoll red can buoy close to port and turn to starboard into the river once the Mid Knoll green conical buoy comes abeam – just south of Martello Tower 'T'.

Going in on the flood, the tide will now be pushing you really hard and, once abeam of Martello Tower 'U', it is necessary to cross towards the Bawdsey shore in order to leave to port the red can buoy Deben, marking a shoal near the Felixstowe Ferry Sailing Club. The only obstacle then remaining is the Horse Shoal, which occupies the centre of the river immediately above the Felixstowe-Bawdsey Ferry. The Horse Shoal is extensive and dries out in parts to a height of about 1m. The main channel is to eastward of the shoal, the channel to port being full of moored craft. It is safer therefore for a stranger to take the main or starboard channel, where there is plenty of water, until the Horse buoy (red can) is reached at the north end of the shoal.

DEPARTURE

While it is easier to leave Woodbridge Haven on the ebb tide, this results in any south-bound yacht having to face the remainder of the ebb after leaving the river. It is usually more convenient therefore to set off from the Haven at about half-flood, depending upon auxiliary power to push a boat over the fast running tidal stream near Felixstowe Ferry. The force of this stream should never be underestimated and, if an exit is to be made during springs, an engine capable of driving the boat at

five knots will be no more than sufficient unless some help can also be obtained from the sails.

MOORINGS

The Felixstowe Ferry Boatyard will usually find a buoy for visiting yachts among the many moorings between the Horse shoal and the Felixstowe bank. One can land from a dinghy at all states of the tide on the convenient steep-to shingle beach by the fishermen's huts on the Felixstowe shore. Some of the huts now house artists and painters rather than fishing nets but there is still a strong fishy connection at The Ferry. Fresh fish, shell fish and smoked fish are usually for sale from a stall near the sailing club and across the road opposite is the Ferry Café serving fish and chips and all day breakfasts. The two pubs, The Ferry Boat and The Victoria, often have fish on their menus.

When anchoring hereabouts, special care must be taken to avoid the nearby moorings, which are laid athwart the stream. Also, it is essential to have ample scope of cable out because of the great strength of the tide – sometimes amounting to five knots. Whether you pick up a mooring or anchor, take care when using a dinghy to get ashore.

BAWDSEY

At Bawdsey, on the north shore opposite Felixstowe Ferry, the former RAF sailing association clubhouse and slipway is used by Bawdsey Haven Yacht Club (a local non-racing club) and by Bawdsey Quay Watersports Centre for sailing courses. On the first floor of the clubhouse is the Boathouse Café, open at weekends

March to November, Tel: 07900 811826. Bawdsey Manor was built in 1886 by the wealthy stockbroker Sir Cuthbert Quilter. Following its purchase by the Air Defence Committee in 1935, Sir Robert Watson-Watt and his team began their historic work on the development of radar at Bawdsey which, during the Second World War, became part of a chain of RAF radar stations and later a training base. The Manor now provides facilities for courses, conferences and functions.

Following the BBC TV *Restoration* programme in 2004, the Bawdsey Radar Group have opened the Transmitter Block where the Magic Ear exhibition can be visited one Sunday a month and bank holidays from Easter to September. For more details go to www.bawdseyradargroup.co.uk or contact the chairman on Tel: 07821 162879.

There has been a ferry between the Felixstowe and Bawdsey shores for hundreds of years. At one time horses used to swim across while passengers used a rowing boat, after which a chain ferry ran from 1894 to 1931. Nowadays a foot passenger ferry service (also takes bikes) operates from the Felixstowe Ferry shore, on demand from April to October, and will also, by arrangement, operate a water taxi for yachtsmen.

For a mile or two above Felixstowe Ferry the Deben looks very much like a river in Essex rather than Suffolk – with low-lying mudbanks and saltings bordered by a sea wall. The channel, which in its centre has no less than 6m at low water, runs rather closer to the west bank up as far as Ramsholt Reach, where a somewhat abrupt change of scenery occurs.

RAMSHOLT

On the east bank the land rises sharply to form a modest cliff topped by a pleasant group of pine trees. Nestling under the cliff, close to the old barge quay, is an inn, the Ramsholt Arms, and there are few places more attractive than this on any East Coast river.

In recent years the trots of swinging moorings at Ramsholt, like everywhere else, have multiplied. The harbour master, George Collins, usually to be found near the quay or on his yacht *Brio*, will advise on the availability of moorings. His mobile telephone number is 07930 304061 and his home number is Tel: 01394 384318.

From the sandy landing place near the old quay a delightful walk leads along the shore and across a meadow up to Ramsholt Church – in fact the whole Bawdsey peninsula is criss-crossed with footpaths and byways. Recently there was a proposal by the local estate's land agents to charge yachtsmen who wished to land at Ramsholt. Fortunately this scheme was strongly opposed by the Fairways Committee, the Deben Association and local clubs led by Robert Simper. The fact that we can continue to go ashore freely here is due to their efforts on our behalf.

The Ramsholt Arms (Tel: 01394 411229) serves meals; but you may need to book in the summer as this is a popular destination for land-based locals and visitors, not to speak of sailing club cruises in company. There is a metered water tap outside the pub (for which you need to purchase a token), but

The moorings at Ramsholt, with the church (centre) and the Ramsholt Arms (right)

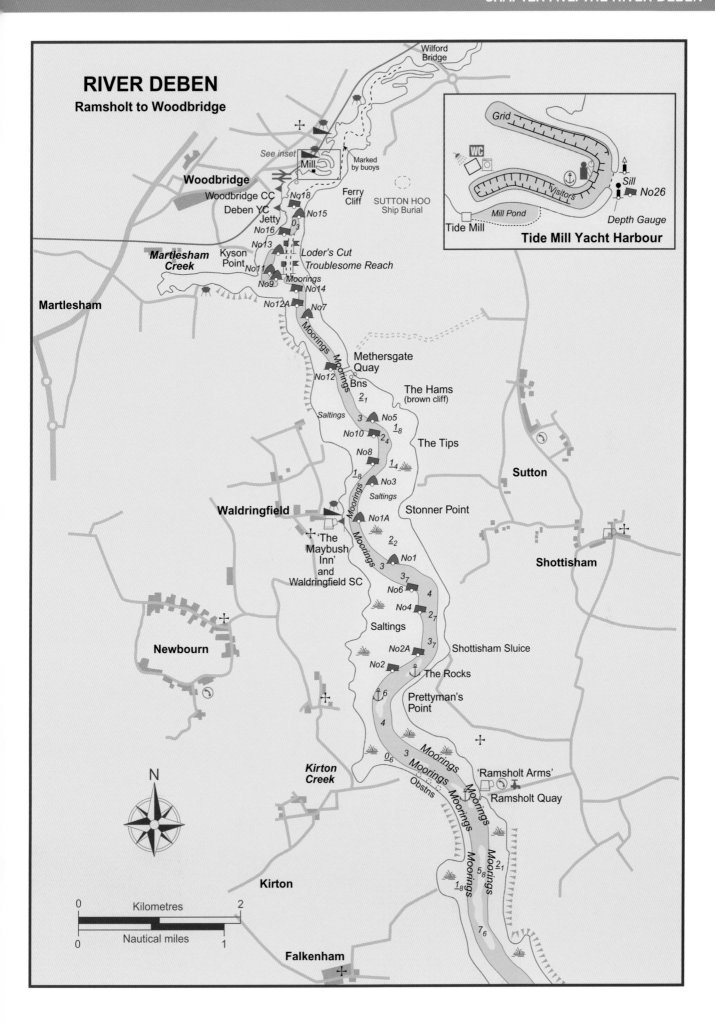

RIVER DEBEN
Ramsholt to Woodbridge

Wilford Bridge

See inset

Mill

Marked by buoys

Woodbridge
Woodbridge CC
Deben YC
Jetty

No18

No15

No16

Ferry Cliff

SUTTON HOO Ship Burial

Martlesham Creek

Kyson Point

No13

No11

Loder's Cut

Troublesome Reach

Martlesham

No9

No12A

Moorings

No14

No7

Moorings

Methersgate Quay

No12

Moorings

Bns

2 1

The Hams (brown cliff)

Saltings

3

No5

1 8

No10

2 4

The Tips

No8

1 4

1 8

No3

Saltings

Waldringfield

Moorings

No1A

Stonner Point

2 2

'The Maybush Inn' and Waldringfield SC

Sutton

Shottisham

3

No1

3 7

No6

4

No4

2 7

Newbourn

Saltings

No2A

3 7

Shottisham Sluice

No2

The Rocks

6

Prettyman's Point

4

Kirton Creek

0 6

3

Moorings

Moorings

'Ramsholt Arms'

Obstns

Ramsholt Quay

Moorings

Kirton

Moorings

Moorings

2 1

5 8

1 8

N

Kilometres

0   2

0   1

Nautical miles

7 6

Falkenham

Tide Mill Yacht Harbour

Grid

WC

Visitors

Sill

No26

Mill Pond

Tide Mill

Depth Gauge

From the quay at Ramsholt there is a pleasant walk to the church

Carrying the tide through the moorings at Ramsholt

the only other facilities at Ramsholt are refuse bins, a public telephone and a post box.

Continuing up-river from Kirton Creek, the channel closely approaches the west bank for a while and then crosses to the east side abreast Ramsholt Woods. There is a very pleasant landing here beneath the trees on a sandy beach known locally as 'The Rocks', so called because of a layer of sandstone rock on the river bed. This septaria is the stone from which Orford Castle was built. There are no roads nearby, but on a fine day there is sometimes a 'traffic jam' of yachts! Yachtsmen who land here are asked to refrain from cutting wood to make fires on the beach – otherwise there will soon be no trees left.

At the top of the Rocks Reach, opposite Shottisham Sluice, is the first of the up-river marks, which continue as buoys or beacons all the way up to Woodbridge. The first two can buoys, 2 and 2a, and all subsequent port hand buoys are numbered evenly, while those on the starboard hand are odd-numbered.

Often to be seen on a mooring off Shottisham Sluice will be Jonathan Simper's Leigh bawley *Mary Amelia* or his father Robert's 1896 lugger *The Three Sisters*. Robert is a local farmer and author of many books about East Anglia and traditional craft.

The next two red cans (4 and 6) mark the mud that stretches out from

the west bank at this bend of the river. Just above these buoys there is a patch of shallow water over a horse (shoal), carrying as little as 1m at low water springs. Above No 6 buoy the channel turns north-west.

A conical green buoy (No 1) is the first to be left to starboard and it marks the downstream end of an extensive tidal island lying between Waldringfield and Stonner Point. At or near high water there is about 1.5m of water between the east bank and the island, but any boat using this route should proceed cautiously and take frequent soundings past Stonner Point.

WALDRINGFIELD

The main channel runs to the west of the island, between two lines of moorings and past green conical buoy No 1A. A gap is left in the moorings opposite

The boatyard at Waldringfield is just upstream of the Maybush Inn

The River Deben at Waldringfield looking east, downriver towards The Rocks and Felixstowe Ferry in the distance

the beach, off the Waldringfield Sailing Club, so that a limited number of visiting yachts can anchor. But when this space is taken up and the fairway opposite the beach is likely to become congested, or racing is in progress, it is better to move either up or down river to anchor with more space, preferably on the west side of the channel. If you require a mooring, Waldringfield Boatyard will be able to advise whether one is available.

Clean landing from a dinghy is possible along the shingle foreshore at almost any time and the Maybush Inn offers splendid views up and down the river.

For about 50 years from the 1840s the fields around the Maybush Inn, and other fields along the banks of the Deben, were dug for coprolite, a mixture of fossilised animal bones and droppings, which was crushed to make fertiliser. This was a booming trade and thousands of tons were shipped to Ipswich by barge until fertiliser began to be imported from abroad. At Waldringfield another flourishing local industry was the making of cement from local river mud, dredged and mixed with chalk. Up to 100 sailing barges a month came into the Deben bringing chalk from the Medway and taking the cement away. Until just before the First World War the fires from the riverside kilns could be seen for miles around.

Continuing up-river from Waldringfield the channel becomes narrower and the mud flats proportionately wider, so that special care must be taken between half-flood and half-ebb when the mud is only just covered.

No 3 buoy, conical green, marks the northern end of the tidal island and, having left this mark to starboard after passing Waldringfield, the next two red can buoys (Nos 8 and 10) identify an extensive spit off the west bank.

Under Ham Woods, described by WG Arnott in *Suffolk Estuary* as '…perhaps one of the most enchanting spots on the river…', there is a low cliff and sandy beach which just invites a picnic – but beware! At high water the beach is hard and sandy, although this hard bottom only extends for a limited distance, after which it abruptly changes to soft mud about a metre deep. If a landing is to be made at 'The Tips', one should return to the dinghy before the mud is uncovered; which happens quickly, for the shore is quite flat hereabouts.

The sandy shore at 'The Tips' resulted from an attempt at the end of the last century by Robert Cobbold to reclaim 150 acres of land from the river. The attempt was stopped by Trinity House, who felt that the scheme would alter the course of the river and interfere with its navigation.

After leaving No 8 and No 10 buoys to port, a green buoy (No 5) is left to starboard below Methersgate Quay, then follows No 12, a red buoy to be left to port opposite the quay.

There are moorings pretty well all the way up from Methersgate Quay to Woodbridge and for the most part they indicate the direction of best water, but additionally there is a closely spaced sequence of channel buoys to guide newcomers through the twists and turns of the Troublesome Reaches. Here even local knowledge is not always enough, as a native of Waldringfield confided to H Alker Tripp (in his book *Suffolk Sea Borders*, 1926), 'Lots of 'em gets stuck wot's used to it, let alone strangers.'

All the navigational and mooring buoys between Methersgate and Woodbridge are under the control of the Kyson Fairways Committee, which decided to name the channel buoys according to the reaches in which they are located. So we now have buoys with names such as Upper Troublesome, Lower Troublesome and Granary Reach; Crummy Moore is named after Major E St F Moore, said to have been a keen local yachtsman.

There are drying moorings and pontoons with water and power at the boatyard on the south side of Martlesham Creek.

One more spherical green (No 13) and one more red (No 16) Granary buoy mark the way to the line of moorings extending down-river from Woodbridge.

Four more port-hand (red can) buoys (Nos 18 to 24) mark the channel between Everson's shed and the entrance to the Tide Mill Yacht Harbour, and are helpful because deeper water changes from side to side of the river hereabouts.

Waldringfield Port Guide – Local tel code 01473	
Water	On quay and at sailing club.
Fuel	Diesel at boatyard, petrol from garage on Woodbridge Road (one mile).
Repairs and chandlery	Waldringfield Boatyard Tel: 736260; slip and 40-ton crane.
Scrubbing posts	Near sailing club.
Transport	Buses to Ipswich.
Telephone	Box near pub.
Yacht club	Waldringfield Sailing Club.
Food and drink	The Maybush Inn, Tel: 736215.

LODERS' CUT

In 1879 a channel was cut to avoid the bend past Kyson Quay. The purpose of Loders' Cut, as the channel is called, was to revive Woodbridge's failing maritime trade. Because it was built not long after the Suez Canal was opened, the Cut was originally marked by the Suez Beacon at its entrance. The plan was not very successful although the Cut remains and can safely be used by shallow draught boats for about 1½ to 2 hours either side of high water. There are port and starboard-hand marks at both ends of the cut, which now has the same water as in the main channel.

Looking across to the Kyson shore from Loders' Cut near high water

A boat leaving the Tide Mill Yacht Harbour. Visitors' berths are round to the left in front of the crane

WOODBRIDGE

Seafaring connections at Woodbridge began with the Anglo Saxons, who arrived by sea and settled in the area. From Tudor times the town was a thriving commercial port and centre for shipbuilding – merchant ships and Royal Naval vessels as large as 600 tons were launched. As well as timber, Suffolk butter was exported and the Deben was busy with vessels engaged in all sorts of trade, including smuggling. After the coming of the railways shipping diminished and the quays silted up.

The poet and philosopher Edward Fitzgerald must have been one of the first yachtsmen on the Deben. Born at nearby Boulge, he returned to live in Woodbridge in 1860 and had a small yacht built which he named *The Scandal* – after the main staple of the town and because she travelled faster than anything on the river, he said. The local auctioneer WG Arnott describes in *Suffolk Estuary* how his mother remembered '…seeing Fitzgerald, complete with old tartan shawl thrown carelessly over his shoulder, walking down The Thorofare in animated conversation with Tennyson.' Together with his skipper 'Posh', 'Old Fitz', as he was known, spent a great deal of time sailing the Suffolk rivers and cruising to Lowestoft, but the Deben was always close to his heart. He is buried in Boulge churchyard.

APPROACHING WOODBRIDGE

There are moorings on both sides of the channel at Woodbridge, but most of the boats take the ground at low water. A few deeper draught craft are located in 'holes' where there is more water; one of these being in midstream abreast of Eversons' building shed, quite close to the re-built bandstand on the river wall promenade. Eversons, which specialises in repairing and maintaining traditional craft, has a jetty and pontoons, half-tide moorings and some fore-and-aft moorings in the aforementioned 'hole'. The clubhouse of the Deben Yacht Club, established in 1838, lies at

The clubhouse of the Woodbridge Cruising Club on the River Wall

The Shire Hall on Market Hill, Woodbridge is home to the Suffolk Horse Museum

the southern end of the River Wall and about halfway between here and the railway station is the Woodbridge Cruising Club whose clubhouse was extended in 2002. The old ferry dock, near the station, is fitted out as a yacht harbour which dries out at low water. However, there are stagings to lie to and the mud is soft; a collection of large traditional craft such as Dutch barges and bawleys is usually berthed here.

Generally, a visiting yacht must expect to come and go on a tide – high water at Woodbridge varies between 30 and 50 minutes later than at Felixstowe Ferry. If you want to stay longer and remain afloat, you will need a berth in the Tide Mill Yacht Harbour, a little further upstream. The old tide mill pool was excavated in the 1960s by Whisstocks, which had been building boats in Woodbridge since 1926, to form a horseshoe-shaped yacht basin where yachts can lie afloat at all states of the tide. The Yacht Harbour has a sill over which there

Woodbridge Port Guide – Local tel code 01394

Tide Mill Yacht Harbour	Tel: 385745; Fax: 380735; VHF Ch 80; email: info@tidemill yachtharbour.co.uk; www.tidemillyachtharbour.co.uk.
Harbour master	Mike Ellis, VHF Ch 80.
Water	Yacht Harbour; stand pipe on Ferry Quay.
Stores	Many shops in town. Early closing on Wednesdays. Budgens in Turban shopping centre 0800-2000 Monday –Saturday, 1000–1600 Sundays. Woodbridge Fine Food Company (deli and much more) just off The Thoroughfare.
Fuel	Diesel and gas from Yacht Harbour and all yards. Petrol from garage on Melton Road.
Chandlery	Small one at Yacht Harbour. Andy Seedhouse (used) Tel: 387833. Classic Marine Tel: 380390.
Chart agents	SCD Ltd, Melton Tel: 382600; www.scd-charts.co.uk.
Repairs	Marine engineer, cranage to 18 tons at Yacht Harbour; Robertsons, Limekiln Quay Tel: 382305, www.robertsons-boatyard.co.uk; Eversons, The Wall Tel: 385786, www.eversonsboats.co.uk.
Sailmaker	Suffolk Sails, Tidemill Way Tel: 386323; www.suffolksails.net.
Rigging	Atlantic Rigging Tel: 610324.
Telephone	Box at station.
Transport	Train service to Ipswich, London and Lowestoft. Buses to Ipswich.
Yacht clubs	Deben Yacht Club, Tel: 386504. Woodbridge Cruising Club, Tel: 382028; www.woodbridgecruisingclub.co.uk
Food and drink	Waterfront Café opposite Tide Mill, Tel: 610333; Riverside Restaurant (next to cinema has dinner and film menu), Tel: 382587; The Captain's Table, Quay Street, Tel: 383145; many hotels, pubs, restaurants and traditional tea-rooms in town.

The Tide Mill Yacht Harbour is a short walk from the centre of Woodbridge

Dinghies can be tied up alongside the Woodbridge Cruising Club pontoon

The toilet, shower and laundry block at the Tide Mill Yacht Harbour

The Riverside Cinema/Theatre also boasts a restaurant

is 1.6m at mean high water neaps and 2.5m at mean high water springs. Craft drawing more than 1.5m (5ft) should not attempt entry after high water on a neap tide. Moorings for waiting yachts, fitted with pick-up buoys and ropes, are placed just outside the entrance where there is an accurate tide gauge. Tidal information regarding the sill can also be found via a link on the Yacht Harbour website.

The pontoon berths in the harbour have been extended in recent years and in 2007 a considerably

The Deben above Woodbridge dries out but is buoyed up to Melton

improved new toilet and shower block with a launderette was opened.

There has been a tide mill where the present Woodbridge Mill stands since 1170. Thanks to an energetic Preservation Society, this last remaining tide mill on the East Coast can be seen in operation, subject to tides, from May to September – details of times are on the notice-board.

Opposite the Tide Mill is the Waterfront Café serving meals made with local produce, and around the ferry dock alongside the railway line is the fascinating yard of Andy Seedhouse who buys and sells mainly second or third-hand small craft and also runs an Aladdin's cave of used chandlery in his headquarters on the Quayside nearby. Just across the railway line is a cinema/theatre and a swimming pool; art galleries and antique shops plus restaurants, cafés and pubs abound in the town; and the Shire Hall on Market Hill is home to the Suffolk Horse Museum.

There are three yards on the west bank of the river above the mill; the first is Robertson's with a slipway and a travel lift. The Granary Yacht Harbour at Dock Lane, Melton, is about a mile above the mill and staff there will send you a sketch chart showing the buoyed channel up to their pontoon berths. The family-run Larkman's yard, at Melton Wharf nearest to Wilford Bridge, mainly uses its 9-ton crane for lifting boats out for their winter lay-up.

A public footpath from Ferry Cliff, opposite the Tide Mill, leads to the site of the Saxon burial ship at Sutton Hoo on the east bank of the river. The burial ground of the Anglo Saxon pagan kings of East Anglia has been called 'page one of English history.' The visitor centre, opened by the National Trust in 2002, includes an exhibition displaying some of the original treasure on loan from the British Museum. For opening hours telephone the National Trust on 01394 389700.

There is always a collection of traditional craft in mud berths at Woodbridge

Halfpenny Pier and the former
Great Eastern Hotel at Harwich

Chapter six
Harwich Harbour

Tides	HW Dover +00.50. Range: springs 3.6m; neaps 2.3m
Charts	Admiralty 1491, 2693, SC5607; Stanfords Chart Pack 6; Imray Y16, 2000 series
Waypoints	**Pitching Ground Buoy** 51°55'.43N 01°21'.05E
	Landguard Buoy 51°55'.45N 01°18'.84E
	Cliff Foot Buoy 51°55'.71N 01°18'.54E
	South Shelf Buoy 51°56'.19N 01°18'.47E
	Guard Buoy 51°57'.07N 01°17'.86E
	Shotley Spit Buoy 51°57'.21N 01°17'.69E
Hazards	Shipping entering and leaving (keep clear of dredged channel)

The earliest indirect reference to a harbour at Harwich is to be found in the *Anglo-Saxon Chronicle* for the year 885: 'The same year sent King Alfred a fleet from Kent into East Anglia. As soon as they came to Stourmouth there met them sixteen ships of the pirates and they fought with them, took all ships and slew the men.

As they returned homeward with their booty they met a large fleet of pirates and fought with them the same day, but the Danes had the victory.'

Some people believe that Bloody Point off Shotley owes its name to the first of these two battles, fought more than a thousand years ago.

Nowhere else on the East Coast is there an expanse of protected deep water as extensive as that formed at the junction of the rivers Orwell and Stour, which emerge to the sea as one between Beacon Cliff and Landguard Point.

The Haven Ports, comprising Felixstowe, Harwich

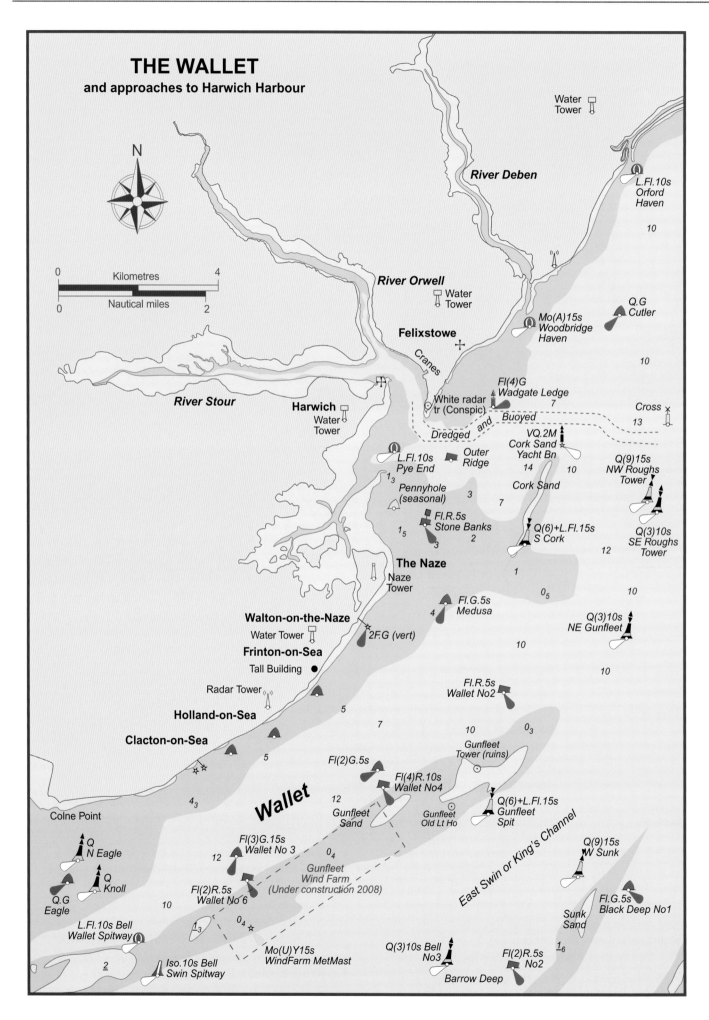

THE WALLET
and approaches to Harwich Harbour

N

Kilometres
0 _____ 4
Nautical miles
0 _____ 2

River Deben

Water
Tower

L.Fl.10s
Orford
Haven

10

River Orwell

Water
Tower

Felixstowe

Mo(A)15s
Woodbridge
Haven

Q.G
Cutler

10

Cranes

Fl(4)G
Wadgate Ledge

7

Cross

River Stour

Harwich
Water
Tower

White radar
tr (Conspic)

Dredged   and   Buoyed

13

VQ.2M
Cork Sand
Yacht Bn

Q(9)15s
NW Roughs
Tower

L.Fl.10s
Pye End

Outer
Ridge

1₃

14

10

Pennyhole
(seasonal)

Cork Sand

3

7

Q(3)10s
SE Roughs
Tower

1₅

Fl.R.5s
Stone Banks

2

Q(6)+L.Fl.15s
S Cork

12

3

1

The Naze
Naze
Tower

0₅

10

Fl.G.5s
Medusa

4

Q(3)10s
NE Gunfleet

Walton-on-the-Naze
Water Tower

2F.G (vert)

10

Frinton-on-Sea
Tall Building ●

10

Radar Tower

Fl.R.5s
Wallet No2

Holland-on-Sea

5

7

10

0₃

Clacton-on-Sea

5

Gunfleet
Tower (ruins)

Fl(2)G.5s

Fl(4)R.10s
Wallet No4

Gunfleet
Old Lt Ho

Q(6)+L.Fl.15s
Gunfleet
Spit

4₃

Colne Point

Wallet

12

Gunfleet
Sand

0₄

Q
N Eagle

Q(9)15s
W Sunk

Q
Knoll

Fl(3)G.15s
Wallet No 3

12

Gunfleet
Wind Farm
(Under construction 2008)

Fl.G.5s
Black Deep No1

Q.G
Eagle

Fl(2)R.5s
Wallet No 6

10

Sunk
Sand

L.Fl.10s Bell
Wallet Spitway

1₃

0₄

1₆

2

Iso.10s Bell
Swin Spitway

Mo(U)Y15s
WindFarm MetMast

Q(3)10s Bell
No3

Fl(2)R.5s
No2

East Swin or King's Channel

Barrow Deep

Looking north over Harwich towards Shotley, with the River Stour branching left and the Orwell to the top right

and Ipswich, between them now handle 357 million gross tons of shipping per year. Some of the world's largest container ships use the berths at the extensive Trinity Terminal at Felixstowe, which is in constant use by day and by night. Meanwhile, many other large commercial ships and ferries will be berthing or leaving the terminal at Harwich/Parkeston in the Stour; others continue up the Orwell to Ipswich Docks.

Further development on the Felixstowe shore will get underway in 2008 when the old P&O ferry terminal and redundant dock basin to the south of the Trinity Terminal are converted to provide an even longer quayside. The Port of Felixstowe will then offer a total of over 4kms of deep water container facilities. In the next few years the entrance to the harbour will undoubtedly become busier, and we may have to watch out for dredgers in the yacht channel while this development is carried out. Whether or not the proposed development of Bathside Bay, on the Harwich side, comes to pass remains to be seen.

It is still imperative for small boat sailors entering or leaving Harwich to stay well clear of the dredged channels, keep to the recommended yacht track, and to maintain a constant look out.

The buoyage and marking of Harwich Harbour and the River Stour are the responsibility of the Harwich Haven Authority. Harbour Operations frequency, VHF Ch 71, is extremely busy at all times and yachtsmen

are asked not to use it. However, it is useful to monitor that frequency in order to anticipate the movements of shipping. On weekends during the summer months the Harbour Patrol Launch will provide assistance and advice to yachtsmen and maintains a listening watch on VHF Ch 71.

APPROACHES

From the south or south-east the harbour can be approached in small craft by two routes, both avoiding the many shoals and banks that lie off the entrance. The course from the south, through the Medusa Channel, is described on page 85 of chapter nine under 'Approaches to Walton Backwaters', and the same directions will serve until the Landguard Buoy (BY N Card Q) is in sight.

Another way into Harwich Harbour from the south-east is through a channel known as the Gullet, passing about midway between the green conical Medusa (Fl G 5s) and the cardinal South Cork buoy (Q (6) + L Fl 15s) and leaving the red can Stonebanks (Fl R 5s) to port.

From the east, the main deep-water channel is exceptionally well marked by pairs of buoys, starting with the cardinal South Shipwash buoy (Q (6) + L Fl 15s) out towards the Sunk. Because of the big ship traffic, yachts must keep to a track south of the dredged channel.

When approaching Harwich Harbour from the Deben or the Alde, the deep-water channel must be crossed as

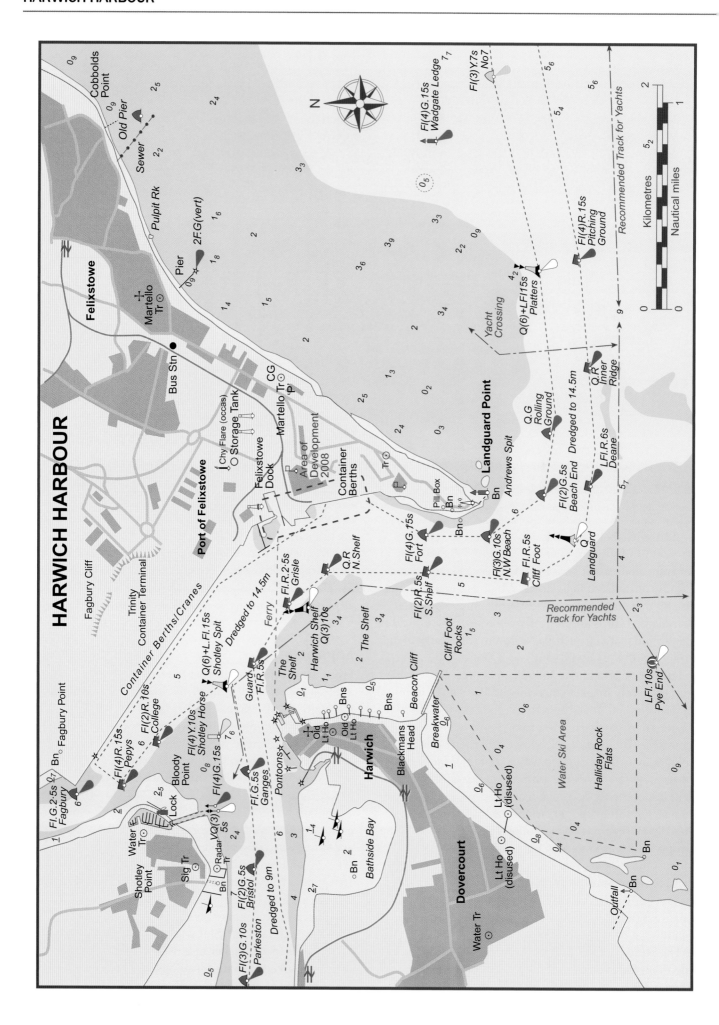

HARWICH HARBOUR

Felixstowe

Port of Felixstowe

Fagbury Cliff

Trinity Container Terminal

Container Berths/Cranes

Fagbury Point

Cobbolds Point

Old Pier

Sewer

Pulpit Rk

2F.G(vert)

Pier

Martello Tr

Bus Stn

Chy Flare (occas)

Storage Tank

Martello Tr

CG

P

Felixstowe Dock

Area of Development 2008

Container Berths

Tr

Pill Box

Bn

Bn

Landguard Point

Andrews Spit

Fl(4)G.15s Wadgate Ledge

Fl(3)Y.7s No7

Fl(4)R.15s Pitching Ground

Q(6)+LFl15s Platters

Yacht Crossing

Recommended Track for Yachts

Kilometres

Nautical miles

Q.R Inner Ridge

Q.G Rolling Ground

LFl.R.6s Deane

Dredged to 14.5m

Fl(2)G.5s Beach End

Fl(3)G.10s N.W Beach

Fl.R.5s Cliff Foot

Q Landguard

Fl(4)G.15s Fort

Q.R N.Shelf

Fl.R.2.5s Grisle

Fl(2)R.5s S.Shelf

Harwich Shelf Q(3)10s

The Shelf

The Shelf

Bns

Bns

Beacon Cliff

Blackmans Head

Cliff Foot Rocks

Breakwater

LFl.10s Pye End

Water Ski Area

Halliday Rock Flats

Recommended Track for Yachts

Dredged to 14.5m

Ferry

Guard Fl.R.5s

Q(6)+L.Fl.15s Shotley Spit

Fl(2)R.10s College

Fl(4)R.15s Pepys

Fl(2)G.5s Bristol

Fl(3)G.10s Parkeston

Dredged to 9m

Radar Tr

VQ(3) 5s

Bn

Water Tr

Shotley Point

Sig Tr

Lock

Bloody Point

Fl(4)Y.10s Shotley Horse

Fl(4)G.15s Ganges

Fl.G.5s

Pontoons

Old Lt Ho

Old Lt Ho

Harwich

Bathside Bay

Bn

Dovercourt

Lt Ho (disused)

Lt Ho (disused)

Water Tr

Outfall

Bn

Bn

Fl.G.2.5s Fagbury

quickly as possible to keep away from the berths at the Port of Felixstowe. The recommended crossing point is from between the south cardinal Platters buoy (Q (6) + L Fl 15s) and the green conical Rolling Ground (QG) buoy, to a point between the red can Pitching Ground buoy (Fl (4) R 15s) and the red can Inner Ridge buoy (QR).

When approaching from the east, yachts must keep to the south of the dredged channel, past the Cork Sand, Pitching Ground and Inner Ridge buoys, before turning to the north, leaving the Landguard and Cliff Foot buoys to starboard.

The old disused leading light towers on the Harwich shore, built in the time of Charles II and still standing, no longer serve as aids to navigation, but the lower one now houses a maritime museum.

The harbour is entered between Beacon Cliff breakwater to the west and Landguard Point, with its

conspicuous radar tower, to the east. The width of the entrance is rather less than a mile, including the water over the Cliff Foot Rocks, located 1.5 to 3 cables off the end of the breakwater. These rocks have as little as 2m over them at low water springs and, when entering the harbour from Dovercourt Bay, they can be avoided by passing within a cable of the beacon on the end of the breakwater. Whenever the latter course is taken, it is important to continue in a north-easterly direction over towards the Felixstowe shore after clearing the breakwater. Any temptation to turn to the north across the Shelf shoal must be resisted until the (seasonal) east cardinal Harwich Shelf buoy (Q (3)10s) has been left to port. The Shelf buoy is not particularly big (to avoid misleading commercial vessels), but as The Shelf shoal has no more than a metre over it in patches at low water springs it is an important mark to locate.

ANCHORAGES

There are several areas within which anchoring is always prohibited because of the necessity to maintain a clear passage for the heavy traffic to and from Ipswich, Parkeston Quay, Harwich and Felixstowe. The principal areas prohibited are:

(1) Anywhere in the fairway or within 200ft thereof between Parkeston Quay and the Rolling Ground buoy.
(2) Between the western edge of the dredged channel and a line joining the Guard and Shelf buoys.

HARWICH QUAY

The UK lighthouse authority, Trinity House, has a long tradition in Harwich – Trinity Pier, the waterfront buildings and buoy store have been its main operations base for nearly 200 years.

Yacht leaving Harwich Harbour having rounded the Harwich Shelf buoy

Outward bound from Harwich. The low and high lights and the church form part of the historic skyline

The Harwich Haven Authority pontoon at Halfpenny Pier

Harwich Haven Authority pontoon mooring berths at Halfpenny Pier can be used by visiting yachts between March and October. Mooring is on a first come first served basis and is free between 0900 and 1600; there is a fee for staying outside these hours which is collected by the pier master. Maximum stay is 72 hours. A swell sometimes makes the pontoon berths uncomfortable; it is advisable to use plenty of fenders which may need adjusting. In good weather it is usually possible for yachts to double or triple berth on both sides of the outer pontoon. Fishing vessels moor inside the pontoon and alongside the quay. Water, showers and toilets are nearby at the head of the pier.

Also at the head of Halfpenny Pier is the Café on the Pier (open daily serving all day breakfasts among other food) and Pier Seafoods, selling fresh fish. A passenger ferry service runs on summer weekends and during school summer holidays from the Pier to Felixstowe and Shotley.

Much of the large expanse of drying mud known as Bathside Bay, to the west of Harwich and north of Dovercourt, is due to be filled in when a new container port is constructed to double existing cargo facilities at Harwich.

HARWICH TOWN

Harwich Town abounds in maritime history. The treadmill crane, on the green near the lighthouses, dates back to the 1660s when Harwich was first a naval base, with Pepys as its MP. When Nelson came to Harwich in the 32-gun frigate *Medusa* in 1801, he was said to have lodged at the Three Cups while checking the coastal gun batteries. To avoid beating out of the harbour when he left, Nelson found a local marine surveyor to pilot his vessel past the Naze and into deep water using what is now known as the Medusa Channel.

Among the many museums open during summer months are the Maritime Museum in the Low Lighthouse, the Lifeboat Museum, the circular Napoleonic Redoubt fort, the Wireless and TV Museum in the High Lighthouse and the RNLI Boathouse museum. Town tours are organised from the Ha'Penny Pier visitor centre. The restored Electric Palace cinema in King's Quay Street shows films at weekends.

The rather imposing Great Eastern Hotel overlooking Halfpenny Pier is now flats. The next door Pier Hotel was once the headquarters of the Royal Harwich Yacht Club, founded in 1843 when one of its chief functions was to organise the Harwich Regatta, attended by royalty, such as the Prince of Wales and the Kaiser, with their great yachts. In *The First of the Tide*, Maurice Griffiths recalls 'It was the custom for yachts of what was known as The Big Class to commence their racing season with the RHYC regatta. The presence of His Majesty's cutter *Britannia* always drew every kind of vessel to watch. What a sight those great racing cutters were as they jilled around by their starting line… but for me perhaps the most impressive sight was *Britannia*'s huge jackyard tops'l, its canvas setting as smooth as a sheet of white paper…'

The circular Napoleonic Redoubt Fort has been restored by the Harwich Society

Harwich Port Guide – Local tel code 01255

Harbour master	Tel: 243030 or 243000.
Harbour operation	Listen on VHF Ch 71; Ch 68 in River Orwell.
Harbour patrol launch	Summer weekends 0800-1800 – provides assistance and advice; VHF Ch 71.
Moorings	Pontoon berths at Halfpenny Pier (free 0900-1600, pay piermaster other times).
Water	Halfpenny Pier.
Toilets, showers, waste disposal	Halfpenny Pier.
Stores	Shops in town, including Co-op. Early closing on Wednesdays.
Fuel	Nearest garage in Dovercourt.
Chandlery	Harwich Chandlers, Kings Head St, Tel: 504061.
Sailmaker	Dolphin Sails Tel: 243366.
Transport	Good train service to London. Buses from quayside to Colchester, Manningtree, Walton-on-the-Naze. Coach service to London. Harwich Harbour Foot Ferry between Harwich, Felixstowe, Shotley (weekends, bank holidays, school summer holidays) Tel: 07919 911440 (mobile).
Yacht clubs	Harwich and Dovercourt Sailing Club; Harwich Town Sailing Club.
Food and drink	The Pier Hotel (bistro and restaurant) Tel: 241212, Halfpenny Pier Café, pubs in town. Fresh fish can be bought from Pier Seafoods.

Harwich Haven Authority's annual Guide to Harwich Harbour and its Rivers *is available free from Navigation House, Angel Gate, Harwich CO12 3EJ, www.hha.co.uk*

The Electric Palace cinema in King's Quay Street

SHOTLEY

On the north shore at Shotley there is good anchorage except in strong southerly or westerly winds. Probably the best spot to choose is inside the trot of moorings situated about two cables south-east of Shotley Pier. Three or four metres with a mud bottom is easy to find here, within a short distance from both the hard and the pier.

The Ganges training base is no more. Only the flag-staff remains to remind us that once a year some brave cadet would stand proudly atop its cap.

The entrance to Shotley Point Marina

SHOTLEY MARINA

To reach the marina from Shotley Spit south cardinal buoy, a yacht should proceed parallel to the deep water channel into the River Stour, passing just south of the seasonal yellow pillar buoy Shotley Horse and then close north of the conical green Ganges buoy to the posts marking the outer end of the dredged channel leading to the marina lock-gates. The port-hand post is yellow and black with east cardinal topmark (VQ (3) 5s) and the starboard-hand post is green with starboard-hand topmark (Fl (4) G 15s).

A special form of indicating signal operates at the Shotley Marina to facilitate keeping to the dredged channel leading to the lock (which is manned 24 hours a day). The INOGON system, as it is called, depends upon the 'passive interaction between the helmsman's line of vision and a mosaic pattern produced by the leading mark.' The practical result is that when a yacht is on the correct bearing, a vertical black line will be seen down the middle of the screen, while any deviation from the correct course will cause the moire pattern to form arrows indicating whether course should be changed to port or to starboard. The density of the arrow pattern will indicate how great the correction should be.

There are waiting pontoons on the port-hand just outside the lock. A passenger ferry service links Shotley with Harwich and Felixstowe, calling at the marina Easter to mid-September at weekends and daily during school summer holidays.

Shotley Point Marina looking across the Orwell to Fagbury Point

The container terminal at Felixstowe now extends as far as Fagbury Point

FELIXSTOWE DOCK

When, in 1886, Colonel Tomline dug out a dock at the end of his private railway, he could never have dreamed of the port of Felixstowe as it is today.

The container terminal, lined with giant cranes, now extends up river as far as Fagbury Point; in 2008 the old P&O ferry terminal and Tomline's long-since redundant dock basin to the south of the Trinity Terminal were being converted to provide an even longer quayside. So nowadays it is hard to imagine that in *We Didn't Mean to Go to Sea* (Arthur Ransome 1937) Jim Brady anchored the *Goblin* off Felixstowe, near the North Shelf buoy, and rowed ashore to get petrol. Left on board, the Walker children '…watched the little black dinghy disappear between the pierheads into Felixstowe Dock.' And so began their great adventure…

Shotley Marina Guide – Local tel code 01473

Shotley Marina	Tel: 788982, VHF Ch 80; www.eastcoastmarinas.co.uk.
Berths	350.
Water	On pontoons.
Fuel	Diesel just inside marina, petrol from garage in Shotley.
Gas	Calor and Camping Gaz from lock control tower (collect at lock gates).
Stores	During summer months, plus off-licence.
Repairs	Full range of services, 30 ton travel-lift, 10 ton crane.
Chandlery	On site.
Transport	Bus service from Shotley to Ipswich. Harwich Harbour Foot Ferry between Harwich, Felixstowe, Shotley (weekends, bank holidays, school summer holidays) Tel: 07919 911440 (mobile).
Telephones	In shower block and in Shipwreck pub lobby.
Food and drink	Restaurant and Shipwreck pub, Tel: 788865, at marina (breakfast available in summer months); Bristol Arms pub in Shotley village, Tel: 787200.

Ipswich Haven Marina looking
across to the Old Custom House

Chapter seven
The River Orwell

Tides	HW Dover +0100. Range: springs 3.7m; neaps 2.3m. HW Ipswich approx 15mins after Pin Mill
Charts	Admiralty 1491, 2693, SC5607; Stanfords No 6; Imray Y16, 2000 series; OS map 169
Waypoints	Pepys 51°57'.74N 01°16'.90E
	College Buoy 51°57'.55N 01°17'.33E
	Orwell No 1 Buoy 51°58'.28N 01°16'.66E
Hazards	Large ships in narrow dredged channel

In his book *Orwell Estuary*, WG Arnott commented on the unchanging nature of much of the river: 'One wonders that the river and its surroundings remain so unspoilt and have suffered so little from the overspill of Ipswich. For this we have largely to thank the much maligned landowners of the estates along its banks. These estates represented a system for which some will say there is little moral justification, but...in the case of the Orwell (it) has saved its banks from spoilation.'

In the year 2000, nearly 50 years later, the river from Collimer Point to the Orwell Bridge is still lined with delightful wooded banks and sandy foreshores, just as Arnott described it in 1954.

The Orwell extends for about nine miles in a general north-westerly direction from the northern side of Harwich Harbour to the docks at Ipswich. Commercial traffic uses the river, some of which is surprisingly large and includes Ro Ro ferries. For the benefit of these ships, up to 20 a week, a dredged and well-buoyed channel is provided by the Ipswich Port Authority. There is an average depth of 7.5m in the main channel, for a width of about two cables, although at high water, with the mud all covered, the width from bank to bank is almost a mile.

On leaving Harwich Harbour, the entrance to the Orwell lies between Shotley Point to the west and the

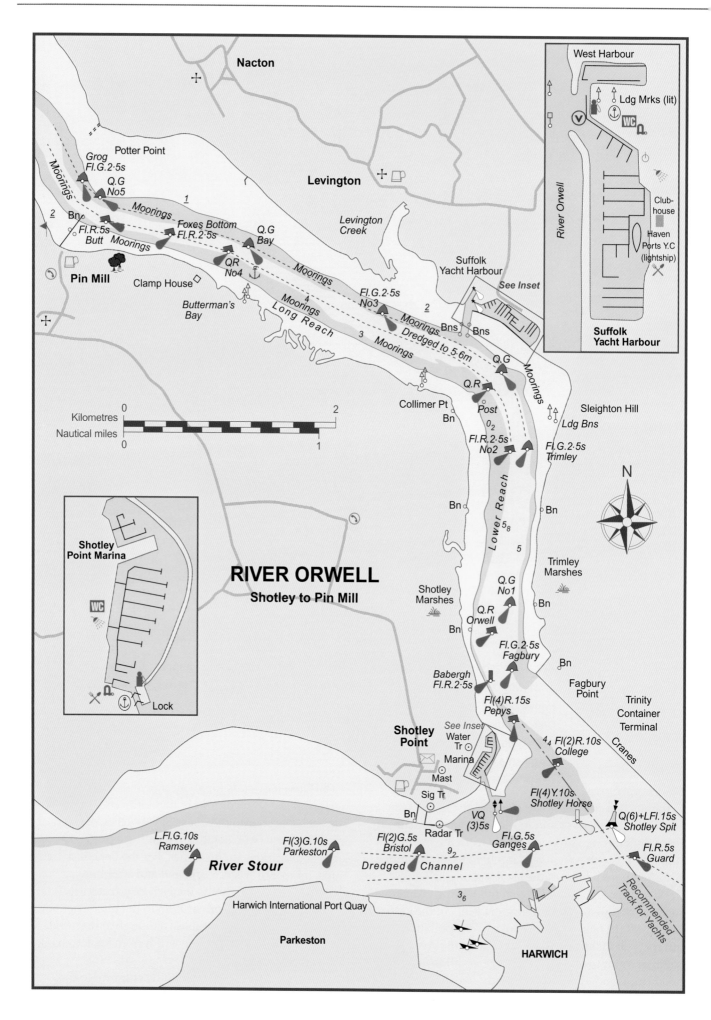

West Harbour

Ldg Mrks (lit)

WC

Club-house

Haven Ports Y.C (lightship)

River Orwell

Suffolk Yacht Harbour

Nacton

Potter Point

Grog
Fl.G.2·5s

Q.G
No5

Levington

Levington Creek

Moorings

1

Bn

2

Fl.R.5s
Butt

Foxes Bottom
Fl.R.2·5s

Q.G
Bay

Moorings

Pin Mill

Clamp House

QR
No4

Butterman's Bay

Moorings

Long Reach

4

3

Moorings

Dredged to 5·6m

2

Bns

Bns

Fl.G.2·5s
No3

Moorings

Q.G

Q.R

Post
0₂

Fl.R.2·5s
No2

Fl.G.2·5s
Trimley

Collimer Pt
Bn

Sleighton Hill

Ldg Bns

Kilometres
0   2

Nautical miles
0   1

Bn

Lower Reach

5₈

5

Bn

Trimley Marshes

Bn

RIVER ORWELL

Shotley to Pin Mill

Shotley Point Marina

WC

Lock

Shotley Marshes

Bn

Q.G
No1

Q.R
Orwell

Bn

Fl.G.2·5s
Fagbury

Bn

Fagbury Point

Trinity Container Terminal

Cranes

Babergh
Fl.R.2·5s

Fl(4)R.15s
Pepys

4₄ Fl(2)R.10s
College

Shotley Point

See Inset
Water Tr

Marina

Mast

Sig Tr

Bn

Radar Tr

VQ
(3)5s

Fl(4)Y.10s
Shotley Horse

Q(6)+LFl.15s
Shotley Spit

L.Fl.G.10s
Ramsey

Fl(3)G.10s
Parkeston

Fl(2)G.5s
Bristol

9₂

Fl.G.5s
Ganges

Fl.R.5s
Guard

River Stour

Dredged Channel

3₆

Recommended Track for Yachts

Harwich International Port Quay

Parkeston

HARWICH

N

Suffolk Yacht Harbour looking east, showing entrance at low water

northern extension of Felixstowe's deep-water container berth quays to the east. The two channel marks indicating the entrance are Shotley Spit buoy (S Card YB Q (6)+L Fl 15s) and the red can College buoy (Fl (2) R 10s) on the west bank opposite the Trinity container terminal. This terminal, the UK's longest continuous quay at 2,354m, can handle two of the largest container ships at the same time. Some of these ships are well over 300m in length so they are unable to turn off the

berths and have to manoeuvre stern first to or from the swinging area east of Shotley Spit and Guard buoys. For this reason the recommended yacht track into the Orwell passes just to the west of the Shotley Spit south cardinal buoy, which is left to starboard.

In the same way, when entering the Orwell from the Stour it is not necessary to round Shotley Spit buoy, instead yachts should round the Shotley Horse yellow pillar buoy (Fl (4) Y 10s) which is laid seasonally to keep small boats clear of the main shipping channel.

EAST SHOTLEY

Many years ago barges used to be seen lying at anchor just inside the river on the western shore, roughly north-east of East Shotley Martello Tower (now topped by a large green water tank). However, the proximity of the extended Trinity container terminal at Fagbury Point on the opposite bank makes the Stone Heaps anchorage less desirable these days.

The red can lit buoys, Pepys and College, up river of Shotley Point Marina, the green conical buoy (Fl G 2.5s) Fagbury, plus the red pillar buoy (Fl R 2.5s) Babergh are maintained by the Harwich Haven Authority, but all of the other buoys in the Orwell are the responsibility of the Ipswich Port Authority. The

College is on the west bank, opposite the container terminal

first pair of their buoys are the Orwell (QR) and No 1 (QG). A telegraph cable crosses the river between Fagbury Point and the Shotley shore, its precise position being indicated by red and white beacons with diamond-shaped topmarks. Other cables cross the river further up and are all marked in the same way, with a beacon on each shore.

Above Fagbury Point the river follows a northerly direction through Lower Reach to Collimer Point. There is low, marshy ground on either side of Lower Reach, but behind the marshes are hills which close in on the river abreast Collimer Point. A little below the point is a pair of lit buoys marking the width of the channel that is dredged to 6m all the way up to Ipswich. The starboard-hand green conical buoy (Fl G 2.5s) is marked Trimley and its pair is No 2 (Fl R 2.5s). Abreast of Collimer Point itself is a second pair of buoys – both of which are lit. There is also a tide gauge on the Point, and inshore of that are the remains of another of the hards that once were in regular use along both banks of the river. On the opposite shore it is also possible to land fairly conveniently just south of a small area of saltings below Sleighton Hill.

After rounding Collimer Point and entering Long Reach, the direction of the river becomes north-westerly and the true character of the Orwell is revealed. From this point on both shores, moorings extend almost all the way upriver to the Orwell Bridge.

Just above Collimer Point, on the north side of the river, is the Suffolk Yacht Harbour at Stratton Hall,

near Levington Creek. The entrance to the harbour is a dredged channel about 30m wide, holding some 2.5m of water at mean low water springs.

The entrance channel is marked at its outer end by a spherical red and white buoy 400m due south of the entrance, and then by port and starboard poles with topmarks. There are leading lights at night (outer Iso Y and inner Oc Y 4s).

Visitors can, if there is space, temporarily leave their yachts at a pontoon (which is also the fuel berth) just inside and opposite the entrance, while reporting to the harbour master for instructions. The harbour has been extended over the years and, with the most recent West Harbour deep water development, now provides 550 permanent berths, with another 50 swinging moorings outside in the river. The focal point of the pontoons is the Haven Ports Yacht Club headquarters on the old Cromer light vessel No 87, where visiting yachtsmen will be made welcome. A mini store next to the chandlery is open daily and there is now a second shower, toilet and laundry block adjacent to the new West Harbour.

From the yacht harbour a pleasant walk of just over a mile, starting out along the seawall footpath beside Levington Creek, will bring you to Levington and the 14th century Ship Inn with its thatched roof, sited on the hill near the village church. The pub serves excellent food, but those with families need to be aware that children are not allowed inside.

Deep draught boats, unsure of the entrance, can

The Kim Holman-designed *Fanfare of Essex* on a mooring in Butterman's Bay. Clamp House can be seen on the shore

The moorings at Pin Mill, with the Butt and Oyster and Alma Cottage at the top of the hard

sometimes find a mooring free near the entrance buoy. Rows of moorings extend above and below the Suffolk Yacht Harbour on both shores.

The next buoy, No 3 (G Con Fl G 2.5s), lies off the entrance to Levington Creek, which is marked by withies. This little drying gutway up to the old wharf

Suffolk Yacht Harbour Port Guide
Local tel code 01473

Yacht Harbour office	Tel: 659465 VHF Ch 80 (daylight hours); www.syharbour.co.uk.
Berths	550.
Water	Near entrance. All pontoons.
Fuel	Petrol and diesel from pumps near entrance, gas from chandlery.
Stores	Mini-market and off-licence (0800-1730 daily) next to chandlery.
Repairs	Shipwrights and engineers on site. Travelhoist, slipway and scrubbing posts.
Chandlery	Store on site, Tel: 659240.
Sailmaker	Quantum Tel: 659878.
Transport	Buses run to Felixstowe and Ipswich (1 mile walk). Local taxi services: Tel: 222222; 407070; 417417.
Yacht clubs	Haven Ports Yacht Club aboard light vessel 87; Tel: 659658 during opening hours.
Food and drink	Bar and restaurant at Yacht Club on light vessel; The Ship Inn, Levington Tel: 659573 (booking not possible). Good food but children are not allowed inside.

at the head of the creek was once regularly used by trading barges but as obstructions in the mud have been reported, it is probably no longer suitable for navigation, except perhaps by dinghy.

Between Levington and Potter Point there is another pair of lit buoys – the Bay is a green conical (QG), while its opposite – a red can buoy No 4 – has a Q flashing red light.

There is the possibility of anchoring on the south side, just below No 4 (QR) buoy near Clamp House, where there will be shelter from the south-west and landing is possible. This time-honoured anchorage, known as Buttermans Bay, is where the grain ships, barques and barquentines used to offload their cargoes into sailing barges. The mooring buoys are now used by the Sail Barge Association. A footpath to Pin Mill leads through the National Trust woods at Clamp House.

Behind the woods on the opposite shore is Broke Hall, the birthplace of Rear Admiral Sir Philip Broke. Broke was Captain of HMS *Shannon*, the frigate that won immortal fame for her capture of the USS *Chesapeake* off Boston in 1813. This battle is considered to be the finest single-ship action in the age of sail, and the victory was due in no small part to Broke's gunnery drill, described as the best of any vessel in the Royal Navy. Broke was severely wounded as he led the boarding party and, after returning to a hero's welcome, he retired from active service to his home in Suffolk.

PIN MILL

For the East Coast cruising man, the Orwell means Pin Mill and it is this unique hamlet, with its waterside inn and the prospect of a collection of Thames barges on the hard, that brings us back time and time again. Arthur Ransome sailed from Pin Mill and described it as '...that most charming anchorage'. The opening chapters of both *We Didn't Mean to Go to Sea* and *Secret Water* are set at Alma Cottage, just up the lane from the Butt and Oyster.

These days it is preferable to find a mooring rather than drop an anchor at Pin Mill. Visitors' buoys are generally located in the trot of moorings nearest to the channel between Fox's Bottom buoy and the end of the Hard. Visitors should pick up a mooring with the name *Ward* on it, which also usually shows a mobile telephone number with which to contact the harbour master Tony Ward. Commercial shipping rounding Potter Point passes very close to the outer rows of moorings and occasionally leaves considerable wash.

As Francis B Cooke wrote so aptly in *Coastwise Cruising* (1929), 'It must not be supposed, however, that there is no mud at Pin Mill, for, as a matter of fact, there is a particularly generous supply at low water.' The very long hard at Pin Mill is still not long enough to provide landing at low water springs. You may have to wait an hour or more to avoid the mud, and boots are advisable. When the tide is rising it is as well to haul the dinghy well up the gulley formed by the Grindle, a stream running down the side of the hard.

The upper hard at Pin Mill is no half-hearted affair, but a fine expanse of firm shingle on which there are sometimes barges undergoing repair. Scrubbing, too, is made easy by reason of the several stout posts that are available. At the top of the hard is the Butt and Oyster Inn – perhaps the most famous of East Coast watering holes – itself awash at high water springs. The hard continues, almost imperceptibly, straight into

a lane that leads up the valley to Chelmondiston.

Visiting yachtsmen are welcome at Pin Mill Sailing Club, whose clubhouse is by the riverside just beyond the yard of Harry King and Sons, builders of *Selina King* for Arthur Ransome and many other wooden boats, several to designs of Maurice Griffiths. The chandlery immediately next door to the Butt has been converted into an art gallery and gift shop.

CHELMONDISTON

Chelmondiston – Chelmo for short – is about three-quarters of a mile from the hard at Pin Mill, and the walk up the lane seems to belong to Devon rather than Suffolk. There is Hollingsworths butcher's and general store, a post office, the Venture pub (formerly the Red Lion), The Foresters Arms, plus a Cantonese take-away in this busy little village.

Above Pin Mill the channel turns more northerly into Potter Reach. Beyond the buoy marking Potter Point, on the eastern shore, is Orwell Park, home to an independent boarding and day school. No 6 buoy (R Can QR) marks the mud off Hall Point, while a green conical buoy (QG) on the other side of the channel is located in Park Bight, together with a continuous line of moorings used by craft based on Woolverstone Marina.

Park Bight marks the east side of the dredged channel

WOOLVERSTONE

The dredged channel now approaches the west bank of the river to within a cable, abreast the Cathouse buoy (G Con Fl G 2.5s). Under no circumstances should a boat anchor inside the buoyed channel, as vessels up to 9,000 tons use the river regularly. The Cathouse is a 200-year-old gothic Folly, built by the riverside in the grounds of Woolverstone Hall. Legend has it that a silhouette of a cat was placed in the window overlooking the Orwell to show approaching smugglers that the coast was clear.

A footpath from Cathouse Hard winds through the 22 acres of Woolverstone Park and along the shoreside to Pin Mill. Francis B Cooke strolled back this way in the 1920s '…admiring the magnificent timber and bracken. We come to a glade and disturb a herd of

Pin Mill Port Guide – Local tel code 01473	
Harbour master	Tony Ward, Tel and Fax: 780621; Mob: 07714 260568; email: moorings.pinmill@ virgin.net.
Water	Alongside clubhouse at Pin Mill Sailing Club.
Stores	General store and butcher at Chelmondiston. Early closing on Wednesdays.
Repairs	Harry King Tel: 780258 or Webbs boatyard Tel: 780291.
Scrubbing post	On hard (for use, consult harbour master).
Transport	Bus service to Ipswich and Shotley from Chelmondiston.
Yacht club	Pin Mill Sailing Club Tel: 780271; www.pmsc.org.uk.
Telephone	In public car park, 100 yards up the lane.
Food and drink	The Butt & Oyster, Tel: 780764; Cantonese Take-Away restaurant Chelmondiston, Tel: 780494; Foresters Arms and The Venture pubs, both situated in Chelmondiston.

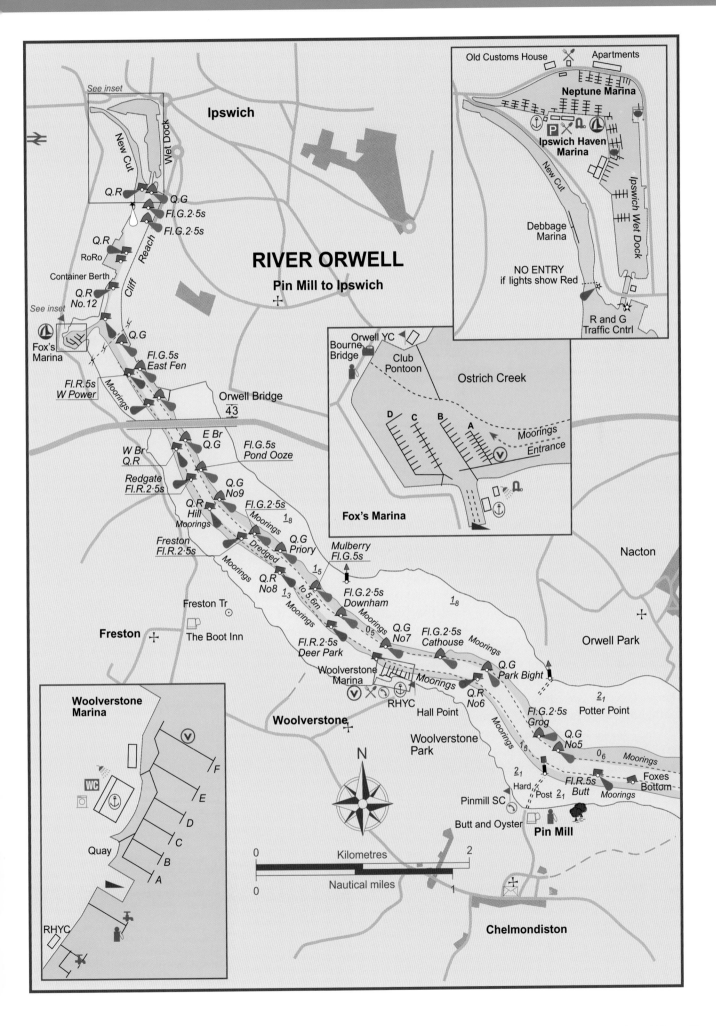

Ipswich

Wet Dock

New Cut

Q.R
Q.G
Fl.G.2·5s
Fl.G.2·5s

Q.R
RoRo
Container Berth
Q.R No.12

See inset

Cliff Reach

Fox's Marina

Q.G

Fl.G.5s East Fen

Fl.R.5s W Power

Moorings

Orwell Bridge
43

RIVER ORWELL

Pin Mill to Ipswich

E Br Q.G
W Br Q.R
Redgate Fl.R.2·5s
Fl.G.5s Pond Ooze
Q.G No9
Q.R Hill
Moorings
Freston Fl.R.2·5s
Fl.G.2·5s
Moorings
Dredged
Q.G Priory
Q.R No8
to 5.6m
1_3
1_5
1_8
Mulberry Fl.G.5s
Moorings

Freston Tr
The Boot Inn
Freston

Fl.R.2·5s Deer Park
Fl.G.2·5s Downham
Moorings
Q.G No7
Fl.G.2·5s Cathouse
Moorings
1_8

Woolverstone Marina
RHYC
Hall Point
Woolverstone
Woolverstone Park

Q.G Park Bight
Q.R No6
Fl.G.2·5s Grog
Q.G No5
2_1 Potter Point
1_6
0_6 Moorings
2_1
Hard
Post 2_1
Fl.R.5s Butt
Foxes Bottom
Moorings
Pinmill SC
Butt and Oyster
Pin Mill

Nacton
Orwell Park

N

0   Kilometres   2
0   Nautical miles   1

Chelmondiston

Inset top right — Ipswich:
Old Customs House
Apartments
Neptune Marina
Ipswich Haven Marina
New Cut
Debbage Marina
Ipswich Wet Dock
NO ENTRY if lights show Red
R and G Traffic Cntrl

Inset middle — Fox's Marina:
Orwell YC
Bourne Bridge
Club Pontoon
Ostrich Creek
D C B A
Moorings
Entrance
Fox's Marina

Inset bottom left — Woolverstone Marina:
Woolverstone Marina
WC
Quay
F
E
D
C
B
A
RHYC

The Royal Harwich Yacht Club pontoons at Woolverstone

timid deer, which speedily seek cover, and in a few minutes we are back at the Butt and Oyster, where we collect our water-jars which we had left to be filled in our absence...'

On the south bank below Cathouse Hard, the Royal Harwich Yacht Club (RHYC) has serviced pontoon berthing for members' yachts. Berths on the outside pontoons are designated for visitors and overnight stays are possible – contact the RHYC berthmaster to arrange a berth. The club was formed in 1845 and by 1848 was holding the first Eastern Coast Regatta in Harwich Harbour, its headquarters for the next 100 years. In 1946 the club moved up-river to its fine present-day site at Woolverstone where its members sail cruisers, dinghies, Ajax keelboats and the 60-year-old RH One-Designs. The RHYC is happy to allow visiting yachtsmen to use its clubhouse and facilities which, during the season, consist of showers, restaurant and a bar.

Immediately upstream, just south of the dredged channel, is the Woolverstone Marina where 235 pontoon berths are accessible at all times. Visitors can berth on the ends of any pontoon or on Pontoon F, the last one upstream. A marina master is on duty seven days a week throughout the year, while facilities include a fuel barge at the end of the short pier, a chandlery and stores as well as the on site Buttermans Bar and restaurant.

No 7 buoy (QG), together with a red can above the marina, mark the commencement of Downham Reach and here the dredged channel becomes less than a cable wide so that the buoys must be strictly observed unless it is near high water. Another green conical buoy, Downham (Fl G 2.5s), marks the eastern edge of the channel through Downham Reach; the western edge is indicated first by Deer Park, a lit red can (Fl R 2.5s), and then by No 8 red can buoy (QR) abreast the prominent tower in Freston Park. Just above No 8 buoy there is a green conical buoy (QG) called the Priory, on the east side of the channel. This is followed by four pairs of lit buoys up to the Orwell Bridge.

Moorings line both banks of the Orwell up to the bridge

Along here are a number of small boat moorings just outside the channel on both sides; they belong to the Stoke Sailing Club whose clubhouse is immediately below Freston Tower. This six-storey Elizabethan edifice was built in 1578 by an Ipswich merchant, Thomas Gooding, possibly as a folly or a look-out, but undoubtedly to show off his wealth. The building has been renovated recently by the Landmark Trust and now provides holiday accommodation, with wonderful views both up and down river. From Freston Hard it is a short walk up the road to the Boot Inn on Freston Hill where they serve freshly cooked food and in front of which buses stop on the Shotley-Ipswich route.

By now the Orwell Bridge will dominate the view ahead, but since it provides a clearance of 125ft (38m) and the width between the only navigable span is 300ft (92m), it should inconvenience yachtsmen very little. No ship can hit any of the eight piers that rise from the river bed because their bases are all protected by artificial islands. Near the bridge are the remains of an old Roman crossing point, originally constructed of shale and stone – a band of shale can still sometimes be seen at low tide.

However, the bridge crosses the navigable channel at an angle so that the pilot of any commercial vessel about to pass under it will have his attention fully occupied without having to worry about any nearby yacht. Common sense therefore dictates that whenever possible the yachtsman should avoid being in the vicinity of the bridge if a commercial vessel is passing through.

There is a pair of lit buoys, West Bridge (QR) and East

Woolverstone Port Guide
Local tel code 01473

Woolverstone Marina (MDL)	Tel: 780206; email: woolverstone @mdlmarinas.co.uk.
Berths	235 plus 100 swinging moorings in river (a water taxi service is provided).
VHF	Ch 80.
Water	From end of pier.
Diesel fuel	From end of pier.
Gas, Calor	From marina master's office.
Repairs	Sea Power Tel: 780090; yard equipped for all services; slipway, mobile crane.
Showers and laundry	On site.
Chandlery	On site 0900-1700 daily, Tel: 780206.
Stores	From Pantry on site.
Yacht clubs	Royal Harwich Yacht Club Tel: 780319; www.rhyc.demon.co.uk. A limited number of visitors' berths on pontoons; showers, restaurant and bar open daily during season except Mondays. RHYC berth master Tel: 07742 145994. Stoke Sailing Club Tel: 780815.
Telephone	Kiosk on hard.
Food and drink	Buttermans Bar at marina Tel: 780803; Royal Harwich Yacht Club restaurant and bar. The Boot Inn, Freston Tel: 780277.

A Royal Harwich One Design just downstream of the RHYC clubhouse and pontoon at Woolverstone

The entrance to Fox's Marina and Ostrich Creek

Bourne Bridge Port Guide
Local tel code 01473

Fox's Marina (Oyster Group)	
	Tel: 689111; VHF Ch 80.
Berths	100.
Water	Marina pontoons; at Orwell Yacht Club.
Stores	Shops nearby.
Petrol and oil	Garage adjacent to clubhouse.
Gas	From marina.
Chandlery	At marina, open seven days a week.
Repairs	Travelifts and extensive facilities at marina boatyard.
Transport	Buses into Ipswich (1½ miles). Good train service from Ipswich to London.
Telephone	At marina, at yacht club, or telephone box nearby.
Yacht clubs	Orwell Yacht Club Tel: 602288; Fox's Marina Yacht Club.

Bridge(QG) very near the bridge where the dredged channel is only about half a cable wide.

Two pairs of lit buoys mark the channel immediately above the bridge. These are followed by a green conical buoy (QG) on the east side and then the No 12 red can (QR), which marks the start of Cliff Reach on the west side. The Orwell Yacht Club has both drying and deep water moorings on the west side of the river up to the West Bank Container Dock; there is a visitor's mooring near No 12 buoy. A red can Factory buoy (Fl R 2.5s) lies off the container Ro-Ro terminal and is followed by several more lit buoys leading right up to the entrance to the Wet Dock.

OSTRICH CREEK AND FOX'S MARINA

Just before the No 12 red can channel buoy, a small RWVS barrel buoy indicates the entrance to Ostrich Creek through which a little stream, Belstead Brook, enters the River Orwell after flowing under Bourne Bridge. Having passed the RWVS barrel buoy, a port-hand beacon indicates the way into the creek, where the Orwell Yacht Club and Fox's Marina are situated.

On the starboard-hand is the Orwell Yacht Club with its series of pile moorings and a double row of boats moored between them. Beyond the posts is the club's floating pontoon, accessible at all times.

Fox's 100-berth marina and boatyard is situated next to Bourne Bridge. Entrance, which can be accessed at all states of the tide, is through a dredged gutway off Ostrich Creek, marked on both sides by beacons.

Approaching the Orwell Bridge, Fox's Marina can be seen through the left-hand span

Fox's 100-berth marina at Bourne Bridge

An abundance of facilities at Fox's include travel lifts, workshops and an extensive chandlery, one of the largest on the East Coast. Also on site at Fox's Marina is Oyster Marine, which builds a range of large, luxurious deck-saloon yachts, some of which can usually be seen afloat in the marina. The Oyster Reach Beefeater pub is nearby.

IPSWICH DOCK

When it was opened in 1850, the Wet Dock at Ipswich was the largest in Europe and right up to the 1930s it was being used by square-rigged grain ships. Now there are two marinas in the dock, and much of the quayside and many of its historic buildings – malt kilns, granaries, flour mills and warehouses – have been or are being developed into residential apartments, restaurants, conference centres and the like. On Neptune Quay, the fine Old Custom House and the ancient Isaac Lord malt kiln building are dwarfed by towering new multi-storey blocks and construction cranes.

The 100-berth Neptune Marina is at Neptune Quay on the Historic Waterfront, to the east of the Old Custom House. Yard facilities include a 40-ton travel hoist.

Run by Associated British Ports, the Ipswich Haven Marina offers 250 pontoon berths and is situated on the south side, opposite the Old Custom House on the peninsula between the New Cut and the Wet Dock. Haven Marina has toilets, shower and laundry facilities, a 70-ton boat hoist, chandlery and a repair shop. The Last Anchor waterfront bar and restaurant is on site.

Both these marinas have shops and restaurants nearby; Ipswich town centre is within a 10-minute walk, as is the mainline railway station.

The peninsula beyond the Haven Marina is also home to Spirit Yachts, builders of modern-day classic wooden yachts, including the elegant 54-footer featured on the Grand Canal in Venice in the Bond movie *Casino Royale*.

The historic Ipswich Wet Dock waterfront

Approaching the Prince Philip Lock into the Wet Dock, the New Cut and Debbages is off to the left

The dock is approached along a closely buoyed channel past the Ro-Ro terminal on the port-hand opposite the grain terminal at Cliff Quay. Commercial vessels use the channel and the berths on either banks on a daily basis, so a good watch must be kept. Yachts should not berth alongside any of the commercial quays without first obtaining permission from the Port Authority.

For most vessels there is 24-hour access to the dock via the Prince Philip Lock. In practice this means the gates will be opened on demand during working hours and at other times by prior arrangement. When planning to enter the dock a yacht should contact Ipswich Lock Control on VHF Ch 68 before passing under the Orwell Bridge. For berthing information contact your chosen marina after passing Orwell Bridge.

The duty officer will give navigation and lock times information. There is a pontoon against which a boat can lie outside the lock while awaiting its opening. Red and green traffic control lights are located on a white pole on the east side of the lock.

NEW CUT

To port of the lock is New Cut, with Debbage's yard just upstream providing drying pontoon moorings, water and diesel fuel, repairs and a 20-ton crane. Shops are nearby and Ipswich station is about half a mile away. There is a water velocity control structure within the entrance to New Cut: when three vertical red lights show, the structure is raised and vessels may not proceed.

IPSWICH

Beginning with the arrival of the Vikings, Ipswich has a long maritime history. When Defoe came in 1668 he described it as 'the greatest town in England for large colliers or coal ships employed between Newcastle and London...' Later, the spritsail barge fleets of Cranfield and Paul carried wheat, while others brought coal or potash for Fisons, loam for the foundries, or cattle feed. Outward-bound they would pick up a (hay)stack, carrots or mangolds

There is a waiting pontoon outside the lock

(mangelwurzels) from little quaysides at farms up and down the rivers and creeks of the East Coast. There are themed walks and signed heritage trails around the Wet Dock, along the riverside and through the lanes and streets of Ipswich. Details of the leisure activities, art galleries, museums or Tolly Cobbold Brewery tours are available from the Tourist Information Centre in St Stephen's Church near the Buttermarket shopping centre. Most are within walking distance of the Wet Dock.

Barges alongside in the Wet Dock

There are heritage trails through the streets and lanes of Ipswich

Ipswich Port Guide – Local tel code 01473

Harbour master	Tel: 211771.
Orwell Navigation Service	VHF *Ipswich Port Radio* Ch 68.
Neptune Marina	Tel: 215204 (dockside), VHF Ch 80, email: enquiries@ neptunemarina.com.
Berths	100 plus visitors.
Ipswich Haven Marina (ABP)	
	Tel: 01473 236644; Fax: 236645; VHF Ipswich Marina Ch 80 or 37; email: ipswichhaven@abports.co.uk.
Berths	250 (30 for visitors).
Repairs	Burton Waters on site, Tel: 225710.
Chandlery	Burton Waters as above (closed Mondays).
Marine engineer	Volspec on site, Tel: 219651.
Marine electronics	R&J Marine, Tel: 214683.
Debbage's Yard	Tel: 601169.
Stores	Nearby and in town centre.
Water	Both marinas.
Fuel	Diesel and gas at both marinas, petrol (own cans) nearby.
Repairs	Travel lift, cranes, shipwrights, engineering, rigging and full yard facilities at Neptune. Hoist and cranage, repairs by arrangement at Ipswich Haven.
Transport	Good train service Ipswich–London (station 10-minute walk from Ipswich Haven Marina).
Telephone	Near Neptune Marina.
Food and drink	The Last Anchor restaurant at Ipswich Haven Marina (Monday-Friday lunch and evening meals; Sunday breakfast and lunch), Tel: 214763 – booking recommended; Salthouse Brasserie, Neptune Quay Tel: 226789; Mortimers Seafood, Duke Street, Tel: 269810; The Galley, St Nicholas Street, Tel: 281131; numerous other pubs and restaurants nearby.

Looking down the Stour from Mistley Quay

Chapter eight
The River Stour

Tides	Wrabness – HW Dover +01.05. Range: springs 3.7m; neaps 2.3m
Charts	Admiralty 1594, 2693, SC5607; Stanfords Chart Pack 6; Imray Y16, 2000 series, OS map 169
Waypoints	**Guard Buoy 51°57'.08N 01°17'.86E**
	Stour No 12 Buoy 51°56'.93N 01°05'.99E
Hazards	Ferries turning off Parkeston Quay

The River Stour has never been as popular with yachtsmen as the Orwell, for several reasons: Parkeston Quay with its attendant movements of large ferries, the absence of any waterside hamlet to compare with Pin Mill, and the difficulty of lying afloat out of the fairway anywhere above Wrabness.

Yet the Stour is quieter and more spacious than the Orwell and, moreover, its twin towns – Mistley and Manningtree – have been called 'two of the best-looking places in Essex.' Archie White summed up the Stour in *Tideways and Byways of Essex and Suffolk*: 'At high water the Stour takes upon itself the aspect of a wide and noble river,' but he goes on to say: 'As a glance at the chart will show, there is but little water above

Wrabness Point. The famous Horlock barges and small coasters trade to Mistley; otherwise the river is bare of craft. More's the pity for it is a beautiful river.'

There are RSPB reserves on the north bank between Shotley and Erwarton Ness and on the south shore between Parkeston and Wrabness. The plentiful mud flats make the river a haven for wading birds and birdwatchers alike.

Frequent ferries and cruise ships operate from the Ro Ro terminals at Parkeston Quay, but it is not difficult to keep clear of them, since even at low water the channel is almost half a mile wide.

However, beyond Wrabness the width of the low-tide channel narrows rather abruptly. Although well

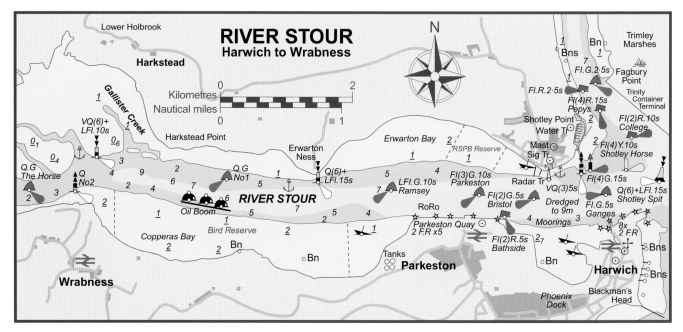

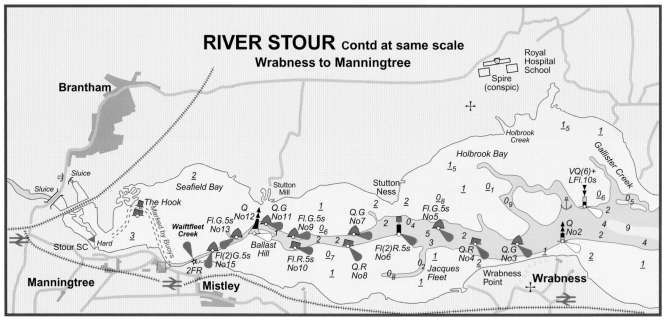

buoyed, it does involve a risk of grounding, particularly when a first passage is attempted whilst the wide mud flats are covered. But this objection is not peculiar to the Stour, since much the same conditions are found in the upper tidal reaches of almost all the rivers of the Thames Estuary.

There is still coaster traffic up the Stour to the Baltic Wharf at Mistley. Vessels as large as 3,500 tons bring granite from China, brick and building blocks from the Netherlands and Denmark, sand from Cornwall, aggregates from Ireland; plus other cargoes such as fertiliser, grain, steel, aluminium and road salt.

CHANNEL WIDTHS

The navigable channel extends from Harwich to Manningtree, some nine miles. The Stour separates the counties of Essex and Suffolk, and its general direction is westerly throughout the eight miles or so to Mistley.

At high tide the river appears to be a mile or more wide throughout the whole of its length. In fact its width at low water, while nearly half a mile abreast Shotley Pier and much the same from there to Harkstead Point, diminishes rapidly thereafter to about two cables off Wrabness Point and up as far as Stutton Ness. Then, along the mile or so of Straight Reach, the channel again narrows to less than a cable just below Ballast Hill. The final reaches between Ballast Hill and Mistley Quay become narrower still – until abreast the quays the channel at low water is less than 50m wide.

There are some small boat moorings in the entrance to the Stour over on the north bank of the river above Shotley Pier, and further rows of moorings on the southern shore across the entrance to Bathside Bay between Harwich and Parkeston Quay. Anchorage is prohibited in the vicinity of Parkeston Quay. The first useful small boat anchorage above Harwich

There is coaster traffic up and down the Stour

Harbour is off Erwarton Ness, about 1½ miles west of Parkeston.

There are three starboard-hand marks between Parkeston buoy and Harkstead Point; first Ramsey green conical buoy (L Fl G 10s), then the Erwarton Ness south cardinal beacon (Q (6)+ L Fl 15s), followed by No 1 green conical buoy (QG). The depth of the water in the channel is never less than 5m, until about a mile below Harkstead Point, when the mid-river water shallows gradually from about 5m to 3.5m abreast the Point.

ERWARTON NESS
With any north in the wind there is a good anchorage off Erwarton Ness about a cable from the derelict quay in line with the south cardinal beacon (Q (6) L Fl 15s). There is good holding in mud, but no protection from

either easterly or westerly winds. Landing is possible near the posts on the foreshore – all that remains of a former quay – between half flood and half ebb. Erwarton village is about a mile away, although the inn, the Queen's Head, is a little nearer.

Continuing upriver, just out of the channel on the port side, about opposite No 1 green conical buoy, is a row of buoys with an oil boom moored between them. To the south, beyond the boom, is the wide expanse of Copperas Bay and the RSPB reserve.

HOLBROOK BAY
Continuing up-river from Erwarton Ness, Harkstead Point is the next low headland on the north shore, while on the south bank, Wrabness Point is notable for its height (40ft) in East Coast waters. Once clear of Harkstead Point and the south cardinal Holbrook beacon (VQ Fl (6) L Fl 10s), the scene to the north will open out to disclose the extensive buildings and conspicuous central spire of the Royal Hospital School. This impressive piece of neo-Wren-style architecture was built in the 1930s when the school moved from Greenwich; and from the high ground at Holbrook it commands sweeping views over the Stour.

When the tide has no more than half flooded, the extensive mud flats of Holbrook Bay cover an area roughly two miles long and a mile deep. Two or three ill-defined creeks lead across these flats, the more important of them being Gallister Creek and Holbrook

There is a good anchorage at Erwarton Ness when the wind is in the north

The moorings at Wrabness

Creek. You may see a small fleet of Cornish Shrimpers with an accompanying RIB in this vicinity, crewed by pupils from the Royal Hospital School learning to sail in Holbrook Bay.

GALLISTER CREEK

Some small boat moorings are situated near the entrance, but there is enough water and just enough space to lie quietly to an anchor a cable or so inside Gallister Creek. For landing it is probably better to use Holbrook Creek.

HOLBROOK CREEK

This creek is marked by withies along its western edge and there is enough depth and space to allow anchoring for a quarter of a mile inside. Any exploring further up the creek should be done just before the mud banks are covered and while the gutway can be followed.

Clean landing is possible at the head of Holbrook Creek near high water, from where Holbrook village is about a mile away.

WRABNESS POINT

The channel runs close to Wrabness Point, past a port-hand north cardinal beacon No 2 (Q) and the Lee No 3 green conical (QG) starboard-hand buoy (formerly known as The Horse buoy). Because of previous dredging for shingle, the holding ground in the channel off Wrabness is not as safe as it used to be and if there is no vacant mooring, it will usually pay to move a bit further upstream towards the next port-hand buoy. In

any case beware of anchoring in mid-channel because of the commercial shipping using Mistley Quay; for anchoring overnight, a riding light is essential.

There are several rows of moorings along the shore at Wrabness extending from just upriver of the No 2 north cardinal beacon up towards the No 4 red can buoy (QR). As there is no yard or club at Wrabness, it would be unwise to leave a boat unattended on a vacant mooring.

The village of Wrabness is reached by climbing a pathway up the cliff and following the lane past the church towards the railway station. The church is one of the two in this district which have their bells in a wooden cage-like belfry in the churchyard.

A television mast on the south side of the river provides a conspicuous mark by day and by night.

When continuing up-river from Wrabness a stranger to the Stour will do well to set off before the mud flats are covered and while the course of the channel is visible as well as the buoys which mark it. In these narrow upper reaches the buoys must be given a wide berth whenever it appears that they are being swept by the tide over the banks they are intended to mark.

From the moorings off Wrabness the channel turns a little north of west for about a mile, past No 4 port-hand buoy (QR) and No 5 conical green buoy (Fl G 5s) to starboard. Jacques Fleet and the bay of the same name are to the south.

The next mark is No 6 beacon (Fl (2) R 5s) with a tide gauge, marking Smith Shoal; it is located about three cables south of Stutton Ness, and the best water here is no more than two cables from the Suffolk shore.

West of Stutton Ness the channel continues for a mile along Straight Reach, becoming narrower and shallower. There are three conical green buoys to be left to starboard and two red cans to be left to port along this reach. Then comes a bottleneck at Ballast Hill, where for a short distance there is a depth of only 1m and a width of less than a cable at low water. The port-hand buoy at Ballast Hill is the north cardinal No 12 (Q).

Use of the sounder offers the best chance of getting through here early on the tide. Once past the shingle patch that forms Ballast Hill, there is an isolated widening and deepening of the channel in Cross Reach. This hole provides the only spot in which a boat drawing 1.5m of water can remain afloat within reasonable distance of Mistley.

After Cross Reach the channel turns south-westerly along Waifffleet Reach and Miller Reach and from hereabouts the warehouses and maltings and the twin towers of the ruined Adam church at Mistley will all come into view.

MISTLEY

In the channel at Mistley the tide runs very hard during the first half of the ebb when the rate can be as high as four knots. At Mistley it is high water 50 minutes later than at Harwich.

Drying pontoon berths at Mistley Marine are at Northumberland Wharf on the port-hand side, downstream of Baltic Wharf, which is the commercial part of the quay. The sailing barge *Victor* plus tug and sundry working craft, some laid-up navigation buoys and a yellow crane can usually be seen on the pontoons

Approaching Mistley from the No 12 buoy at Ballast Hill

and slipway at Mistley Marine. It may be possible to moor on the pontoons or temporarily alongside the *Victor*, but visiting yachtsmen are advised to contact David Foster at Mistley Marine beforehand.

Tucked away at the downriver end of Baltic Wharf is the disused shed and slipway where many of the famous Horlocks of Mistley barges were built. Originally wood and later steel barges such as *Redoubtable, Adieu, Xylonite, Portlight, Repertor* and *Reminder* all slid down the ways here, and several of these are still sailing.

In *Down Tops'l*, published in 1951, Hervey Benham wrote: 'Mistley, with its sister town of Manningtree, just up the river, casts a spell on every sailorman. Here the maltings line the quay, where the railway trucks shunt sleepily, and behind the road rises sheer over the roofs of the maltings and one looks out on eye-level with the fluttering bobs of the barges at the quay.'

The quay is still working commercially, although

Mistley Marine, where it is sometimes possible to lie alongside the barge *Victor*

Approaching Manningree after rounding the red can Hook buoy

the fine maltings buildings lining the quayside have been converted to luxury riverside apartments. There is often a distinctive aroma of malt extract in the air, wafting across the river. This emanates from the local maltsters Edme Limited, a reminder that in the 19th century Mistley was the centre of the malting trade in East Anglia.

At the top end of the quay is a vegetarian café serving breakfast, lunch and afternoon tea (closed Mondays) alongside the Mistley Workshops and art gallery. It is possible to moor temporarily alongside the quay hereabouts but the quayside itself is not very yacht friendly. About 50m off the quay at Mistley beware of a mud and shingle bank, often covered with swans, walking.

A stroll away in the High Street is the Swan Basin and fountain, once part of an elaborate but failed sea-water spa scheme which Robert Adam was commissioned to design in 1774. Opposite the Basin is The Mistley Thorn hotel and restaurant.

While you are ashore, it is worthwhile walking to the top of Furze Hill to enjoy the fine view of the river from there; or to see the famous towers, all that remains of the Adam church, along the road towards Manningtree.

ABOVE MISTLEY

With local knowledge, Manningtree can be reached in craft drawing as much as 2m, provided the buoys are carefully observed and you are prepared to take the ground soon after arrival at Manningtree. The quay is not so extensive as at Mistley and there is no water at all at low tide.

In a shallower draught boat, drawing no more than 1m, it is also possible, just before high water, to take the North or Second channel across Seafield Bay direct from Ballast Hill to the bend in the channel known as the Hook. But if you are sailing across the flats off Mistley, look out for the wreck that lies there. The local centreboard classes belonging to the members of the Stour Sailing Club race around

a course which takes them right across Seafield Bay to within a cable or so of the Suffolk shore.

The channel is marked with small port and starboard-hand buoys from above Mistley Quay. After passing some moorings, usually with smacks on one or two of them, the channel leaves the Mistley shore in a north-westerly direction for about half a mile before turning back to the south-west in a big sweep around The Hook, marked by a red can buoy with a topmark. From hereon there are moored boats on either hand up to and beyond the quayside at Manningtree, and if in doubt about the channel, it is best to keep close to these moorings.

At Manningtree, the Stour Sailing Club provides a visitor's mooring – a white buoy located in the creek near the bottom of the hard. Visiting yachtsmen are made very welcome at the clubhouse, which incorporates a shower facility. Several shops and a supermarket are situated close to the waterside.

It is only a 10 or 15 minute walk to Manningtree from Mistley along a pleasant riverside road.

Mistley/Manningtree Port Guide
Local tel code 01206

Mistley Marine	Drying moorings by arrangement – contact David Foster Tel: 392127; VHF Ch 80; email: davidfoster05@aol.com.
Water	From Mistley Marine.
Stores	Several shops in main street near the quay. Early closing on Wednesdays.
Fuel	Diesel from Mistley Marine, petrol from garage.
Repairs	Lift out and cranage.
Transport	Trains to London from main line station at Manningtree.
Yacht club	Stour Sailing Club, Quay Street, Manningtree Tel: 393924; www.stoursailingclub.co.uk.
Food and drink	The Mistley Thorn, near quayside Tel 392821; Mistley Quay Café Tel: 393884.

The quayside at Manningtree

Stone Point is a popular landing place

Chapter nine
Walton Backwaters

Tides	Stone Point HW Dover +0040. Range: springs 3.6m; neaps 2.1m
Charts	Admiralty 2695, SC5607; Stanfords Chart Pack 6; Imray Y16, 2000 series; OS map 169
Waypoints	**Stone Banks Buoy 51°53'.19N 01°19'.22E**
	Pye End Buoy 51°55'.04N 01°17'.88E
Entrance	www.eastcoastrivers.com for downloadable sketch plan of entrance

The map that Arthur Ransome's *Swallows and Amazons* drew of their secret waters would still serve quite well for navigating the Walton Backwaters, for little has changed except the number of boats. All the creeks give good protection in almost any weather, and the Backwaters are an excellent base from which to make a number of modest cruises to the nearby Stour, Orwell or Deben.

APPROACHES

The entrance to the Backwaters is located about half a mile off the Dovercourt foreshore and half a mile or so south of the mouth of Harwich Harbour. Whether approaching from the north or the south, it is necessary to find Pye End buoy (RW Sph L Fl 10s) marking the northern extremity of an area of hard sand known as Pye Sand and the Sunken Pye.

When approaching Harwich from the south through the Wallet and the Medusa channel, the most prominent landmark is the Naze Tower, erected by Trinity House in 1720 and standing 160ft above the cliffs just north of Walton-on-the-Naze.

Another conspicuous landmark was added in 1992 in the form of the 187ft radar mast located on the cliff-top between Frinton and Clacton.

The Medusa buoy (G Con Fl G 5s) lies just over two miles east of Walton pier and, from a position midway between the pier and the Medusa, the Naze Tower will

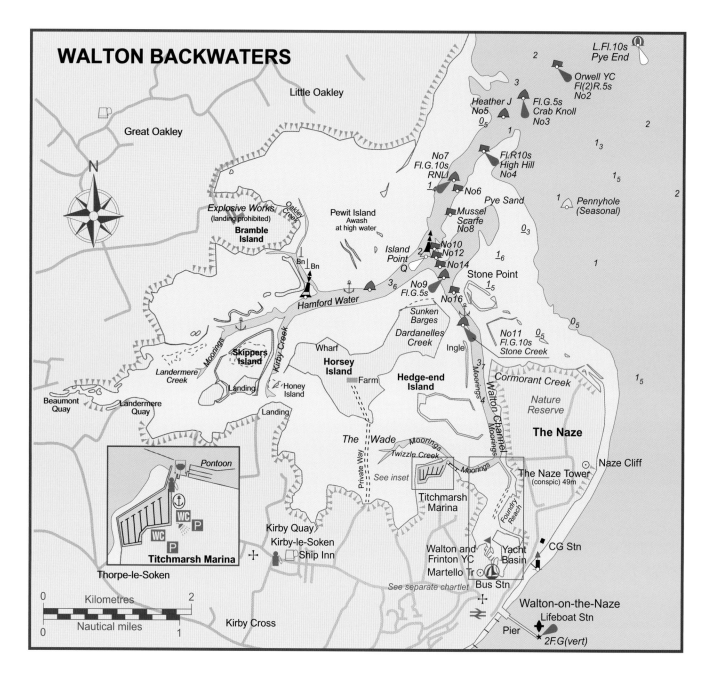

WALTON BACKWATERS

Little Oakley

Great Oakley

2 L.Fl.10s Pye End

Orwell YC Fl(2)R.5s No2

3

Heather J No5 0₅

Fl.G.5s Crab Knoll No3

1 1₃

2

No7 Fl.G.10s RNLI 1₄

Fl.R10s High Hill No4

1₅

No6

Pye Sand

1 Pennyhole (Seasonal)

2

Explosive Works (landing prohibited) **Bramble Island**

Oakley Creek

Pewit Island Awash at high water

Mussel Scarfe No8

0₃

Bn Bn

Island Point Q

No10 No12 2

No14

1₆

1

Hamford Water

3₆

No9 Fl.G.5s

No16

Stone Point 1₅

0₅

Skippers Island

Kirby Creek

Wharf **Horsey Island**

Sunken Barges Dardanelles Creek Ingle

No11 Fl.G.10s Stone Creek

0₅

Landermere Creek

Landing

Honey Island

Farm

Hedge-end Island

Moorings

Cormorant Creek

1₅

Beaumont Quay

Landermere Quay

Landing

The Wade

Moorings Twizzle Creek

Moorings

Walton Channel Moorings

Nature Reserve

The Naze

Naze Cliff

Pontoon

Private Way

See inset

Moorings

The Naze Tower (conspic) 49m

WC P

WC P

Titchmarsh Marina

Titchmarsh Marina

Foundry Reach

CG Stn

Thorpe-le-Soken

Kirby Quay Kirby-le-Soken Ship Inn

Walton and Frinton YC Martello Tr

Yacht Basin

Bus Stn

Walton-on-the-Naze Lifeboat Stn

0 Kilometres 2

See separate chartlet

0 Nautical miles 1

Kirby Cross

Pier

2.F.G(vert)

The Stone Banks buoy off Pennyhole Bay

bear approximately north-west while the next mark, the Stone Banks red can buoy (Fl R 5s) with topmark, will lie about three miles away to the north-north-east. Any less than a mile offshore around the Naze will probably have you bumping the bottom. There is considerable erosion of the cliffs, and as a result a shoal patch seems to be spreading out beneath the tower.

Another problem hereabouts is the multitude of lobster pots that are set by inshore fishermen. However hard one tries, it is difficult to avoid them in poor visibility and practically impossible at night. So if you find your progress seems slower than usual, see whether you have a line and pot caught by your rudder or prop.

In good visibility such landmarks as the tall spire of St Nicholas Church at Harwich and the large cranes at the Port of Felixstowe will be seen before the Stone Banks buoy comes up. This buoy, as its name suggests,

Looking up Hamford Water from over Stone Point, the entrance to the Walton Channel bottom left

marks a number of isolated clumps of stones and rocks with no more than 2m over them at low water springs. A course only slightly west of north from the Stone Banks buoy will bring Harwich breakwater (awash at high water) in view ahead. The Pennyhole (seasonal) yellow racing buoy is located in Pennyhole Bay, about one mile to the west-north-west of the Stonebanks buoy.

When about a mile from the breakwater and the entrance to Harwich Harbour, it should be possible in conditions of reasonable visibility to spot the Pye End buoy (RW Sph LFl 10s) which is located approximately one mile due south (°M) from the end of the breakwater and is now the responsibility of the Harwich Harbour Board. See the Harwich Harbour chart on page 60.

The buildings along the shore of Dovercourt Bay provide a background which makes it rather difficult to locate the buoy. Dovercourt Bay is a designated area for powered craft which launch from a ramp at Harwich Green.

The shallowest part of the approach to the Backwaters is the area known as the Halliday Rock Flats off Dovercourt, where there can be less than 1m in places during low water springs. This shoal water may prevent many craft from attempting the entrance before two or three hours of flood. It is spring tide high water hereabouts at approximately midday and midnight. Springs rise 4m and neaps 3m.

When approaching the Backwaters from the north,

the well-buoyed big-ship channel should be crossed as quickly as possible and then followed, outside it, as far as the Landguard buoy (North Card YB Q) from which a course of approximately 245°M will lead to the Pye End buoy less than a mile away. This same course, if continued, should find the No 2 red can buoy Fl (2) R 5s at the entrance to the channel into the Backwaters.

For almost a century the narrow channel into the Walton Backwaters over the Pye Sands has been marked by navigation buoys supplied and maintained

It is essential to locate the Pye End Buoy before entering the Backwaters

by the Walton and Frinton Yacht Club. This started when barges were trading up to the two mills and the foundry at the head of Foundry Reach near the town, and also up to the farm wharves at the head of the various creeks in the Backwaters. Today this facility is enjoyed by local users and visiting yachts alike, but the cost to the club runs into several thousand pounds per year. In order to ease the cost of laying and maintaining them, the club relies on sponsorship from local firms, donations and club funds.

To assist local craft using the channel at night, No 2 Orwell Yacht Club red can, No 3 Crab Knoll green conical, No 4 High Hill red can, No 7 green conical, the north cardinal Island Point buoy and the next two green conicals are all lit.

However, even in bright daylight, the newcomer will look to the south-west from abreast the Pye-End buoy and find it difficult to believe that any kind of deep-water channel lies ahead. But after sailing in a generally south-westerly direction for a quarter of a mile or so, the next buoys – No 2, a red can buoy Fl (2) R 5s, and No 3 (Crab Knoll), a green conical buoy Fl G 5s, will come into view. The Dovercourt shore shelves gradually and is the safer side to work until this first pair of buoys have been reached, after which the channel becomes narrower and deeper and the sand is steep-to on either hand.

The next green conical buoy, No 5, is about half a mile further to the south-west, marking the western edge of

the channel where it narrows to a bottleneck, little more than a cable wide, at a point known as High Hill. This is identified by a lit red can buoy bearing that name (Fl R 10s). There are 8 or 9m of water in the channel here, but since the sand on either side is quite steep-to, short boards are essential whenever it is necessary to turn to windward, and continuous use of the echo-sounder is the only sure guide to the limits of the channel when the tide has covered the banks and there are no ripples. It is also as well to remember that spring tides run out of here at 2.5 knots during the first part of the ebb.

From High Hill onwards, the channel widens to two or three cables and is marked on the west side by No 7 green conical buoy (Fl G 10s) and on the east side by red cans (Nos 6 and 8). From hereabouts it is usually possible to see the north cardinal Horsey Island Point buoy (Q) at the junction of Hamford Water and the Walton Channel.

ENTRANCE TO WALTON CHANNEL

When bound for the Walton Channel there are three more red can buoys, Nos 10, 12 and 14, to be left to port round Mussel Scarfe. This series of buoys should not be passed too closely because under certain conditions of tide and westerly wind they can be over the bank they mark. Neither should the Island Point buoy be approached too closely when entering or leaving the Walton Channel, as there is an extension of the mud bank to the east, just south of the buoy. A green conical buoy, No 9 (Fl G 5s), marks this hazard.

Yacht leaving the Backwaters having rounded red cans 14, 12 and 10. The sunken barges on the Horsey Island shore can be seen behind

Walton and Frinton Yacht Club clubhouse at the head of Foundry Reach

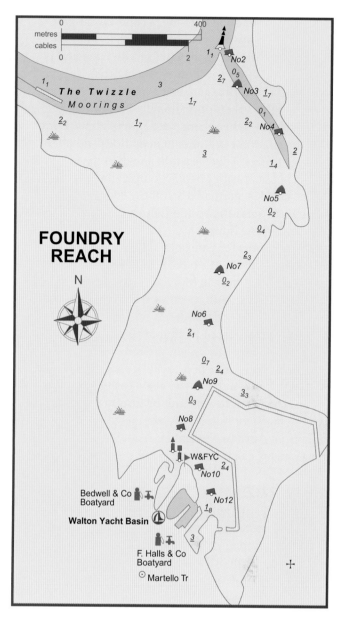

The last port-hand buoy, No 16, marks the western edge of Stone Point. There is sometimes an outer (more northerly) port-hand buoy indicating the south-west end of a channel known as 'The Swatch', which is occasionally used (near high water) by local craft bound for the fishing grounds off the Naze.

STONE POINT

The steep-to shingle bank at Stone Point provides a popular landing place at all states of the tide, while the anchorage nearby offers excellent protection. It is not advisable to anchor in the fairway where the depths are considerable and the ebb runs hard in midstream, as much as three knots during springs. It is preferable to anchor close to the east bank, where there is a slight contra-flow eddy during the first part of the ebb.

On a fine day in summer, Walton Stone Point gets very busy as it is a good spot for a bathe and picnic, but be aware that it is adjacent to a privately-owned bird sanctuary and nature reserve. Unfortunately some unthinking people light fires, leave rubbish, disturb nesting terns and trample down the plants and grass that are so important to the wildlife of the area. If this kind of thoughtless behaviour were to continue, Stone Point might be prohibited to yachtsmen. Fortunately the Point is under the management of the Walton and Frinton Yacht Club, which needs our support. Should you intend to come to Stone Point as part of an organised group or club cruise, the Walton & Frinton Yacht Club would appreciate being contacted in advance of your visit.

After the Ingle lit green conical, the Walton Channel is not buoyed between Stone Point and the Twizzle. The best water is to be found between the moorings, except near the mouth of Stone Creek, where mud extends to the west and the channel is nearer the Horsey Island shore, marked by the aforementioned Ingle buoy. The depths in the channel decrease from 7m off Stone

Point to rather less than 5m where the Walton Channel changes direction and name and becomes the Twizzle, at the entrance to which there is a shoal area. This is marked by a north cardinal buoy, The Spit. This buoy and the nearby red can buoy No 2 are the first of a series of numbered port and starboard-hand buoys laid by the Walton & Frinton Yacht Club to mark Foundry Reach all the way up to its clubhouse and yacht basin.

WALTON AND FRINTON YACHT CLUB

The landing at the clubhouse, built in 1920 on the site of an old windmill, can be reached by dinghy for all but two hours on either side of low water. Visitors to the Backwaters are always welcome at the club – ask for the resident steward and he will sign you in. The bar and restaurant are open at lunchtime and evenings on most days of the year, the rest of the club and toilet facilities are accessible at all times. The Walton and Frinton Yacht Club has a fleet of about a dozen recently restored Jewel class one-designs; 40 of these 14-footers were originally built for the club by James and Stone of Brightlingsea soon after the Second World War.

The limited access yacht basin is adjacent to the Walton and Frinton Yacht Club in Mill Lane and is run by the Walton and Frinton Yacht Trust. This yacht basin has a retaining gate that is opened around the time of high water (approximately 20 minutes after HW Harwich) when there is a depth of about 1.6m over the sill in the entrance at neap tides and about 2.3m at springs. There is a tide gauge to the left of the gate. It is not always possible to open the gate on very low neap tides, particularly if these coincide with high barometric pressure, besides which it is opened only during working hours.

Arrangements for gate opening should be made in advance with Bedwells (see Port Guide opposite), one of the two boatyards in Mill Lane – the other is Frank Halls. Inside the basin, yachts are moored fore-and-aft between staging and buoys.

The seaside resort of Walton-on-the-Naze with its shops, pubs, restaurants, ten-pin bowling and good beaches, is less than a mile away. It should be noted that there is no bank in the town, just a cash machine at the Co-op. The Naze Tower, built by Trinity House in 1720 as a daymark for sailors, has been restored and is open daily from April to November; it now houses a local museum, art gallery and tea shop.

THE TWIZZLE

The Twizzle, or Twizzle Creek, which runs in a generally westerly direction, is really a continuation of Walton Channel, offering complete protection in an average depth of 2m at low water except near its entrance. Craft are moored on both sides of the

Walton-on-the-Naze Port Guide
Local tel code 01255

Walton Yacht Basin	Contact Bedwells Tel: 675873.
Yacht club	Walton and Frinton Yacht Club, Mill Lane Tel: 675526; www.wfyc.co.uk.
Water	From alongside the clubhouse.
Stores	Shops ¼ mile from clubhouse. Early closing on Wednesdays (there are no banks in town).
Fuel	Diesel from yard, nearest petrol from garage in Frinton or Kirby-le-Soken.
Repairs	Yards in Mill Lane: Bedwells Tel: 675873; Franks Halls Tel: 675596.
Chandlery	At boatyards.
Transport	Trains to London via Colchester. Buses to Colchester, Clacton and Harwich.
Food and drink	Bar and restaurant at yacht club (lunchtimes and evenings).
Telephone	At clubhouse.

Twizzle; after enquiry at the clubhouse or one of the local yards, it is sometimes possible to borrow one of the moorings for a short period. Those marked with a 'B' belong to Bedwells, while those with an 'H' are owned by Halls.

TITCHMARSH MARINA

The Titchmarsh Marina (450 boats) is on the south side of the Twizzle, a little to the west of Colonel's Hard. Dredging over the years since this marina was established means that there is now 1.3m of water over the entrance sill at low water springs. A pontoon is situated outside in the Twizzle, part of which is owned by the marina, where boats can lie while they wait for water over the sill. The Coastguard boat *Hunter* is based here.

The marina is a fair way from the town of Walton-on-the-Naze, so you may need to

Some of the recently restored Jewel One Designs racing from the club

Looking across Titchmarsh Marina and the Twizzle to the Walton Channel and Pennyhole Bay beyond

call a taxi; it is as well to know that there are no banks in the town although there is a cash point in the Co-op. There are good facilities on site, including a chandlery and the Harbour Lights bar and restaurant, which overlooks the pontoons and provides breakfasts, bar meals, restaurant with silver service and, in summer, barbecues on the terrace. A limited selection of basic stores is available at the chandlery.

The Twizzle is navigable at low water by craft drawing 1m as far as the western end of Hedge End Island. Further west, the Twizzle becomes a narrow, winding gutway through the extensive mud and saltings of Horsey Mere. The withies here indicate oyster layings rather than a channel. The creek finally peters out to the east of the rough roadway known as the Wade, which crosses Horsey Mere to join the mainland with the farm on Horsey Island.

There are oyster beds at the extreme western end of the Twizzle, so care must be taken not to go aground in this area.

Those who have read Arthur Ransome's *Secret Water* will no doubt remember the exciting race the 'Explorers' had when they crossed the Wade during a rising tide.

It is possible to sail straight across Horsey Mere from the Twizzle to Kirby Creek, provided the boat does not draw more than about 1m and the trip is made about an hour before high water, on a day near to, but before, spring tides.

As with all the other creeks and inlets that make up the Backwaters, undoubtedly the best way to explore is by dinghy, preferably a sailing one.

Titchmarsh Marina Port Guide
Local tel code 01255

Harbour master/marina office	
	Tel: 672185; VHF Ch 80; www.titchmarshmarina.com.
Water	On pontoons.
Stores	Small selection at chandlery.
Diesel	Fuel pontoon just inside marina entrance (open daylight hours).
Gas	From harbour master.
Chandlery & Cycle hire	Tel: 679028.
Repairs	35-ton travel-lift, French Marine Motors Tel: 850303;
Electronics	Hurst Marine Services Tel: 673171.
Food and drink	Harbour Lights restaurant and bar Tel: 851887 (open all week).
Taxis	Walton Taxis Tel: 675910.

HAMFORD WATER

Hamford Water is also known as the West Water. It runs in a generally south-westerly direction from the Island Point buoy moored off the mud spit extending from the north-eastern corner of Horsey Island, to the north-eastern end of Skipper's Island, where the channel divides. There is plenty of water in this main reach of Hamford Water – 7m near the entrance and 5m about a mile inside, but depths are variable. The width of the channel is nearly two cables at low water and the north side of it is marked by a green conical buoy.

This is a very popular anchorage, with both excellent protection and holding, unless you are unlucky enough to drop your hook on top of one of the massive growths of pipe weed that have infested these waters in recent years. When any kind of anchor lands on a patch of this stuff its holding power becomes negligible. It is therefore a good idea to test (under power if necessary) that your anchor is holding before settling down for the night and certainly before leaving the boat.

The full-time Walton Backwaters warden is often on duty in the Tendring District Council launch, *Limosa*; one of his duties is monitoring the growing colony of around 70 harbour and grey seals which can be seen in and around Hamford Water.

OAKLEY CREEK

Oakley Creek branches to the north, out of Hamford Water and between Bramble and Pewit Islands. The spit off the western side of the entrance is marked by the Exchem east cardinal buoy. There is enough water for light draught craft to lie afloat for nearly a mile within, but it is probably best to resist any temptation to anchor here because the creek is used once or twice a week by freighters which load at the wharf belonging to the Exchem explosives factory at Oakley, where landing is strictly prohibited. At the head of Oakley Creek there is a jetty on marshland owned by English Nature and managed by the Little Oakley Wildfowlers Association. Although some small boats are kept here, landing is discouraged.

LANDERMERE CREEK

By continuing west along Hamford Water, a boat drawing up to 2m can safely reach the division of the channel where Landermere Creek turns towards Landermere Quay. Several moorings lie just beyond

here but there is usually enough space and depth to anchor clear of them. Landing from a dinghy is feasible at the quay from about half-flood.

At around high water it is possible to take a dinghy beyond Landermere up The Cut to Beaumont Quay. The quay was built in 1832 using stone from the old London Bridge, brought to the Backwaters by barge. A limekiln, which can still be seen, a coal store and a granary were built and for the next 100 years or so the quay was a bustling place with cargo such as chalk, coal, wheat and ragstone (for walls and roads) being loaded and unloaded. The local barges were the *Beaumont Belle* and the 28 ton *Gleaner*, built specially for The Cut. Another little barge, the *Hector*, was based at Landermere Quay.

An overhead power cable now spans the cut and prevents boats with masts from reaching the quay. However, a few years back the little barge *Cygnet* did berth alongside the quay, having lowered her gear first, with a token cargo of thatching reed from her home port of Snape.

KIRBY CREEK

This creek joins Hamford Water on its south side, about a quarter mile beyond Oakley Creek, and offers a quiet anchorage, although there are some moorings in the creek. The Naze Oyster Company has some of its layings in Kirby Creek and, like anywhere else that oysters are cultivated, a yachtsman is responsible if, by anchoring or grounding, he damages any of the stock. Noticeboards to this effect will be seen at the entrance to the creek.

If for some reason conditions in Hamford Water are uncomfortable, yachtsmen may be able to anchor just within Kirby Creek and above the layings, but then they must beware the treacherously long spit of mud that extends from the north-east end of Skipper's Island.

Skipper's Island is used by the Essex Naturalists' Society, whose members have erected an observation tower from which they can watch the many species of birds that come to the Backwaters. A landing can be made at a wooden staithe on the mainland opposite the south-east corner of the Island. This is a good landing except right at low water, and the walk along the sea wall to Kirby-le-Soken is about a mile and a half. In the village there is a shop and post office, garage and two pubs.

From abreast the wooden staithe, Kirby Creek turns sharply to the east, to emerge into Horsey Mere, before turning south again up to Kirby Quay. The quay can be reached by dinghy towards high water, and the tortuous gutway is plentifully marked by withies, which are no doubt understood by local sailors but at first acquaintance are only likely to baffle the uninitiated. The house on the quay was originally a granary dating back to the time when barges traded up the creek; the village and The Ship inn (Tel: 01255 674256) are just a short walk away.

Looking north over Kirby Creek where it joins Hamford Water with Skipper's Island to the left and Horsey Island to the right

The pontoon berths at Brightlingsea

Chapter ten
The River Colne

Tides (Brightlingsea)	HW Dover +0.55. Range: springs 4.6m; neaps 2.6m (HW Colchester approximately 20mins after HW Brightlingsea)
Charts	Admiralty 3741, SC5607; Stanfords Chart Pack 4; Imray Y17, 2000 series; OS map 168
Waypoints	**Knoll Buoy 51°43'.88N 01°05'.06E**
	NW Knoll Buoy 51°44'.35N 01°02'.17E
	Inner Bench Head Buoy 51°45'.96N 01°01'.75E
	Brightlingsea Spit Buoy 51°48'.08N 01°00'.70E
Hazards	Knoll, Colne Bar and Bench Head shoals near low water

The gentle wooded slopes that line the banks of the Colne below Wivenhoe give the river a pleasant rural feel which is unspoiled by the moorings and marinas that characterise many other local rivers. Colchester has been de-registered as a port and the Hythe and quays have been redeveloped for housing or leisure use. So, although the ballast quay at Fingringhoe is still busy with sand barges, by and large the river is as peaceful and quiet as it has ever been.

The River Colne is smaller and more intimate than its close neighbour, the Blackwater. Both these rivers join the sea at the NW Knoll buoy, midway between Colne Point to the east and Sales Point to the west. The distance from the Knoll buoy to the Hythe at Colchester is about 11 miles, most of which lies in a north-north-westerly direction.

APPROACHES FROM SEAWARD

When approaching the Colne from the south through the Swin Spitway or from the north, up the Wallet, make for the Knoll buoy (North Card Q) and then leave both the Eagle (G Con QG) and the Colne Bar

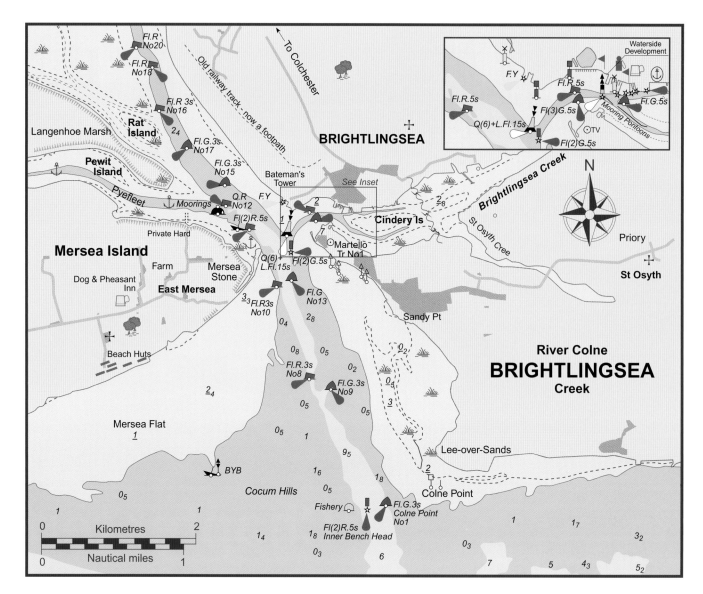

The Colne Bar buoy

(G Con Fl (2) G 5s) buoys close to starboard before shaping a course of 350°M into the entrance of the river. From a position near the Bar buoy a group of three more buoys will usually be seen in daylight – the Fishery buoy (Sph Y), the Colne Point buoy (G Con) and the Inner Bench Head (R Can Fl (2) R 5s).

Shoal draught boats can, provided it is not too near the time of low water, cross Colne Bar north of the Eagle and as much as a mile inside the Bar buoy. When coming south a sudden increase in depths will indicate when the bar has been crossed.

From the Inner Bench Head light buoy inwards, the channel is buoyed on both sides – even-numbered red cans to port and odd-numbered green conical buoys to starboard. There is a depth of some 9m between the first pair of channel buoys, and there is not much less than 6m anywhere within the channel until abreast the entrance to Brightlingsea Creek. However, carefully observe the buoys on both hands since the water shoals quite rapidly, particularly to the west.

When sailing to the Blackwater from the Colne it is safe, except near low water, for craft drawing 2m or less to cross from the deep water of the Colne on a course that has St Peters Chapel (near Sales Point) bearing 240°M. This will lead about midway between the Bench Head and Cocum Hills shoals.

In clear weather, from a position abreast the Inner Bench Head, it is possible to see Brightlingsea Church tower on high ground, due N (°M), from a distance of four miles. The conspicuous new (2007) apartment development, Waterside Marina, on the site of the former James and Stone shipyard in Brightlingsea, may also help the newcomer get his bearings.

BRIGHTLINGSEA CREEK

When approaching Brightlingsea Creek, stand well off the green conical buoy Colne No 13 (Fl G). The buoy marking the spit on the north side of the entrance is a yellow and black south cardinal (Q Fl (6)+L Fl 15s). To starboard a beacon (Fl (2) G 5s) marks the shallows off the St Osyth shore; there is a tide gauge on the beacon showing the least depth in the channel. The entrance between these two marks is very shallow, with not much more than 1m best water at low water springs.

The correct course into the creek itself is 42°M and by day this line is indicated by two leading marks (red and white stripes) known locally as the 'cricket stumps' and set up on poles in the town. Batemans Tower, a restored folly and local landmark used by

Colne Yacht Club on race days, shows a yellow light at night. A green conical buoy (Fl (3) G 5s) inside the entrance is intended to keep you off the spit that extends from St Osyth Stone Point, while a red can (Fl R 5s) marks the northern edge of the channel. Deeper water between these two buoys is to be found to the south; then head for the Fishermen's Pontoon which should be left close to starboard.

Two rows of pontoons extend upstream in the South Channel just beyond the fishing boats with Cindery Island to the north. Some local Brightlingsea boats have permanent berths and it is the custom for regular berth holders to leave a note when they vacate their mooring saying whether they will be back that day. However, do not leave your boat unattended on any berth without checking first. Brightlingsea is a popular port of call in the summer months so it is advisable to enquire beforehand as to availability of berths, although individual berths cannot be booked.

At springs the tide runs hard and extra care should be taken while berthing and turning in the vicinity of the pontoons and moorings.

At all reasonable times the harbour master, Bernard Hetherington, can be found in his launch; he can also be contacted by phone or on VHF. From April to October on weekends from Friday evening to Sunday night, plus

Brightlingsea looking north-east with Cindery Island and the pontoons in the South Channel and St Osyth Creek leading off in the top right

weekdays in school summer holidays, there is a regular and inexpensive water taxi service to the Colne Yacht Club pontoon.

The Brightlingsea Harbour Commissioners patrol launch *Dracula* is used on the Colne while the smaller harbour master's launch operates a foot and cycle ferry service between St Osyth Stone and East Mersea Stone between Easter and October. A fisheries patrol vessel also operates out of Brightlingsea.

The North Channel, which holds very little water, runs to the north of Cindery Island and on up to the head of the creek where there is a jetty that until recently was used by sand barges. Once or twice a week freighters still load scrap metal for Spain using Oliver's Quay, a commercial wharf beyond the Colne Yacht Club. Some of this traffic can be at night, so there are no moorings to the north of Cindery Island and a fairway must be maintained here at all times.

Brightlingsea has long provided excellent facilities for the traditional yachtsman. There is a fine hard on which almost any boat can stand upright against one of the several posts available. Arrangements for using the posts should be made with the hard master whose office is near the yacht club jetty; he is in attendance from Monday to Friday in the mornings only. To the west of The Hard and the scrubbing posts, the Town Causeway has recently been upgraded into an extensive pontoon with an all-tide hammerhead. Waiting alongside is limited and yachts must not be left unattended. Some of the finance for this pontoon was provided by the developers of the adjacent Waterside Marina apartment blocks.

The Colne Yacht Club, just east of The Hard and beyond the Anchor Hotel building (now flats), has a catwalk and pontoon as well as a clubhouse with commanding views. Visiting yachtsmen are welcome, and meals and showers can usually be obtained. Just beyond the yacht club pontoon is the Aldous Heritage

A starboard-hand beacon marks the shallows off the St Osyth shore

Smack Dock, headquarters of the Colne Smack Preservation Society and home to a fleet of restored fishing craft, many of which were built in Brightlingsea over 100 years ago.

'In years gone by Brightlingsea men went far afield,' wrote Archie White in *Tideways and Byways in Essex and Suffolk*, '…across to Terschelling for oysters… in vessels specially built for the job… highbowed, with powerful shoulders and running to over sixty feet in length…fitted with wells in which oysters were kept alive.' These 'skillingers' were away for months at a time and it was said that 'the men in them never went ashore from the time they left Brightlingsea until they came back.'

Shipbuilding, spratting and scalloping may have finished but some of the traditional skills are being kept alive by sailors such as Jimmie Lawrence, the local sailmaker, whose restored bawley *Saxonia* is available for charter out of Brightlingsea.

The North London SA sails Wayfarers and Lasers from its residential base in the Old Custom House close to The Hard. Courses and informal sailing breaks are provided for school, youth and community groups from North London and further afield.

The south cardinal Brightlingsea Spit buoy and the leading marks on the shore

Brightlingsea Port Guide – Local tel code 01206

Brightlingsea Harbour Commissioners

Harbour master	Bernard Hetherington Tel: 302200, Mob: 07952 734814; VHF Ch 68.
Hard master	Tel: 303535.
Water taxi	VHF Ch 37; Tel: 07733 078503.
Water	Tap at top of hard; or Colne Yacht Club pontoon, but only by arrangement.
Waste	Rubbish disposal at top of Colne Yacht Club jetty; afloat pump-out by arrangement.
Stores	Shops in town, short walk.
Chandlery	French Marine Motors engineers and chandlery Tel: 302133.
Petrol and diesel	From chandlers (cans).
Repairs	Brightlingsea Boatyard in North Channel Tel 821211.
Sailmaker	James Lawrence, Tower Street, Tel: 302863.
Transport	Buses to Colchester, whence good train service to London.
Yacht clubs	Colne Yacht Club: water, showers, toilets, restaurant and bar. Tel: 302594; www. colnesailingclub.org.uk. Brightlingsea Sailing Club.
Telephone	At top of hard.
Food and drink	Shellfish and fish restaurant; fish and chip shop; Chinese take-away on waterside; plus other pubs, restaurants and take-aways nearby.

ST OSYTH CREEK

Above Brightlingsea there are two tidal islands – West and East Cindery Islands, dividing Brightlingsea Creek into two branches, abreast the junction with St Osyth Creek. This latter creek is no more than a mile long and is very narrow, particularly near the entrance where the best water (perhaps as much as 1.5m at low water) will be found between a tiny hummock of land known as Pincushion Island and the south bank. Shallow draught boats or dinghies can safely reach the head of the creek for about an hour or so either side of high water. The creek is sparsely marked by withies.

St Osyth village, pronounced 'Toosey' by locals, is worth visiting to see the remains of the Abbey, which started life in the 12th century as a priory but became rich and had a later upgrade. Beside the quay, originally medieval and busy long ago with limekilns and maltings, is the St Osyth Boatyard (Tel: 01255 820005) which has a crane and slip. This is a popular venue for owners of Essex smacks and is also home to the boatyard owner's *Edme*, a sailing barge built by

Canns of Harwich in 1898. She was named after the malt extract company in the hope of gaining work with them, which she did. *Edme* is one of two engine-less sailing barges on the East Coast, the other being the *Mirosa*. Two other barges, *Thalatta* and *Vigilant*, are also based here.

A weather-boarded tidemill, which used to stand on a causeway damming the head of the creek, was still working up until the 1930s, but was finally demolished after a gale took off its roof about 40 years ago.

MERSEA STONE POINT

Opposite the entrance to Brightlingsea Creek is Mersea Stone Point – the eastern extremity of Mersea Island. There is a good landing on the shingle here, and one can walk to the Dog and Pheasant, about a mile away.

Good holding ground in 5m, well protected from all but southerly or south-easterly winds, can be found clear of the few moorings and between the point and the old wreck that dries out just below the entrance to Pyefleet Creek. This wreck, of a ship called *Lowlands*, is marked by a red can buoy (Fl (2) R 5s).

Since chartered sailing barges and coasters frequently bring up off the entrance to Brightlingsea Creek, it is essential to use a riding light when anchored at night.

PYEFLEET CREEK

A cable or two above the wreck on the west side of the river is the entrance to Pyefleet Creek, which provides an excellent anchorage with good protection. In fact, an anchorage in Pyefleet is usually more comfortable than a berth within Brightlingsea Creek, because of the swell that often enters the creek at the turn of the tide.

Pyefleet Creek is one of the most popular Saturday night anchorages on the whole of the East Coast. Perhaps this is because it offers that sense of remoteness for which so many of us feel a need. There are no landing places and no cars in sight and, although there may be 20 or 30 craft at anchor, everyone (except the waterskiers) is there for the peace and quiet and acts accordingly.

Oysters are still cultivated in Pyefleet Creek, as they were when the Romans were at Colchester. Every October the Mayor, accompanied by officials of the Colchester Oyster Company, celebrates the start of a new season while moored in the Creek. At weekends during the summer it is possible to buy cooked crabs and lobsters at the Colchester Oyster Company shed (Tel: 01206 384141), which is open all day on Sundays and early on Saturday mornings. However, do remember that the hard and the East Mersea foreshore hereabouts are private.

The deep water in the entrance to Pyefleet is indicated by a line of mooring buoys, belonging to the Oyster Company, which are often used by smacks and bawleys. There is plenty of room and plenty of water

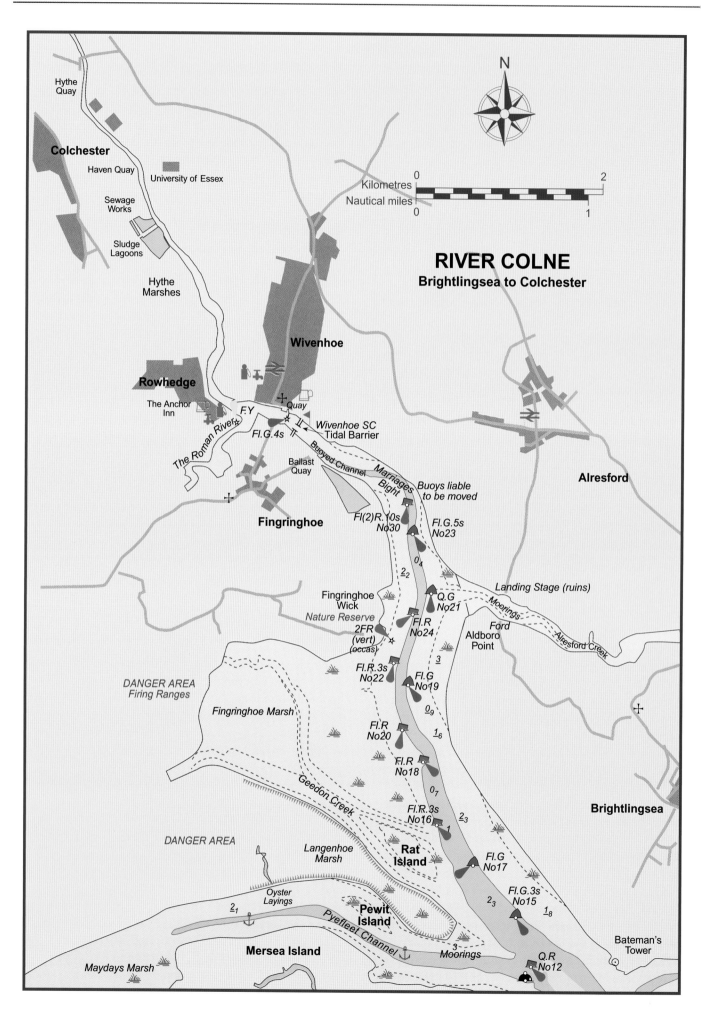

Hythe
Quay

Colchester

Haven Quay

University of Essex

Sewage
Works

Sludge
Lagoons

Hythe
Marshes

N

0   Kilometres   2
Nautical miles
0   1

RIVER COLNE
Brightlingsea to Colchester

Wivenhoe

Rowhedge

The Anchor
Inn

The Roman River

F.Y

✠ Quay

Wivenhoe SC
Tidal Barrier

Fl.G.4s

Ballast
Quay

Buoyed Channel

Marriages
Bight

Buoys liable
to be moved

Fingringhoe

Fl(2)R.10s
No30

Fl.G.5s
No23

0₄

Alresford

2₂

Landing Stage (ruins)

Q.G
No21

Moorings

Fingringhoe
Wick

Ford
Aldboro
Point

Alresford Creek

Nature Reserve

Fl.R
No24

2FR
(vert)
(occas)

3

Fl.R.3s
No22

Fl.G
No19

DANGER AREA
Firing Ranges

0₉

Fingringhoe Marsh

1₆

Fl.R
No20

Fl.R
No18

Brightlingsea

Geedon Creek

0₇

DANGER AREA

Fl.R.3s
No16

2₃

1

Langenhoe
Marsh

Rat
Island

Fl.G
No17

Oyster
Layings

Fl.G.3s
No15

2₃

1₈

2₁

Pewit
Island

Pyefleet Channel

Mersea Island

3 Moorings

Bateman's
Tower

Q.R
No12

Maydays Marsh

for a mile or more up the creek, and yachts may bring up either just within the entrance or anywhere up to or even above Pewit Island, with its old oyster packing shed. Great care must be taken to avoid anchoring or grounding on any of the oyster layings (beds) in the Pyefleet. Craft drawing up to 2m can remain afloat as far up as Maydays Marsh, where the channel divides; the southern branch leading to the Strood which joins Mersea Island to the mainland.

The only disadvantage of the Pyefleet anchorage is that no supplies are available nearer than Brightlingsea, which can seem a long way when a strong wind is blowing up or down the Colne.

Returning to the Colne river buoyage, a red can buoy, No 16 (Fl R 3s), marks the mud spit formed by the small creek which enters the river north of Rat Island. Above Rat Island the channel continues in a north-north-westerly direction before turning north-easterly round Aldboro Point. Three red cans and a green conical buoy mark the course of the channel round this bend.

ALRESFORD CREEK

Fingringhoe Marshes, part of which is a nature reserve controlled by the Essex Wildlife Trust, are now on the port hand and a disused jetty will come into view on the same shore. Much of this marsh area is used by the MOD as firing ranges – when firing is in progress, red flags are flown. The next starboard-hand buoy (No 21 green conical QG) will be found off the entrance to Alresford Creek. The entrance is marked by a pair of small pillar buoys, with further pairs of similar buoys marking the gutway. For a quarter of a mile inside the creek there are small boat moorings up to a ford, at which landing can be made on either bank. From the ford up to Thorington Mill at the head of the creek it is a little over a mile, but most of the creek dries out at low water. Out in the river there is enough water for large boats to lie afloat at low water out of the channel opposite Aldboro Point.

Above Alresford Creek the channel continues in a northerly direction and is well marked with both lit and unlit buoys round the sweeping bend known as Marriages Bight. The mud flat stretching from the Fingringhoe shore is extensive and the narrowing channel leads right over to within half a cable of the pleasantly wooded Alresford shore, before turning north-westerly again towards the other bank.

The next channel buoys are located just below the ballast quay on the Fingringhoe shore (from which small sand barges operate). Above this point the best water lies roughly midway between the banks, and the buoyage sequence is liable to change. There are fore-and-aft mooring trots on either hand just below the Wivenhoe Tidal Barrier, which will now be seen. This is normally open and if so causes no problem. However, if three FR (vert) lights show on the north pier, up or downstream, either the gates are shut or a large

vessel is negotiating the barrier. Immediately below the barrier on the starboard-hand is Wivenhoe Sailing Club which, with its slipway and pontoons, has access from around one hour before to one hour after high water on average tides. Yachts of up to 6ft draught can lie in soft mud alongside and visitors are welcome to stay overnight. Nineteen Wivenhoe One-Designs were built for club members before the Second World War; 16 of these 15ft clinker-built centreboarders have been restored or re-built in recent years and can often be seen sailing on The Colne.

WIVENHOE

The river front at Wivenhoe has a pleasant and unusual atmosphere, especially at high water with the sun shining on the quayside houses. Most of the boats at Wivenhoe dry out at about half-ebb, when they settle in soft mud.

The village became a yachting centre after the local boatbuilder and smuggler, Sainty, had been commissioned to build the famous *Pearl* for the Marquis of Anglesey in the 1820s. Many more successful schooners, yawls, cutters, fishing smacks and other craft were then launched from yards in Wivenhoe in its heyday, including Sir Thomas Brassey's *Sunbeam*, Edward Fitzgerald's *Scandal* and the lovely clipper-bowed 40-rater *Creole*. During the Second World War huge sheds were built by Vospers to house MTBs. One of the last craft to be launched at Wivenhoe was the Jubilee Sailing Trust's *Lord Nelson*, a training ship for disabled sailors, built at James Cook's yard in the 1980s.

Many Colne men were crew on the gentlemen's yachts that fitted out at the local yards, and in the 1920s Captain Albert Turner from Wivenhoe was professional skipper of King George V's racing cutter *Britannia* until the death of her owner in 1935.

Wivenhoe Sailing Club is located just below the tidal barrier on the east bank

The waterfront at Wivenhoe

Wivenhoe Port Guide – Local tel code 01206

Water	From quayside hose.
Fuel	Garage ¾ mile (cans).
Stores	Local shops, including a post office. Early closing on Thursdays.
Transport	Train service to Colchester and London.
Yacht club	Wivenhoe Sailing Club, open Friday evenings and Sunday lunchtimes, or when tide suits (showers, toilets, telephone etc); Tel: 822132.
Essex Wildlife Trust, Fingringhoe	Tel: 729678.

Across the river from Wivenhoe is the entrance to Fingringhoe Creek or the Roman River – a reminder that the Romans settled in these parts 19 centuries ago. In the summer months a ferry service runs between Rowhedge, Fingringhoe and Wivenhoe from about two hours before to two hours after high water.

ROWHEDGE

Up-river on the west bank is Rowhedge, described by Hervey Benham as '...once the roughest of all the Colne and Blackwater villages.' Alain Gerbault's famous *Firecrest* was built here in 1892 – at a time when some

40 smacks sailed out of Rowhedge mixing fishing with salvaging, wrecking – and yachting in the summer! The Dixon Kemp-designed *Firecrest* was one of hundreds of vessels built in the village – the Rowhedge Ironworks built minesweepers and MFVs and later maintained RNLI lifeboats. Today, as at Wivenhoe, there are new houses on the quayside and scarcely any signs remain of the once strong maritime links of this Colne-side village.

Access to the quay at Rowhedge, near the riverside pub, is possible from about 2 hours before and 1½ hours after high water. A small pontoon off the quay makes it easier to get ashore and is also used by the Wivenhoe ferry; or it is sometimes possible to lie alongside the quay itself near the Green.

The remaining three miles of river between Rowhedge and the road bridge above the Hythe at Colchester should only be attempted after about four hours of flood. The best water, which will vary from 2m to 3m at the top of the tide, will generally be found midway between the banks. At night, during high water, one bank is lit by a continuous line of street lamps.

COLCHESTER

Colchester is a de-registered port and the Hythe quayside area has been developed. Brightlingsea Harbour Commissioners now has responsibility for buoyage in the River Colne.

The Hythe at Maldon

Chapter eleven
The River Blackwater

Tides	Nass Beacon – HW Dover +00.30. Range: springs 4.6m; neaps 2.6m. (HW Maldon approximately 25mins after HW West Mersea)
Charts	Admiralty 3741, SC5607; Stanfords Chart Pack 4; Imray Y17, 2000 series; OS map 168
Waypoints	Bench Head Buoy 51°44'.69N 01°01'.10E
	Nass Beacon 51°45'.84N 00°54'.84E
Hazards	Thirslet Spit

Arnold Bennett owned a Dutch barge-yacht called *Velsa*, which he kept in Walton Backwaters but also sailed to other Essex and Suffolk rivers as well as to Holland. In the *Log of the Velsa* (published in 1914) he wrote: 'Time was when I agreed with the popular, and the guide book, verdict that the Orwell is the finest estuary in these parts; but now I know better. I unhesitatingly give the palm to the Blackwater. It is a noble stream, a true arm of the sea; its moods are more various, its banks wilder, and its atmospheric effects much grander. The season for cruising on the Blackwater is September, when the village regattas take place and the sunrises over leagues of marsh are made wonderful by strange mists.'

The entrance to both the Blackwater and the Colne is generally considered to be at the Bench Head buoy, some 15 miles down-river from Maldon. Coming up from the south, most yachts follow the example of the sailing barges when they were trading in days gone by, and go through the Swin Spitway.

The deepest water through this swatch is in a line between the Swin Spitway buoy, a safewater pillar buoy with spherical topmark (Iso 10s Bell), to the south-east of the swatch, and the Wallet Spitway safewater spherical buoy (L Fl 10s Bell), a mile away to the north-north-west. See Ray Sand and Swin Spitway chart on page 116. Quite often a yacht gets a fair wind through

Tollesbury looking north-east across Shinglehead point and Great Cob Island; Mersea Island top left, Sales Point to the right

the Spitway when entering the Blackwater, but if ever it is necessary to beat through, then very short boards and constant use of the sounder are essential because the water shoals on to the Buxey Sands on the one hand and the Gunfleet Sands on the other.

From the Spitway, your course is changed to bring the Knoll buoy north cardinal (Q) close to port after about two miles. Then, about a mile away is the Eagle conical green (QG), to be passed close to starboard. With Eagle abeam, the red can of the North-West Knoll buoy (Fl (2) R 5s) will usually be visible and is passed close to port. After this, without altering course appreciably, the green conical Bench Head buoy (Fl (3) G 10s) can be left to starboard at the entrance to the Blackwater.

With the Bench Head astern, a newcomer will find it difficult to identify anything, except the conspicuous Nuclear Power Station at Bradwell, but a course of 295°M from the Bench Head will lead to the Nass beacon. This course is in fairly deep water – for the East Coast at least – and when the tide is running up against a westerly wind it is easy to tell where the channel lies because of the rougher water. After a while St Peter's Chapel should become visible on Sales Point to the south-west, and at about the same time the trees and higher ground at West Mersea will take shape. The safest course is roughly midway between these two shores.

It should be noted that as a result of the Bradwell Power Station being decommissioned, in early 2008

the lights went out so we can no longer rely on the building being conspicuously lit at night.

The Nass beacon, marking the entrance to Mersea Quarters, is a yellow and black steel post topped by a solar panel and a quick flashing light, so that it is

The Nass Beacon marks the entrance to Mersea Quarters and Tollesbury Creek

often easier to find by night than by day. There is little water near the Nass beacon – perhaps no more than 2m at low water springs. During the season there are a couple of mooring buoys in the vicinity of the beacon which are used by committee boats starting races for the West Mersea clubs. It should be noted that many Blackwater Joint Racing Committee racing marks exist in the estuary, one of which is named 'MG' in memory of Maurice Griffiths, who lived the last years of his life on Mersea Island. These marks, often small yellow pillar buoys with numbers on them, are regularly used throughout the season for local club racing, regattas and class championships.

A series of four starboard-hand green can buoys mark the way through Mersea Quarters from the Nass beacon, the last of these, No 7, off Cobmarsh Island, being lit (Fl (1) G 6s). To port are three red can buoys. After the third red can, a lit black and yellow east cardinal buoy marks the Quarters Spit on the north side of Tollesbury Creek. These navigation buoys are laid by the West Mersea Yacht Club.

WEST MERSEA

West Mersea is probably the most popular sailing centre on the River Blackwater and consequently it tends to be crowded. When Archie White, the marine artist, wrote: 'The creeks are crowded with yachts and smacks, the channels are narrow, and there is more mud than water...', he summed up Mersea rather nicely. One of the few East Coast sailing centres without a marina, Mersea retains a timeless quality, which could be why the magician of the swatchways himself, Maurice Griffiths, chose to spend the latter part of his life on Mersea Island.

The West Mersea Town Regatta day, usually in August, was described by the late John Leather in *The Salty Shore* as '...the greatest survivor of informal waterborne fun in Essex, with ex-fishing smacks and bumkins coming to the line and rolling the clock back, followed by the latest fashions in hulls and sail plans of plastic hulled offshore racers and cruisers, class by class ...some classes are still often decided by popular consent in the public bar rather than by formulae...'

These days restored and re-built smacks from Mersea, Maldon, Tollesbury and the Colne are a common sight out on the Blackwater and, on regatta days particularly, the old rivalry between the villages is still intense.

MOORINGS

The best ploy for visiting yachtsmen is to pick up a vacant buoy temporarily and contact the West Mersea Yacht Club boatmen, Jeff or Steve Wass, who will advise further. Although there are no moorings actually designated for visitors, Jeff will usually be able to find you a vacant buoy, probably in the Salcott Channel or the Thornfleet. West Mersea Marine, based at Victory

West Mersea Port Guide – Local tel code 01206	
Moorings/Launch services	
	West Mersea Yacht Club Boatmen Jeff and Steve Wass VHF Ch M, callsign *YC One* or Mob: 07752 309435. West Mersea Marine Launch Mob: 07810 705111; Peter Clarke's Tel: 385905.
Water	Can be obtained at outer end of pontoon landing.
Stores	Limited at Fleetview Stores near pontoon Tel: 382643; shops include Tesco, Co-op, Boots, post office, banks and laundry in West Mersea village; early closing on Wednesdays.
Fuel	Cans, from Underwoods garage in village.
Gas	Wyatts Chandlery (see below).
Repairs	Peter Clarke's Boatyard: slipways, cranage, hoist, chandlery Tel: 385905; West Mersea Marine Tel: 382244, Mob: 07810 705110.
Marine engineers	AB Clarke's near pontoon, Tel: 382706; Malseed Marine Engineering, Coast Road, Tel: 382457, Mob: 07860 727476; West Mersea Marine Engineers Tel: 384350.
Chandlery	Wyatt's Chandlery Tel: 384745; Peter Clarke's Tel: 385905.
Sailmakers	Gowen Ocean Tel: 384412.
Scrubbing posts	On foreshore (contact West Mersea Yacht Club).
Transport	Buses to Colchester whence trains to London.
Yacht clubs	West Mersea Yacht Club, Tel: 382947. Restaurant and bar weekends; lunchtimes and Wednesday evenings during week. Dabchicks Sailing Club Tel: 383786. Bar usually open Wednesday and Saturday evenings; Saturday and Sunday lunchtime.
Telephone	Near Victory Inn on Coast Road.
Food and drink	West Mersea Yacht Club and Dabchicks Sailing Club (see above); all-day breakfasts at Waterfront Café, Tel: 386061, Coast Road beyond Firs Chase; The Coast Inn, Coast Road, Tel: 383558; Victory Hotel, Coast Road, Tel: 382907; The Company Shed, Tel: 382700 (near Wyatts Chandlery) oysters and shellfish, bring your own bread and wine; West Mersea Oyster Bar, Victory Dock, Tel: 381600.

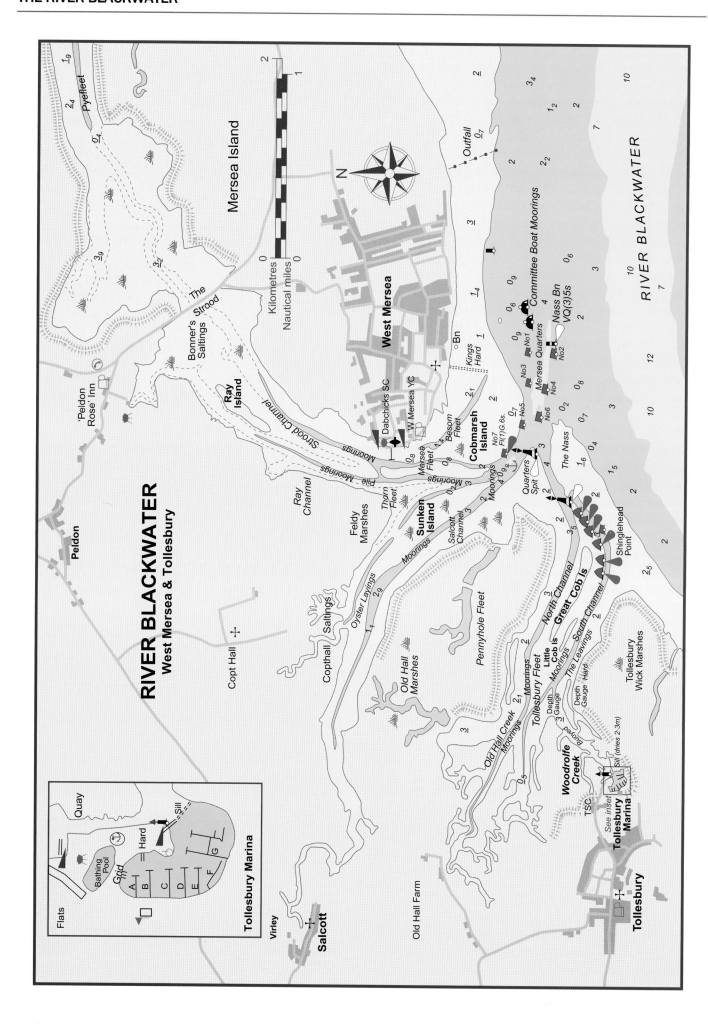

RIVER BLACKWATER
West Mersea & Tollesbury

Mersea Island

Pyefleet

West Mersea

Peldon

'Peldon Rose' Inn

Bonner's Saltings

The Strood

Ray Island

Strood Channel

Ray Channel

Pile Moorings

Dabchicks SC

W Mersea YC

Mersea Fleet

Besom Fleet

Kings Hard

Cobmarsh Island

Thorn Fleet

Sunken Island

Salcott Channel

Feldy Marshes

Moorings

Quarters Spit

The Nass

Nass Bn
VQ(3)5s

Committee Boat Moorings

Mersea Quarters

Outfall

RIVER BLACKWATER

Copt Hall

Copthall Saltings

Oyster Layings

Old Hall Marshes

Pennyhole Fleet

Tollesbury Fleet

Little Cob Is

Great Cob Is

North Channel

South Channel

The Leavings

Shinglehead Point

Old Hall Creek

Moorings

Depth Gauge

Depth Gauge Hard

Tollesbury Wick Marshes

Woodrolfe Creek

Tollesbury Marina

Buoyed

Sill (dries 2·3m)

TSC

Tollesbury

Old Hall Farm

Virley

Salcott

Kilometres
Nautical miles

Tollesbury Marina

Quay

Flats

Bathing Pool

Grid

Hard

Sill

A B C D E F G

Packing Shed Island, with the moorings in the Fleet and Mersea Island itself beyond

Dock, manages moorings and operates a launch service; and Peter Clark of The Boatyard on Coast Road may also be able to help with visitors' moorings.

It is not advisable to anchor further in than the Quarters because of the extensive moorings, and also there are oyster layings in Mersea Fleet running between Cob Marsh Island and Packing Marsh Island, as well as the Salcott Channel up to the little villages of Salcott and Virley.

Sabine Baring Gould, once rector at East Mersea, wrote a haunting Victorian melodrama set around The Ray and its salt marshes. In the story, the heroine Mehalah is married with a ring of iron to the evil Elijah Rebow in the tiny church at Virley. The Rev Baring Gould is perhaps better known for writing the words for the hymn *Onward Christian Soldiers*.

Space is so scarce at Mersea that moorings are laid well inside Salcott Creek and at low water in any of the creeks there is very little room to manoeuvre.

For getting ashore, contact the West Mersea Yacht Club launchmen or West Mersea Marine, which also operates a launch service.

The all-tide pontoon landing is the centre of sailing life at West Mersea – a hub of activity with sailing folk coming and going according to the tide – much as the village fishermen must have done when the posh pontoon was just a muddy hard.

TOLLESBURY

Tollesbury Creek leads directly out of Mersea Quarters and soon divides into the South Channel, which holds the more water, and the North Channel, with the Cob Islands (Great and Little) between.

The east cardinal Quarters Spit buoy indicates the junction of the Creek with the Quarters. The spit extending from Great Cob Island is marked by another lit black and yellow east cardinal, indicating the entrance to the South Channel. The channel is then

marked by a series of six green starboard-hand lit buoys and one red port-hand buoy. Keep close to these until you reach a line of moorings which indicate the way through The Leavings (where the Tollesbury fishing smacks were left while their crews went ashore) to the entrance of Woodrolfe Creek. There is a hard nearby from which it is about a mile walk along the sea wall to the marina and Tollesbury village.

Near the entrance to the creek, which dries out, there are three waiting buoys marked 'Marina' where you can lie afloat. A tide gauge here shows the depth of water over the sill at the marina. The sill has some 2m of water over it at high water springs and about 1.5m at neaps.

The way up Woodrolfe Creek to the marina is marked initially by four pairs of red and green traffic cone-like buoys (lit at night); after which keep to the centre, passing the ex-Trinity House light vessel (used by Fellowship Afloat as a residential outdoor and sailing centre) in the saltings on your starboard hand. On the bend where the creek turns to starboard, you will see the marina entrance to the south of the Woodrolfe Boatyard buildings.

Having entered the basin, moor temporarily at the jetty beneath the crane. While in the yacht harbour, visiting yachtsmen are welcome at Tollesbury Cruising Club where facilities include a heated, covered swimming

Woodrolfe Creek and the light vessel at Tollesbury

pool, tennis courts and restaurant. The long established Tollesbury Sailing Club has its clubhouse nearby in Woodrolfe Road; its members cruise and race and the club organises the annual Tollesbury Smack and Classic Boat Regatta.

The Count de la Chapelle, a famous and well respected gentleman wildfowler, lived in Tollesbury. His record of weekend bags between 1904 and 1918 included '1322 Dunlin, many dozens of which were killed by punt guns for the market'; he noted that 'certain old fishermen in Tollesbury considered a stew of the blackheaded gull a luxury.' In 1894 the Count had a beamy 32ft gunning yacht designed and built by John Howard, the Maldon barge and smack builder. *Scoter* was sailed in winter (with a swivel gun and a punt on deck) as well as in summer up and down the East Coast, with a fisherman as a hand. She was a centreboarder, later much admired by Maurice Griffiths who wrote in *The First of the Tide* that '… this gaff cutter was to influence my ideas for designing shallow draft cruising yachts for many years to come.'

The Old Hall and Tollesbury Wick grazing marshes are managed by the RSPB and Essex Wildlife Trust respectively and attract thousands of wildfowl every winter, but all that is aimed at the birds nowadays is a pair of binoculars.

Many Tollesbury men sailed as hands on the big gaff cutters of the Edwardian era. Edward Heard captained several of them including, in 1930, *Shamrock V*, the last of Sir Thomas Lipton's America's Cup challengers, after which he went on to skipper the J-Class cutter *Endeavour* for Thomas Sopwith.

THE BLACKWATER

On leaving the Quarters and rounding the Nass into the deep water of the Blackwater, the course when proceeding up to Osea Island or Maldon is approximately 250°M.

BRADWELL CREEK

About a mile up-river from the Nass, on the south shore, is Bradwell Creek. The entrance is difficult to see but is in fact only about a quarter of a mile south-west of the Barrier wall off the Nuclear Power Station.

Entrance to the creek is marked by a substantial north cardinal beacon (Q) bearing a tide gauge that shows what water there is over the sill into the marina. Because of silting near the end of Pewet Island, the creek is only accessible within four hours either side of high water. The beacon is considered to be a port-hand mark in the River Blackwater. However, it MUST be left to starboard on entering the creek.

From the beacon a line of orange can buoys indicates the port side of the gutway and a line of withies marks the other side. Best water will be found near the withies.

When the last of the can buoys has been left to port, the channel changes direction towards the south-east, as indicated by two orange-painted triangular topped leading marks that will be seen rather low down in the saltings under a concrete slabbed section of the sea wall. After steering on these beacons for about a cable, the last mark – a green conical buoy – should be left to starboard before continuing along the line of moored craft that extends past the old quay. A concrete slip is situated near the quay end.

At the quay itself, a few gnarled old tree-trunk piles are all that remain to remind us of the days when the creek was busy with Clem Parker's barges, loading from his farms on the surrounding Dengie marshes. Of the Parker fleet, which was said to be the best kept of any, Hervey Benham wrote '…the racer *Veronica* was the fleetest; indeed she was perhaps the fastest flat-bottomed craft ever launched…'

There are still two scrubbing posts alongside the public ramp which were erected by the Bradwell Quay Yacht Club. The club is quite willing for visitors to use them provided they book a time and pay a small fee. Visiting yachtsmen are welcome to use the nearby clubhouse facilities, which include a bar, a barbecue unit and decking area. The Bradwell Quay Yacht Club stewardess can provide meals at reasonable prices particularly for groups, class associations or

Tollesbury Port Guide – Local tel code 01621

Tollesbury Marina/Woodrolfe Boatyard	Tel: 869202; Fax: 868489; VHF Ch 37 or 80; email: marina@woodrolfe. demon.co.uk; www.tollesbury-marina.co.uk.
Berths	240.
Water	On pontoons.
Showers and laundry	On site.
Stores	Shops in village, a 10-minute walk away. Early closing on Wednesdays.
Fuel	Diesel and gas from pontoon, petrol from garage in village.
Chandlery	At yard.
Repairs	Three slipways, lifts, cranage, workshops.
Transport	Bus to Colchester rail station.
Yacht clubs	Tollesbury Cruising Club (in marina), Tel: 869561; Tollesbury Sailing Club, www.tollesburysc.co.uk; bar open Wednesday, Friday, Saturday evenings as well as Sunday lunchtimes.
Food and drink	Tollesbury Cruising Club restaurant offers home cooking. The Hope and the King's Head pubs in High Street.

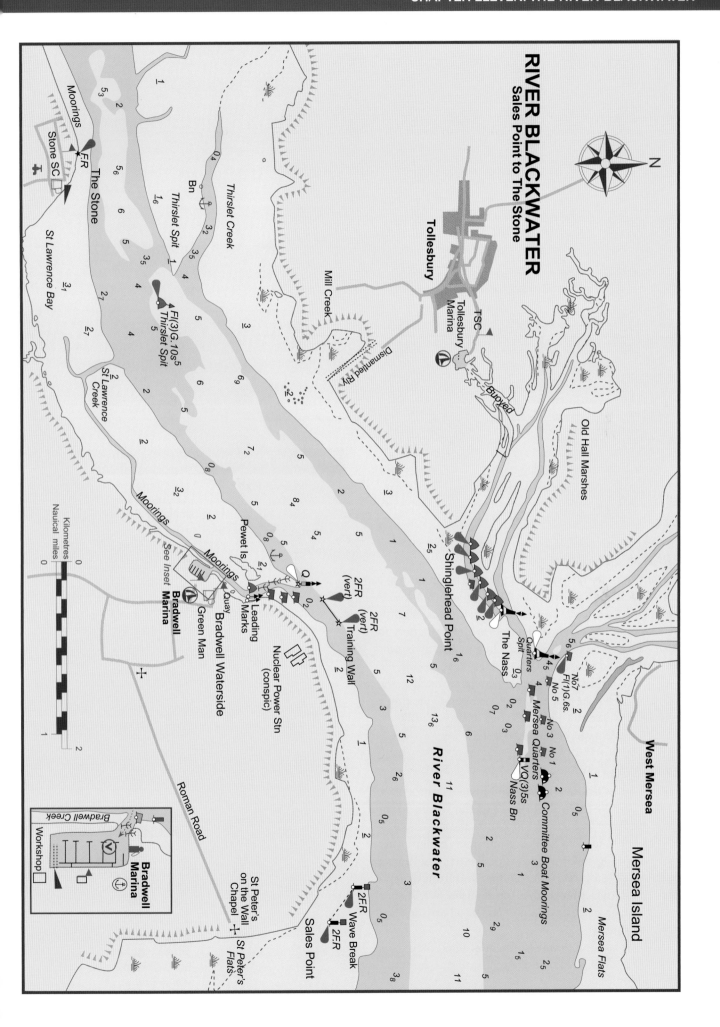

RIVER BLACKWATER
Sales Point to The Stone

N

Moorings

Stone SC

The Stone

F.R

St Lawrence Bay

Thirslet Spit

Thirslet Creek

Bn

Fl(3)G.10s
Thirslet Spit

St Lawrence Creek

Tollesbury

Tollesbury Marina

TSC

Buoyed

Dismantled Rly

Mill Creek

Old Hall Marshes

Shinglehead Point

The Nass

Quarters Spit

Mersea Quarters

No7
Fl(1)G.6s

No5

No3

No1

Committee Boat Moorings

VQ(3)3s
Nass Bn

West Mersea

Mersea Island

Mersea Flats

Moorings

See Inset

Moorings

Bradwell Marina

Green Man

Quay

Bradwell Waterside

Pewet Is

Leading Marks

Q

2FR (vert)

2FR (vert)
Training Wall

Nuclear Power Stn
(conspic)

River Blackwater

Roman Road

St Peter's on the Wall Chapel

St Peter's Flats

Sales Point

Wave Break

2F.R

2F.R

Kilometres

Nautical miles

Bradwell Creek

Workshop

Bradwell Marina

The entrance to Bradwell Marina is marked by an orange buoy, followed by posts on either hand

club visits, so long as she is given ample notice.

The Essex County Council has its Field Studies and Sailing Centre here at Bradwell Waterside, and there is usually a good deal of youthful activity afloat and ashore as a result.

BRADWELL MARINA

The entrance to the marina is indicated by an orange can buoy – Bradwell Marina – and the way in is marked by posts on either hand. Depths in the marina are slightly more than in the creek, and access is approximately four hours either side of high water. Once inside, a visitor should berth on the ends of the first two pontoons.

Bradwell Cruising Club clubhouse is situated in the marina and its bar and restaurant is open to visiting yachtsmen. Essential supplies such as bread, milk, bacon, eggs etc can be obtained here.

BRADWELL

The village of Bradwell (Bradwell Juxta-Mare) is about a mile from the marina; St Peter's on the Wall, a Saxon chapel built by St Cedd in 654 AD on the site of the Roman shore fort of Othona, is a further straight mile along an old Roman road towards the sea. This ancient building, possibly the oldest in England from which Christianity was preached, has been used over the centuries as a mariners' beacon and as a barn, and was re-consecrated in 1920.

In 2007 planning permission was granted for a 10-turbine wind farm on a site a little to the south of the Roman road.

Just north of the chapel is the isolated headquarters

Bradwell Port Guide – Local tel code 01621	
Marina, Port Flair	Tel: 776235; Fax: 776393; www.bradwellmarina. com; VHF Ch M or 80.
Coastguard	Tel: 776310.
Water	In marina or from Bradwell Quay Yacht Club (near top of hard).
Fuel	Diesel, petrol, bottled gas at marina.
Stores	Basic supplies from Bradwell Cruising Club restaurant.
Repairs	At marina, slip up to 20 tons, hoist up to 16 tons.
Transport	Railway station Southminster; buses to Maldon; taxis Tel: 772999.
Telephone	At Bradwell Cruising Club clubhouse.
Laundry	At marina.
Food and drink	Bar and restaurant at Bradwell Cruising Club, Green Man pub restaurant (Tel: 776226) just up the road from Waterside.
Yacht clubs	Bradwell Cruising Club (marina) Tel: 892970. Bradwell Quay Yacht Club. Visitors welcome, bar open weekends and Bank Holiday evenings, barbecue unit available, meals provided by arrangement. Tel: 01245 258420 (Gerry Askham, BQYC Commodore) or www. bqyc.org.uk.

The Port Flair Marina at Bradwell

of the Christian Community of Othona. Hidden behind low trees, on the edge of the saltings to the south is a cottage where once lived Walter Linnet, last surviving professional wildfowler on the Blackwater, who earned a living with his guns and punts into the 1950s. The cottage, in which Walter's father, 'Old Linnet', and his grandfather before him, lived a remote and self sufficient life, is now used by the Essex Naturalist's Trust, which also manages the Bradwell Cockle Spit and the saltings nearby.

THIRSLET CREEK AND GOLDHANGER CREEK
Out in the river again, the next thing to watch for is the green buoy (Fl (3) G 10s) marking a spit of hard sand that protrudes into the river on the north side at the entrance to Thirslet Creek.

Until the Thirslet buoy is located, there is nothing to indicate how far into the river the spit extends, and many yachts have sailed headlong on to the hard sand while aiming, as they thought, straight up the middle of the river! When coming down-river, a safe course

The Thirslet buoy marks a hard spit of sand

results from steering on Bradwell Power Station. Although the water is deepest along this northern shore, the sand is dangerously steep-to and care must therefore be taken not to stand over too far. It is safer to keep well over to the south shore until abreast St Lawrence Bay.

A couple of miles above Thirslet Creek, also amid the northern flats, is the entrance to Goldhanger Creek, marked by a green conical buoy. This also serves as a main river channel buoy and must, therefore, be left to port when entering the creek. A reasonably hard foreshore exists near the top of Goldhanger Creek, but this is only really accessible by dinghy since there is very little water at the head of the creek, even at high water springs. A path along the sea wall can be used to reach the village and the Chequers Inn a mile or so away, where the pub cellar is reputed to have been used for hiding smuggled goods. There are oyster layings in the creek.

For those who appreciate the quiet of remote anchorages, there is enough water in which to lie afloat overnight for half a mile or more within the entrances to both Thirslet and Goldhanger Creeks.

STONE ST LAWRENCE
Over on the south shore is Stone St Lawrence, easily located by the many boats moored in the bay as well as the bungalows and caravans on shore. Stone Sailing Club at the top of the shingle beach is home to fleets of performance dinghies and catamarans which use the wide expanses of the Blackwater for their racing. Powerboat racing also takes place in the region of St Lawrence Bay.

Another club, Marconi Sailing Club, has its clubhouse half a mile further up-river and at night a fixed white light is shown from a corner of the building. There are four rows of moorings with one or two at the upriver end. Here water is obtainable at the top of the slip. On the south side a red port-hand lit buoy, Marconi (Fl (2) R 3s), marks the river where it narrows between Stangate Point and Osea Island.

Coming up-river, Osea Island has been likened to '…an atoll plucked from the Southern Seas,' and on a hot summer's day it can often appear '…as a mirage floating in air, pearly-grey and lovely, shimmering in the warmth of the day,' (Archie White, *Tideways and Byways in Essex and Suffolk*).

From St Lawrence Bay the remains of the little pier at Osea Island can be seen in daylight and its two fixed green lights at night. It is safe for any but deep draught boats to set a course direct to the end of the pier. Larger boats must watch out for a shallow patch known as the Barnacle just east of the pier, and once up-river of the pier, it is not advisable to cut inside any of the buoys marking the rather shallow island shore.

OSEA ISLAND

The southern side of Osea Island has been used as an anchorage for centuries. Almost certainly the longboats of the Vikings lay there before the battle of Maldon in 654 AD and throughout the 19th century collier brigs would have waited off the island for water to take them up to the Hythe at Maldon.

'According to Tide' is what it says on the Osea Island post box, the reason being that communication by land can only take place at low water across a causeway. This is probably why, in 1903, a member of the East End brewers family Charringtons bought the island to create a home for alcoholics, although curing the inmates was made more difficult by the Maldon fishermen who profited by smuggling in illicit drink by boat. A hundred years later a rather more upmarket 'therapeutic retreat' has opened on Osea – it also deals with drug addiction and other disorders, and its clients are flown in by helicopter.

During the First World War Osea was used as a Royal Naval Base: jetties, slipways and berths were built for motor torpedo boats and fast minelayers. Designed by Thornycroft, with hydroplane hull forms that could reach speeds of up to 55mph, they took part in many heroic actions including attacks on Ostend and Zeebrugge in 1918.

LAWLING CREEK AND MAYLANDSEA

Half a mile or so across the river from Osea lies Lawling Creek, the entrance to which is marked by the next port-hand buoy after Marconi, red can No 2 (Fl R 3s). Once over the shallow bar (1m low water springs) and past the large red buoy with *Blackwater Marina* notice on top, there is usually a pair of small red and green spherical buoys, followed by two more greens. But these are liable to be altered so more useful are the mooring buoys – showing a letter C – that have been laid in the middle of the channel; these provide a quiet berth in plenty of water. A yacht can reach the marina at Maylandsea for about half the tide, but in a dinghy it is possible at almost any time.

As well as the many swinging moorings that extend throughout the length of the creek, the Blackwater Marina has serviced floating pontoons and a launch service is available. All forms of repair and rigging can be undertaken; there are three slipways and Thames barges and smacks use the dry dock at the yard fairly regularly.

MAYLAND

In the 1930s small plots of land were sold in Mayland for holiday chalets and around this time George Cardnell, from a local farming family, started building yachts at nearby Steeple which were hauled by horse-drawn carts to the creek. During the Second World War George and his brother Tom established their yard beside the creek where they built motor torpedo boats, fast motor launches and MFVs for the Admiralty. Boats built at Cardnells yard after the War included many Kim Holman designs – the offshore racer *Grenade*, plus several Stellas and Twisters – on the site which is today occupied by Blackwater Marina.

Maylandsea Bay Port Guide Local tel code 01621	
Blackwater Marina	Tel: 740264; www.black watermarina.co.uk; VHF Ch M.
Water	From pontoons at yard.
Stores	Limited provisions available from nearby shops.
Services	Shower and toilet facilities.
Fuel	Diesel and Calor at yard.
Repairs	Yard with slipways, hoists, dry dock and workshops.
Chandler	At yard.
Transport	Bus services to Maldon and Chelmsford.
Telephone	At marina clubhouse.
Yacht clubs	Maylandsea Bay Yacht Club; Harlow Blackwater Sailing Club.
Restaurant/bar	Blackwater Marina.

Marconi Sailing Club at Stansgate has one or two visitors' moorings

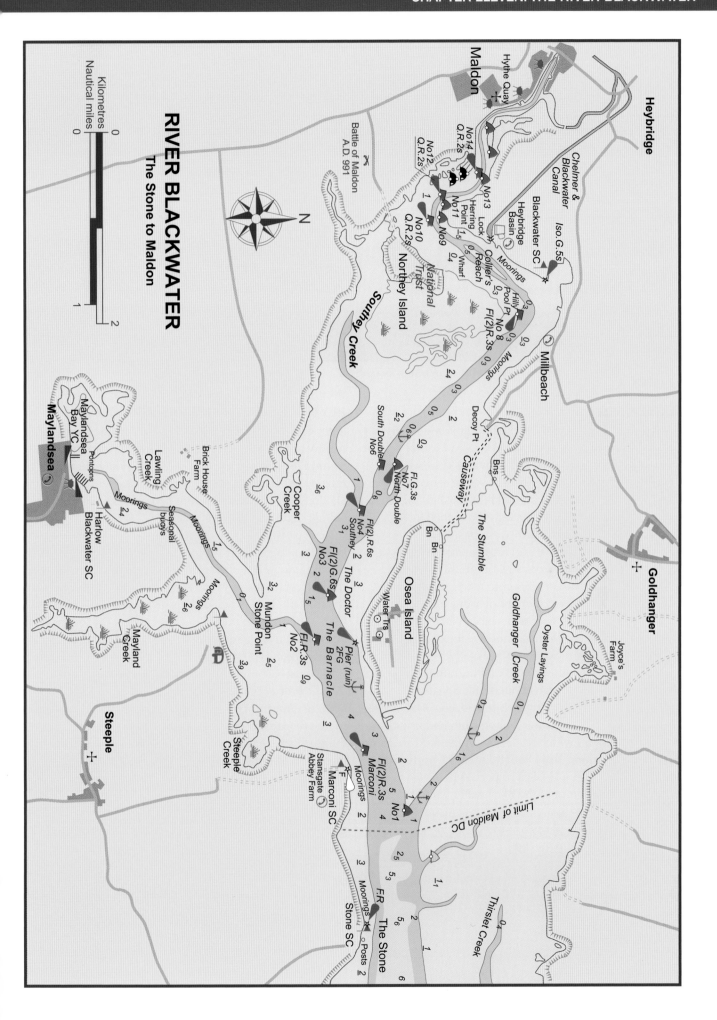

RIVER BLACKWATER

The Stone to Maldon

Kilometres
Nautical miles

Heybridge

Maldon

Hythe Quay

Chelmer &
Blackwater
Canal

Battle of Maldon
A.D. 991

No14
Q.R.2s

No12
Q.R.2s

No13

Herring
Point

Lock

No11

No9

No10
Q.R.2s

No8
Q.R.2s

Collier's
Reach

Hilly
Pool Pt

Fl(2)R.3s

Wharf

Heybridge
Basin

Blackwater SC

Iso.G.5s

Millbeach

National
Trust

Northey Island

Southey Creek

Moorings

Decoy Pt

The Stumble

Causeway

Bns

Bn

Bn

South Double
No6

North Double
No7

Fl.G.3s

Osea Island

Water Trs

The Doctor

Fl(2).R.6s

Southey

Fl(2)G.6s
No3

Cooper
Creek

Brick House
Farm

Lawling
Creek

Maylandsea
Bay YC

Maylandsea

Harlow
Blackwater SC

Moorings

Seasonal
buoys

Moorings

Moorings

Mayland
Creek

Mundon
Stone Point

Fl.R.3s
No2

The Barnacle

Pier
(ruin)
2FG

Steeple
Creek

Steeple

Marconi SC

Stansgate
Abbey Farm

Moorings

Fl(2)R.3s
Marconi

No1

Goldhanger

Goldhanger Creek

Oyster Layings

Joyce's
Farm

Limit of Maldon DC

Thirslet Creek

Moorings

The Stone

Stone SC

F.R

Posts

The southern side of Osea Island has been used as an anchorage for centuries

ABOVE OSEA

It is a good thing for yachtsmen that the Maldon District Council buoy the Blackwater above Osea Island because the channel follows a much less obvious course in the upper reaches of the river. Just above the remains of Osea Pier a green conical buoy (Fl (2) G 6s) guards a mudbank – known as the Doctor. Above the Doctor the channel turns to the north-west, past Southey, a port-hand red can buoy (Fl (2) R 6s) at the entrance to Southey Creek. If a boat draws 4 or 5ft, this is about as far up-river as she can expect to reach and remain afloat at low water. Two more buoys, one a green conical (Fl G 3s) and the other a red can (No 6) are known locally as the Doubles, and are located just above the entrance to Southey Creek.

By this time the maltings and mill buildings beyond Mill Beach should be seen about a mile ahead, and to the west of them a long, low, white building. This is the clubhouse of the Blackwater Sailing Club and it will serve as a mark on which to steer until the red can buoy (Fl (2) R 3s) marking Hilly Pool Point at the northern end of Northey Island is seen to port. A light (Iso G 5s) is shown from the roof of the Blackwater Sailing Club.

The green conical buoy No 3 is known as The Doctor

HEYBRIDGE BASIN AND CHELMER CANAL

After rounding Hilly Pool Point and turning sharply southwards into Collier's Reach, the cluster of houses round Heybridge Lock will come into view about half a mile away. There are densely packed half-tide moorings all along the Heybridge shore between the Blackwater Sailing Club and the lock entrance.

From an hour before to an hour after high water a boat drawing 6 or 7ft should have no great difficulty in getting into or out of Heybridge Lock. Because of the need to retain water in the canal during the summer months, the lock is worked for only one hour before high water during neap tides. At springs the lock will be worked over a longer period. Prior notification and confirmation with the lock-master is required if the lock is to be used at night.

It is never very easy to tell whether the lock gates are open or shut until close to and in line with them, but there are traffic lights on the west side of the lock. From the starboard-hand green conical buoy Lock Approach, the entrance gut is marked by withies which should be left to about a boat's width to port.

Locking out normally occurs first. The gut is narrow so do not attempt the approach channel until a single green light is displayed and all boats have left the lock and cleared the entrance. When you are inside the lock the lock-keeper will allocate you a berth; in busy times this may involve rafting up with other boats. In summer when sailing club cruises in company and rallies often visit the Basin, it is advisable to check beforehand to see if there are spaces.

The Basin is managed by Essex Waterways (a subsidiary company of Inland Waterways), which took over from The Chelmer and Blackwater Navigation Company in 2005. There are about 150 permanent berths in the Basin; those for visitors are immediately inside the lock, with adjacent facilities – toilets, showers and laundry.

A daily launch ferry service operates in summer up the canal to Heybridge and Maldon where there are shops and superstores. A licence is necessary for boats navigating the canal.

As well as two pubs – the Old Ship at the top overlooking the lock and the river, and the Jolly Sailor nestling below the seawall – there is a waterfront tea-room run by the local Tiptree Jam Company (on the former boatyard and chandlery site).

The Basin has always been a stronghold for traditional boats and there are usually several old-timers together with local smacks undergoing restoration work alongside the towpath or in mud berths or dry docks outside the lock. Peter Brookes, who restored many West Solent One-Designs and other classic boats, has now returned to New Zealand but shipwrights are still at work here: the most recent project being the re-build of the sailing barge *Dawn*, completed in 2008.

Heybridge Basin and the 14-mile Chelmer and Blackwater Navigation Canal were constructed in 1797 for the purpose of lightering coal into Chelmsford – hence Collier's Reach. In the 1950s imported Baltic timber was lightered up the canal to Sadds timber yard at Heybridge, many of the lighters being de-rigged sailing barges (one of which, the *Mirosa*, features on the front cover of this edition, happily re-rigged and still sailing). For a few years there was a thriving trade in live eels from Holland. This slippery cargo was decanted from the holds of small motor ketches off Osea into special floating tanks which were then towed up to the Basin. There was talk at the time of diamonds being smuggled in with the eels.

From off Heybridge Basin, the river continues in a south-westerly direction for about a quarter of a mile before turning north round Herring Point. To the

south is the tidal causeway connecting Northey Island with the mainland; the causeway is believed to be the site of the Battle of Maldon. Access to the National Trust-owned island can be arranged by contacting the National Trust warden.

From here up to Maldon the winding channel is well marked with conical green buoys on the starboard side and red cans on the port-hand side.

Heybridge Basin Port Guide
Local tel code 01621

Lock-keeper	Martin Maudsley Tel: 853506; Fax: 859689; Mob: 07712 079764; VHF Ch 80, callsign *Heybridge Lock*.
Essex Waterways	www.waterways.org.uk/ essexwaterways ltd.
Visitors' berths	Immediately inside inner gates; some rafting up.
Water and electricity	At visitors' berths.
Services	Toilets, showers and laundry.
Stores	Basin Pleasure Boats, Tel: 07835 657462, summertime launch/ferry service daily to shops, Tesco at Heybridge/ Maldon.
Fuel	Petrol and gas from garages at Heybridge.
Transport	Infrequent buses to Maldon.
Telephone	110 yards from lock.
Yacht club	Blackwater Sailing Club, Tel: 853923 (quarter of a mile from lock).
Repairs	Stebbens Boatyard, Tel: 857436.
Food and drink	The Old Ship, Tel: 854150; The Jolly Sailor, Tel: 854210; The Lock Tearoom, Tel: 226616; Fish and chip shop plus take-aways in Heybridge.

The green conical Lock Approach buoy off Heybridge Lock

MALDON

Towards the top of the tide you can sometimes find yourself approaching the town in company with one or more sailing barges, not to speak of smacks, river cruise boats and other yachts. Bear in mind that the barges come alongside the quay with their bows pointing downstream and will therefore need room to manoeuvre.

Apart from one or two holes, the river dries out almost completely at Maldon, and the local boats take the mud. In 1892 H Lewis Jones wrote in *Swin, Swale and Swatchway* '...it is rather an undertaking to stay at Maldon Hythe...'

Nowadays the visitors' pontoon at the north end of Hythe Quay is accessible about 1½ hours either side of high water. The pontoon is about 70ft long and if you are prepared to take the mud, and probably raft up, you can stay overnight. This is a delightful spot to stop over but it can get crowded – as there is no longer a Maldon District Council River Warden, it is usually a case of first come first served. Facilities on the quay include toilets, showers, washing machines, dryers; however, keys will need to be obtained from a barge skipper. Garbage disposal is nearby.

For a short stay you may be able to lie alongside one of the barges, but your yacht should not be left unattended. Several barges are based at Hythe Quay,

A statue of Byrhtnoth stands at the end of the Promenade

Maldon Port Guide – Local tel code 01621

River bailiff	Nigel Harmer (Bailiff's Hut) Tel: 875837; Mob: 07818 013723.
Water	Standpipe on quayside near pontoon.
Stores	Many shops in town. Early closing on Wednesdays; Tesco at Fullbridge (10-15 minute walk).
Fuel	Diesel and petrol from Promenade Garage (own cans), Tel: 852821.
Repairs	Yards and slips above The Hythe.
Chandlery	Maldon Chandlery, North Street, Tel: 08707 777089.
Sailmaker	Taylors, The Hythe.
Transport	Bus to Chelmsford main line railway station.
Yacht clubs	Maldon Little Ship Club, The Hythe, Tel:854139; Maldon Yacht Club.
Food and drink	Queen's Head and Jolly Sailor on The Hythe; pubs and restaurants in High Street; local oysters and seafood at Essex Oyster and Seafishing Company behind Cook's Yard on quayside (occasionally during summer).
National Trust Northey Island	Tel: 853142.

including the Thames Sailing Barge Trust's *Centaur* and *Pudge*; the charter barges *Reminder, Repertor* and *Hydrogen* ca.: be seen alongside regularly, and the Thames Sailing Barge Heritage Centre has a permanent exhibition aboard the *Glenway*. The annual Blackwater Barge Match usually takes place in early June.

Maldon's name derives from Maeldun, Anglo Saxon for cross on a hill top. Here the Saxons built a fort to defend the River Blackwater against marauding Norsemen – to whom they finally succumbed in 991 at the Battle of Maldon. As you pass the western end of Northey Island, give a thought to the heroic defence by Byrhtnoth's men against the Danes a thousand years ago. A splendid statue of a defiant Byrhtnoth (by the internationally renowned, and locally based, sculptor John Doubleday) stands at the end of the Promenade.

The town went on to prosper as a fishing and trading port, the Royal Charter was granted, and ships were built such as the 48-gun *The Jersey*, which served with Blake in the Mediterranean. She was launched at the yard where, several hundred years later, John Howard created a succession of beautiful Maldon barges and smacks. At that same yard during the last century, Dan Webb built the famous little Blackwater sloops, many of which are still sailing today.

The waterfront at Burnham-on-Crouch

Chapter twelve
The River Crouch

Tides	HW Dover +1.10. Range: springs 5.0m; neaps 3.2m (HW at Whitaker Beacon approximately 20mins before HW at Burnham-on-Crouch)
Charts	Admiralty 3750, SC5607; Stanfords Chart Pack 4; Imray Y15, 2000 series; OS map 168
Waypoints	**Wallet Spitway Buoy** 51°42'.87N 01°07'.30E
	Swin Spitway Buoy 51°41'.95N 01°08'.35E
	Whitaker Bell Buoy 51°41'.43N 01°10'.51E
	Whitaker Beacon 51°39'.65N 01°06'.17E
	Ridge Buoy 51°40'.13N 01°04'.87E
	Sunken Buxey Buoy 51°39'.54N 01°00'.59E
	Outer Crouch Buoy 51°38'.38N 00°58'.48E
	Buxey Beacon 51°41'.16N 01°01'.29E
Hazards	Shoal water between Swin Spitway and Whitaker Beacon

Some people say Burnham's popularity as a sailing centre has declined, but if you arrive in the Crouch during Burnham Week, you'll be thankful the place is no more popular than it already is. Archie White wrote of Burnham Week being '…a positive orgy of swiftness lasting a whole week at the latter part of the season.

What with the rapid gunfire ashore and the falling masts of contenders afloat, the affair resembles an old-time naval engagement. During regatta week the river is almost impassable to humble cruisers…'

As a river, the Crouch can hardly be described as beautiful. Its higher reaches are certainly more pleasant

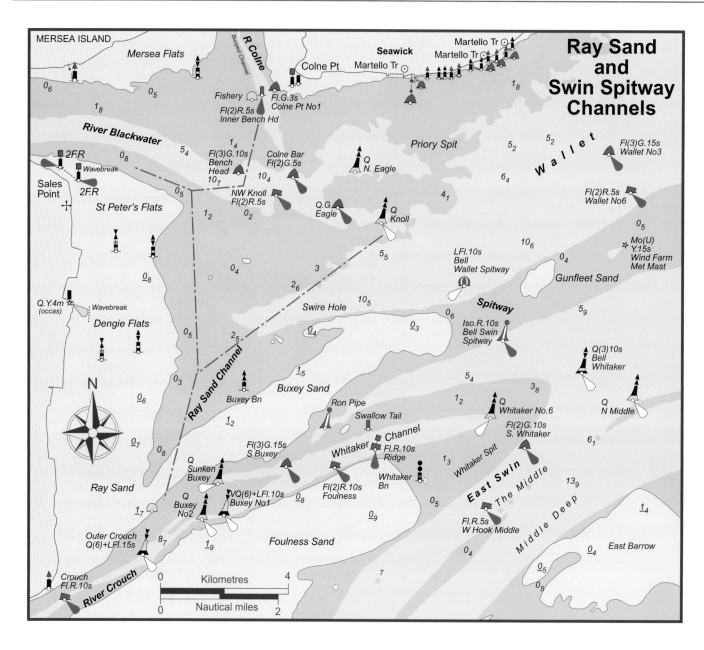

Ray Sand and Swin Spitway Channels

MERSEA ISLAND
Mersea Flats
R Colne
Seawick
Colne Pt
Martello Tr ⊙
Martello Tr ⊙
Martello Tr ⊙

Buoyed Channel
Fishery
Fl.G.3s
Colne Pt No1
Fl(2)R.5s
Inner Bench Hd

0₆
0₅
1₈

River Blackwater
5₄
0₈

2F.R
Wavebreak
Sales Point
2F.R
St Peter's Flats

1₄
Fl(3)G.10s
Bench Head
10₇

Colne Bar
Fl(2)G.5s
10₄

Q
N. Eagle

Priory Spit
5₂
5₂
Wallet
6₄

Fl(3)G.15s
Wallet No3

NW Knoll
Fl(2)R.5s
1₂
0₂

Q.G.
Eagle

Q
Knoll

4₁

Fl(2)R.5s
Wallet No6
0₅

0₈

Q.Y.4m ☆
(occas)
Wavebreak
Dengie Flats

0₄
2₅

3
2₆

Swire Hole
10₅

0₄

LFl.10s
Bell
Wallet Spitway
Ω

10₆
0₄

Gunfleet Sand

Mo(U)
Y.15s
Wind Farm
Met Mast

5₉

N
0₆
0₇
0₈

0₅
0₃
0₄

Ray Sand Channel

Buxey Bn
Fl(3)G.15s
S.Buxey

1₅
1₂
Buxey Sand

0₆

Ron Pipe
Swallow Tail

Whitaker Channel
Fl.R.10s
Ridge

0₆

Iso.R.10s
Bell Swin
Spitway

0₃

Q(3)10s
Bell
Whitaker

5₄
3₈

Q
Whitaker No.6
Fl(2)G.10s
S. Whitaker

Q
N Middle

6₁

1₂

Q
Sunken Buxey

VQ(6)+LFl.10s
Buxey No1

0₈

Fl(2)R.10s
Foulness

Whitaker Bn

1₃

Whitaker Spit

East Swin
The Middle
13₉

Q
Buxey No2

1₇

8₇
1₉

Ray Sand

0₉
0₅

Fl.R.5s
W Hook Middle

0₄

Middle Deep
1₄

Outer Crouch
Q(6)+LFl.15s

Foulness Sand

7

0₅
0₅

0₄
East Barrow

Crouch
Fl.R.10s
River Crouch

0
Kilometres
4

0
Nautical miles
2

---

than the five or six miles between Burnham and Shore Ends, where nothing much can be seen above the bordering sea walls except for a short while at high tide. Yet, because of these unobstructed shores, the Crouch offers racing yachtsmen the best possible sport and, with the smaller River Roach entering at right angles, a variety of courses can be laid to suit all wind conditions.

BUOYAGE OF RIVER CROUCH

Buoyage and marking of the River Crouch is the responsibility of the Crouch Harbour Authority. All the buoys were lit in the 1980s when there was considerable commercial traffic to and from Baltic Wharf, Wallasea. Shipping subsequently declined and some buoys were removed. However, in the early years of the 21st century the importing of timber and steel to the wharf is on the increase again; much of the timber goes to the site of the 2012 Olympics building project in East London. Vessels from 80m to 120m in length come in and out of the river a couple of times each week under

pilotage; details of ship movements are posted on the Crouch Harbour Authority website.

From Battlesbridge, the navigable limit of the river, down to Shore Ends where the Crouch clears the land, is approximately 15 miles. From Shore Ends out to the Whitaker bell buoy, marking the extremity of the Whitaker Spit, is another nine or 10 miles.

Excluding the top-of-the-tide entrance through Havengore Creek and the River Roach, there are two approaches to the Crouch: through the Whitaker Channel from the Swin or the Spitway and through the very shallow Ray Sand (Rays'n) Channel between Dengie Flats and the Buxey Sand. The deep water approach will be considered first.

When coming from the north through the Swin Spitway, shape a course of 180°M from the Wallet Spitway buoy towards Whitaker No 6 buoy and, to avoid the eastward-extending Swallowtail shoal, continue until the Ridge buoy (red can with topmark) bears 255°M before altering course to pass just north of

The Swin Spitway safewater buoy

the Ridge buoy. From the Ridge and Foulness buoys, a course should be set to Buxey No 1 buoy, leaving the green conical South Buxey buoy to starboard.

The channel between the Ridge and Swallow Tail is wide and deep, but the channel to the north of the Swallow Tail, along the south-east shore of the Buxey Sand, is often used when sailing between the Spitway and South Buxey buoys. As a result a safe water mark, Ron Pipe (formerly North Swallow), has been established here. The buoy is an unlit pillar buoy, red and white vertical stripes with a red ball topmark.

The Sunken Buxey shoal is marked on both sides, and many yachtsmen prefer to pass to the south of it, leaving the south cardinal, Buxey No 1 (VQ (6) + L Fl 10s) buoy to starboard and the north cardinal Buxey No 2 (Fl R 10s) to port. This way in is probably easier with a fair wind or under power, but when beating, the northern side of the shoal will allow longer boards.

When coming from the south round the Whitaker Beacon, deep water will be found about midway between Whitaker No 6 north cardinal and the Ridge buoy, and when the latter bears 255°M, alter onto that course.

Continue as described above, and once the Outer Crouch buoy (South Card Q (6) + L Fl 15s) has been located, a course should be shaped to leave it close to starboard and thence into the river.

To the south of the Crouch approaches, the MOD carries out regular gunnery and explosives exercises across the ranges on both Foulness and Maplin sands between The Whitaker and Shoeburyness. On a more peaceful note, you may also see numbers of seals in this vicinity on either the Buxey or Foulness sands.

THE RAY SAND CHANNEL

Moderate draught yachts bound from the Blackwater to the Crouch can, at the right state of the tide, come through the Ray Sand or Rays'n Channel. There is little or no water in the southern end of the swatchway at low water springs, in fact it is possible at low water extraordinary springs to walk virtually dry footed from the mainland to the Buxey Sand.

The time-honoured Buxey Beacon still stands where it did when Maurice Griffiths wrote *The Magic of the Swatchways*, but no longer with its easily recognised sign-post topmark. Instead, a north cardinal mark tops the beacon which, like the Whitaker, has a tripod base. Trinity House has now disowned this and several other beacons in the Thames Estuary, so we must hope that local authorities or yacht clubs will see that they are maintained in future.

The Dengie Flats were once used as a dive-bombing range and four derelict target craft still remain as a reminder. These wrecks are marked by unlit beacons; the two inshore having west cardinal topmarks and the outer two with east cardinal topmarks.

When bound from the Wallet past the Knoll buoy, the best course to hold into the Rays'n will be 235°M. The North Buxey buoy is no longer there to guide you, but sudden changes in depth near the Swire Hole should serve to locate you on the chart. When the Buxey Beacon bears 180°M, change course to 215°M to pass it about half a mile away to port.

Finally, when the conspicuous pylons on Foulness Island come to bear 210°M, change on to this course until the deeper water of the Crouch is found – about a mile to the west of the Sunken Buxey buoy, with its double cone (north cardinal) topmark.

Shallow draught boats, using a rising tide, can often sneak through the Rays'n closer inshore by following a course approximately 185°M and about a mile to seaward of the outer pair of wrecked target vessels. This is the area in which to change course to about north, if bound from the Crouch to the Blackwater.

A small spherical yellow buoy is laid seasonally in the southern entrance to the Rays'n by the Burnham yacht clubs and is intended to indicate a way through the swatch. The latest position of the Rays'n buoy was 51°39'.07N 00°59'.29E, but it is liable to be moved or to go missing off station. There was a shallow patch to the west of this buoy, which is best treated as if it were an east cardinal mark. Even so, do not expect to find any clear cut channel or gutway.

THE RIVER CROUCH

About 1½ miles south-west of the Outer Crouch buoy and just inside the river itself is the Crouch red can buoy (Fl R 10s). After the Crouch buoy direction is changed to a westerly course, which can be held up-river as far as the junction of the River Roach about three miles away. Halfway between the Crouch buoy and the entrance to the Roach is the red and white spherical Inner Crouch buoy (L Fl 10s), which can be passed on either hand. Two racing buoys may be seen on the northern side of the channel, just below the entrance to the Roach, and these should be left to the north to be sure of missing the mud of Redward Flats. The yellow spherical Branklet Spit buoy marks an arm of mud that extends north-easterly from Wallasea Ness. West of Branklet Spit the deepest water is to be found near the north bank of the river. However, because the south shore is steep-to, it is often the safer one to work.

A north cardinal buoy – Horse (Q Fl) – just west of the entrance to the River Roach, was originally intended to mark the southern end of a dredged channel leading to the Burnham Fairway buoy; but it is doubtful whether the channel still remains.

On the south side of the river, six breaches in the seawall, associated with the Wallasea Wetlands Project, are marked by a series of beacons. Starting at Breach No 2 the beacons are steel tubular piles carrying red port-hand topmarks and they indicate the riverward extent of underwater hazards or obstructions in way of the breaches. It is advisable not to stand in on this shore because at low water springs there can be shallow water north of the beacons.

Some of the northern part of Wallasea Island was opened to the sea in 2006 as part of a DEFRA Managed Re-alignment scheme that is now being managed by the RSPB, which plans to transform much of the arable farmland on the island back into coastal marshland in partnership with the owners. This major development may eventually involve several further breaches being made in the seawall to the south of Wallasea Island in the River Roach.

BURNHAM

Burnham-on-Crouch has long been considered as the Cowes of the East Coast. When the Great Eastern branch railway line was built in the 1890s, boat owners migrated to Burnham from the then busy and dirty Thames and found the Crouch to be a better location for both cruising and racing. Thus it was that a quiet oyster-fishing village turned rapidly into a popular yachting centre, and has remained so to this day.

According to Francis B Cooke '...a year or two before the outbreak of the Great War ...there were more than eight hundred craft... lying off the town.' Boatyards, sailmakers, chandleries and stores flourished, and fleets of the elegant East Coast One-Designs, followed by the Royal Burnham and the Royal Corinthian One-Designs were launched. In the 1960s, Tucker Brown, whose

The River Crouch looking east, with Burnham Yacht Harbour and the town to the left and Essex Marina to the right

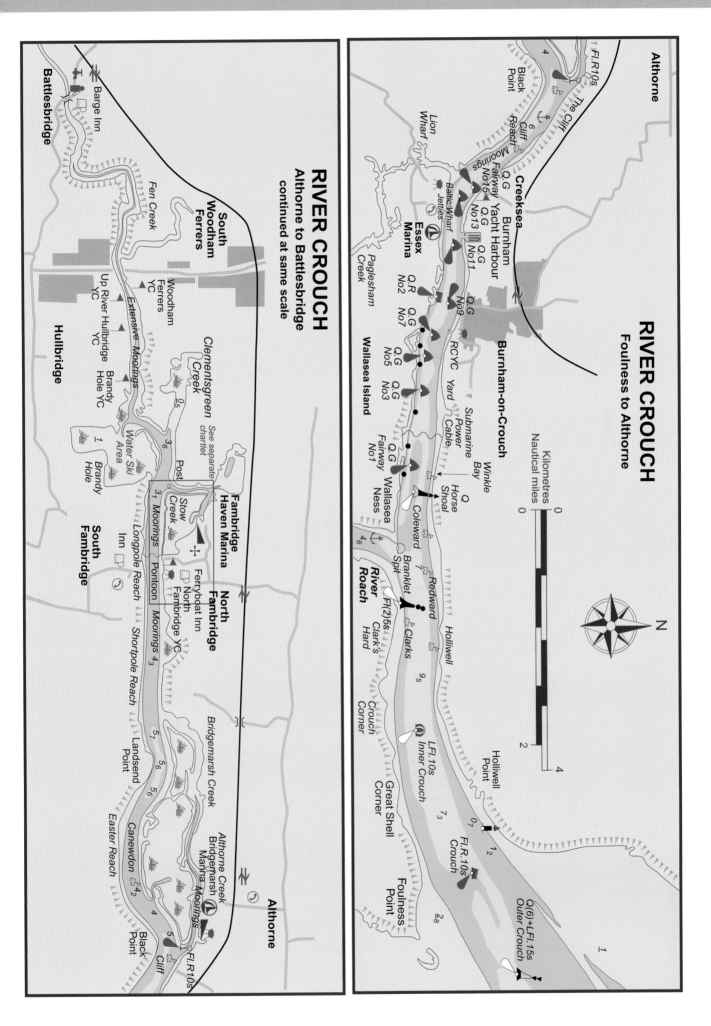

RIVER CROUCH
Foulness to Althorne

Kilometres
Nautical miles

N

Althorne

Black Point

Cliff Reach

The Cliff

Fl.R10s

Creeksea

Fairway Moorings

Q.G No15

Q.G No13

Q.G No11

Burnham Yacht Harbour

Lion Wharf

Battle Wharf Jetties

Essex Marina

Burnham-on-Crouch

Paglesham Creek

Wallasea Island

Q.R No2

Q.G No7

Q.G No5

Q.G No3

Q.G No9

RCYC

Yard

Submarine Bay

Power Cable

Winkle

Q Horse Shoal

Fairway No1

Wallasea Ness

Coleward

Branklet Spit

Redward

Holliwell

River Roach

Clarks

Fl(2)5s

Clark's Hard

Crouch Corner

Inner Crouch

LFl.10s

Great Shell Corner

Holliwell Point

Fl.R.10s Crouch

Foulness Point

Q(6)+LFl.15s Outer Crouch

RIVER CROUCH
Althorne to Battlesbridge
continued at same scale

Battlesbridge

Barge Inn

Fen Creek

South Woodham Ferrers

Woodham Ferrers YC

Up River Hullbridge YC

Brandy Hole YC

Extensive Moorings

Clementsgreen Creek

Hullbridge

Water Ski Area

Brandy Hole

See separate chartlet

Post

Stow Creek

Moorings

Pontoon

Ferryboat Inn

North Fambridge YC

Fambridge Haven Marina

North Fambridge

South Fambridge

Inn

Longpole Reach

Shortpole Reach

Moorings

Landsend Point

Bridgemarsh Creek

Canewdon

Easter Reach

Black Point

Cliff

Fl.R10s

Althorne

Althorne Creek

Bridgemarsh Marina Moorings

premises now house the local museum, produced a galaxy of Stellas, and Priors built offshore racers such as Maurice Laing's *Vashti*. Nowadays Petticrows turn out glassfibre Dragons that are sold worldwide – the Burnham Dragon fleet is one of the strongest in the UK.

Approaching Burnham from the river, after the featureless seawall scenery in the lower reaches of the Crouch, you cannot fail to notice the clubhouse of the Royal Corinthian Yacht Club. This edifice dominates the eastern end of the town's skyline from miles away. When it was built in 1931, J Wentworth Day, that staunch defender of traditional Essex, described it as '....a cross between a football grandstand and a town hall of Teutonic conception...' The concrete and plate glass construction seems out of keeping with the mellow Georgian houses further along the red brick quayside, yet it has become an integral part of Burnham's waterfront image and is now a listed building.

The many yacht moorings off Burnham commence just above a group of four yellow spherical buoys marking submerged cables carrying 33,000 volts. The Burnham Fairway is on the south side of the river and, although narrow, it is well marked by eight starboard-hand buoys (QG) and one port-hand can buoy (QR). There is at least 4m of water throughout the length of the Fairway and the south shore is steep-to. When it becomes necessary to beat up-river and boards on the port tack are extended in among the moored craft, a close watch should be kept on the effects of the tide, for the ebb at spring tides can run at three knots past Burnham.

Anchoring is prohibited in the fairway, and the multitude of moorings makes it very difficult to bring up to an anchor anywhere in the area. For brief stops you may be able to use one of the pontoons along the waterfront: from the east these are at Rice & Cole's, the Royal Corinthian Yacht Club, the Royal Burnham Yacht Club, the public pontoon at the Town Steps, Prior's, and the Crouch Yacht Club. You can usually find a buoy off one of the clubs or yards, although during Burnham Week (which always starts near the August bank holiday weekend) this would need pre-booking. The Royal Corinthian Yacht Club has a visitor's mooring sited directly off its clubhouse, but if this is occupied, enquiries will usually lead to the provision of some other vacant buoy. It should be noted that the tide runs fast through the moorings, particularly on a spring ebb, so for longer stays the visiting yachtsman would be well advised to head for the 350-berth Burnham Yacht Harbour, accessible at all states of the tide, at the western end of the town.

The entrance is marked by a yellow pillar buoy with X topmark (Fl Y 5s) and a couple of posts with red and green flashing lights.

The little town is a pleasant place, there are facilities for yachtsmen close at hand and many of its people are in some way connected with sailing. During the summer months a ferry connects Burnham with Wallasea Island. The service runs to the Essex Marina from a pontoon at the old Town Steps, on the Quay opposite The Anchor Hotel and just upriver from the Royal Burnham Yacht Club. This landing pontoon, which has a hammerhead, can be used by visiting yachts on a short term basis.

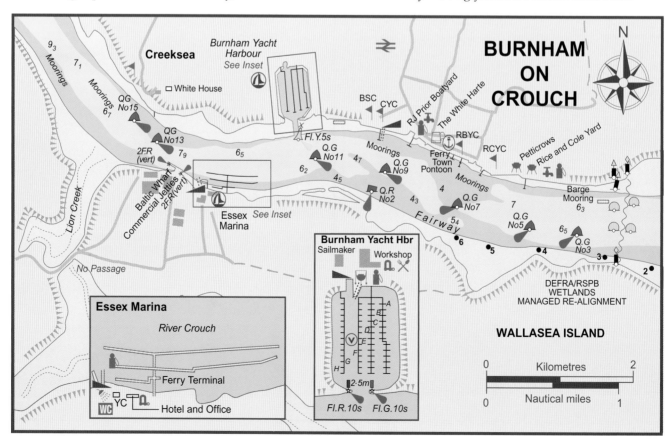

The Town Landing pontoon

The Royal Corinthian Yacht Club

The Burnham Yacht Harbour is at the western end of the town

Burnham-on-Crouch Port Guide
Local tel code 01621

Crouch Harbour Authority	
Harbour Master	The Quay Tel: 783602, 0930-1130 Monday-Friday; email: info@crouchharbour.org; www.crouchharbour.org. CHA launch *Watchful* weekends 0900-1700; VHF Ch 16 and M (ex-37). 24-hour emergency Mob: 07724 561453.
Burnham Yacht Harbour	Tel: 782150; Fax: 785848; VHF Ch 80.
Berths	350 at Yacht Harbour.
Swinging moorings	Rice & Cole, Sea End Boathouse, Tel: 782063; RJ Prior & Sons Tel: 782160.
Water	Yacht Harbour, Rice & Cole pontoon, stand-pipes near most landing places.
Stores	Co-op near Yacht Harbour open late most evenings and Sunday mornings. Shops, including Tesco Express, in High Street. Early closing on Wednesdays.
Fuel	Diesel from yacht harbour; petrol from Essex Marina fuel barge at Wallasea or garage in town; gas from chandlery at yacht harbour.
Repairs	100 ton slipway, 30 ton hoist, engineers, riggers at Yacht Harbour; Rice & Cole, Sea End Boathouse.
Chandlery	Marine Store at Yacht Harbour, Tel: 783090. Fairways Yacht Chandlery, The Quay, Tel: 782659.
Sailmakers	Lonton & Gray, 61c High Street, Tel: 786200. Wilkinson Sails Tel: 786770.
Transport	Regular trains to London Liverpool Street via Wickford, some through trains (station about 10 minutes walk from yacht harbour).
Yacht clubs	Royal Corinthian Yacht Club Tel: 782105. Royal Burnham Yacht Club Tel: 782044. Crouch Yacht Club Tel: 782252. Burnham Sailing Club Tel: 782624.
Telephone	Near White Hart.
Food and drink	Swallowtail lounge bar and restaurant at Yacht Harbour, Tel 785505; bar and restaurant at Royal Corinthian and Crouch Yacht Clubs; White Hart Tel: 782106 and other pubs on Quay and High Street; Contented Sole, Tel 782139, specialises in seafood; Dengie Shellfish stall near War Memorial off High Street.
Ferry	Wallasea Island to Town Quay (Easter to end of September) Tel: 01702 258666; www.ladyessex.com.

The Quay at Burnham is lined with mellow Georgian houses

WALLASEA BAY

On the opposite shore and about a mile up-river from Burnham is Wallasea Bay. Here again the moorings are numerous, but this time located along the south as well as the north side of the river. Essex Marina at Wallasea Bay has 400 pontoon berths and swinging moorings, along with shoreside toilet, shower and laundry facilities. The fuel barge is located on the upriver or western end of the inshore pontoon near the slipway. The marina bar and restaurant on site has good views across the river to Burnham and from Easter to September there is a ferry service from the marina to Burnham Town Quay.

The western end of Burnham Fairway is marked by the No 13 buoy off the Baltic Wharf, which handles imported timber and is strictly commercial, with no facilities to the public. There is shallow water on the north side of the river just below Creeksea, where the Creeksea Sailing Club has a small, low profile boathouse and races Phantom dinghies.

The river now turns north-westerly through Cliff Reach; so called because of the modest (40-50ft) cliff just above Creeksea. Cliff Reach is important to the

yachtsman in as much as it provides shelter from south-westerly winds, when most of the other reaches in the Crouch are made uncomfortable. Towards low tide a good look-out should be kept for a line of concrete sinkers that can be found along the low water line below the cliff.

At the top of Cliff Reach the main stream turns south-westerly round Black Point, where the shore is steep-to, into Easter Reach. A yellow racing buoy marked 'Cliff Reach' is usually located off Black Point. A minor branch of the river continues north-west into Althorne Creek.

ALTHORNE CREEK

The entrance to the creek is identified by a port-hand spar (Fl R 10s) and a series of three red can buoys. The course when entering is roughly N (°M), leaving the beacon and the first red can close to port.

At Bridgemarsh Marina, Tel: 01621 740414, there are over 100 boats moored to pontoons between piles along the centre of the creek, both above and below the spot where there was once a ford leading on to Bridgemarsh Island. There are some visitors' moorings, while on the north bank is a yard comprising two docks, a slipway, a crane and pontoons equipped with water and power, with toilet and showers provided. Althorne station is only about a quarter of a mile away, whence it is no more than an hour to Liverpool Street station in London, or a few minutes to Burnham-on-Crouch station.

It is possible in a small craft, with a rising tide and a commanding wind, to sail behind the island through Althorne Creek and Bridgemarsh Creek to join the Crouch again some two miles further up-stream. However, the channel is extremely narrow and tortuous and it should be noted that the creeks and lagoons within Bridgemarsh Island are private.

From the Cliff Reach buoy the river flows south-westerly through Easter Reach, where during the summer the last of the racing buoys – Canewdon – is located in mid-stream in about 5m at low water. Then, from abreast the point where Bridgemarsh Creek emerges from behind the western end of the island, the river flows westerly for two or three miles straight through Shortpole and Longpole Reaches up to and beyond North and South Fambridge. There is no less than 4m of water in mid-channel up as far as North Fambridge.

NORTH FAMBRIDGE

Francis B Cooke (whose many books on small boat cruising have become collectors' items) contributed an autobiographical note entitled: *Birth of a Great Yacht Station* to *Yachting Monthly* on the occasion of his 100th birthday:

'Anyone seeing Fambridge today for the first time

Wallasea Bay Port Guide – Local tel code 01702	
Essex Marina	Tel: 258531; VHF Ch 80; www.essexmarina.co.uk.
Water	From pontoon.
Stores	Shop near boatyard.
Fuel	Petrol and diesel from fuel barge, Calor Gas.
Chandlery	On site.
Repairs	Yard with slipway up to 100 tons, 70 ton hoist.
Food and drink	Bar and restaurant nearby.
Transport	Bus from Loftman's Corner (two miles away); Rochford rail station; Southend airport.
Yacht club	Essex Marina Yacht Club.
Telephone	Western end of sea wall.
Ferry	Wallasea Island to Town Quay (Easter to end September) Tel: 258666; www.ladyessex.com.

The Essex Marina at Wallasea Bay

could hardly imagine what a delightful waterside hamlet it was when I first discovered it (in 1893). The only buildings near the water were Fambridge Hall, the old Ferry Boat Inn, a tiny school, a row of four or five small timber built cottages, an old barn and the little church nestling among the trees. The road leading down to the Ferry hard was just a narrow country lane, with wild roses blooming in the summer. My friends the Viner brothers had decided to spend the summer there and asked me to join them. I readily agreed and we arranged with the landlady of the Ferry Boat Inn to board there. She agreed to take us for twelve shillings a week and hoped she was not charging too much, but of course that would include our laundry.'

When Cooke first sailed to Fambridge '...there were only four boats stationed there.' He only intended to stop for one night but as it turned out he was destined

The North Fambridge Yacht Club

to sail from there for 20 years. He and his above-mentioned friends commuted to London from the nearby station. They eventually took rooms at the Railway Cottages when getting their own meals became 'rather irksome.' In summer they slept on board, going for a sail in their 'little old tore-outs' in the evenings if there was any wind.

The Fambridge Yacht Club was founded at around this time and its clubhouse, still in use on the riverbank, is based on a galvanized iron building that started life as a mobile hospital unit for the Crimean War.

There are four lines of moorings off North Fambridge Yacht Station, with a fairway between them. The moorings are administered by the Yacht Haven Group, which manages the North Fambridge Yacht Station and the Fambridge Haven Marina in Stow Creek (formerly known as West Wick Marina). The only possible places to anchor are above or below these moorings, but there is plenty of water (2.5m) even at low water springs.

Landing is possible at the 120m deep-water hammerhead pontoon which extends into the river from near the North Fambridge Yacht Club clubhouse. The pontoon has a sizeable extension from the hammerhead downriver, on both sides of which a number of visiting yachts can be accommodated. In 2008 a large slipway was under construction just upriver of this pontoon. Landing on the south bank is not easy.

There is water on the pontoon and shower and toilet facilities ashore at the Yacht Station, from which it is a short walk to the Ferry Boat Inn. Overnight or short stay swinging moorings are also available for visitors and a water taxi operates on weekends from June to October.

The Fambridge Haven deep water hammerhead pontoon at North Fambridge

North Fambridge Port Guide
Local tel code 01621

NORTH FAMBRIDGE YACHT STATION
Tel: 740370; email: fambridge @yachthavens.com; www.yachthavens.com.

Water	On pontoon.
Repairs	18 ton boat lift; Bosun's stores.
Yacht clubs	North Fambridge Yacht Club.
Food and drink	Ferry Boat Inn Tel: 740208.
Water taxi	Weekends June to October.

FAMBRIDGE HAVEN (FORMERLY WEST WICK) MARINA
Stow Creek Tel: 740340; VHF Ch 80.

Berths	180 at marina.
Water	On pontoon.
Stores	Convenience store at chandlery.
Fuel	Diesel at marina; Calor and Camping Gaz at reception.
Repairs	Facilities and 25 ton hoist and mobile crane.
Chandlery	On site.
Transport	Trains hourly to London from Fambridge station (one mile).
Yacht club	North Fambridge Yacht Club,
Food and drink	Bistro at marina; Ferry Boat Inn Tel: 740208.
Essex Wildlife Trust	Warden at Blue House Farm reserve, Tel: 740687.

North Fambridge Yacht Station houses the archives of the Society for Sailing Barge Research in a building in the boatyard.

The grazing marshes south of the railway station in Fambridge are part of Blue House Farm, a working farm owned by the Essex Naturalists Trust. Access to the nature reserve is from the public footpath along the seawall, a short walk from the marina and Yacht Station. From April to October there is a permissive path to the bird hides that overlook the fleets.

STOW CREEK – FAMBRIDGE HAVEN MARINA
Rather less than a mile above Fambridge, Stow Creek enters the river from the north side.

The entrance is marked with a single pile beacon, known as Stow Post, and this should be left to port when entering. The channel is then marked by buoys for about a quarter of a mile up to the entrance to Fambridge Haven Marina (formerly West Wick Marina). White on white leading lights on the shore indicate the course up the centre of the creek by night. Access is possible for yachts of up to 2m draught at most states of the tide, although deeper draught boats may be restricted at low water springs. A depth of 1.5 to 2m is maintained in the marina by dredging.

Above Stow Creek the river narrows and shallows fairly rapidly. Clementsgreen Creek is navigable only around high water and, since it is dammed, it is of little interest to yachtsmen.

BRANDY HOLE
From abreast Clementsgreen Creek the river turns south-westerly through Brandy Hole reach into Brandy Hole Bay, which is a water-skiing area and very busy at weekends. Moorings begin again off Brandy Hole Yacht Club and continue for a mile or more up to the entrance to Fenn Creek, just above the ford at Hullbridge. There are drying pontoons off Brandy Hole Yacht Club. Anywhere along here a boat will take the ground for an hour or two either side of low water. Watch out for a spit extending from the north bank just above Brandy Hole Yacht Club.

HULLBRIDGE
Hullbridge Yacht Club lies half a mile above Brandy Hole Yacht Club, and here there is a jetty and slipway. Shallow draught boats can lie against the jetty, which has a tide gauge at each end marked in feet. Water is available from the rear of the clubhouse where there are showers and toilets (keys in office); and there are scrubbing posts which can be used, tide permitting, by arrangement.

The other yacht club on the southern shore at

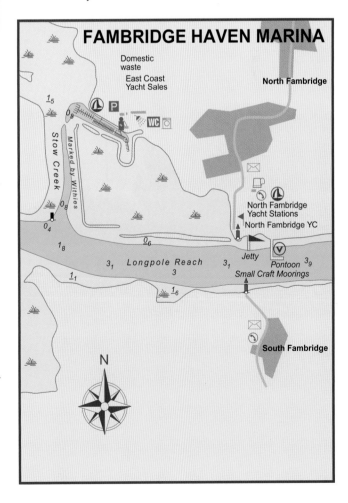

FAMBRIDGE HAVEN MARINA

Hullbridge (Brandy Hole) Port Guide
Local tel code 01702

Water	At Hullbridge hard and at clubhouses.
Stores	At Hullbridge village.
Fuel	Garages (one mile).
Repairs	Boatyard adjacent to Brandy Hole Yacht Club.
Transport	Buses from Hullbridge to Southend (from The Anchor pub).
Yacht clubs	Brandy Hole Yacht Club, Tel: 230320, VHF Ch 37; Up River Yacht Club Tel: 231654; Hullbridge Yacht Club; Woodham Ferrers Yacht Club.

The drying pontoons off Brandy Hole Yacht Club

Hullbridge is the Up River Yacht Club, which has dinghy sailors as well as a cruising membership, while on the north bank near the road down to the ford is the Woodham Ferrers Yacht Club. There are public launching sites on both sides of the river at the ford in Hullbridge.

High water at Hullbridge is 25 minutes later than at Burnham.

BATTLESBRIDGE

Above Hullbridge the river becomes very narrow and tortuous, and in places is no more than 10 or 12m wide between the retaining walls, although there are some moorings in Long Reach. At springs, a boat drawing 2m can take the tide right up to Battlesbridge, where there is an antiques centre based in the old mill buildings and a typical Essex weather-boarded pub, The Barge, near the quayside. Unless the return trip is commenced almost immediately, it would be best to moor alongside the concrete landing quay, or a small pontoon on the south bank.

In their heyday the mills at Battlesbridge were owned by the Meeson family who maintained a fleet of sailing barges all of which, according to Hervey Benham, had a reputation for being well found. 'Anything those barges wanted they had, and those over 100 tons were all three-handed. Meesons also had the noted little *Rainbow* built … a stumpie of only 15 tons, the smallest of all the miniatures, she spent her time scooting about the Crouch and Roach.'

Hullbridge Yacht Club boasts a jetty, slipway and scrubbing posts

The pontoon at Paglesham Waterside dries out but is fine for this lifting keel Parker yacht

Chapter thirteen
The River Roach and Havengore

Tides	Paglesham – HW Dover +1.10. Range: springs 5.0m; neaps 3.2m
Charts	Admiralty 3750, SC5607; Stanfords Chart Pack 4, Imray Y 17, 2000 Series, OS map 178
Waypoints	**Branklet Spit 51°36'.98N 00°52'.15E**
	South Shoebury Buoy 51°30'.44N 00°52'.40E
Hazards	Havengore route – except on rising tide

Yachtsmen who are based on the Roach consider it to be a better river than the Crouch. Its several changes of direction offer a wider variety of sailing and its upper reaches have remained quite unspoilt. Another advantage is that Havengore is nearby to provide us with a back door to the Thames and Medway or even across the estuary to the (North) Foreland.

From its junction with the River Crouch, about three miles inside Shore Ends, the Roach winds for some six miles in a mainly south-westerly direction up to its tidal limit at Stambridge Mill. Apart from the lower reaches below Paglesham, the Roach is very narrow at low water and not many craft use the river above Barling Ness.

What does make the Roach interesting to many yachtsmen is the network of subsidiary creeks which link the river with the sea over the Maplin Sands. The best-known and most important of these small channels is Havengore Creek which, passing Rushley and Havengore Islands, leads through a lifting bridge at its eastern end to the Thames Estuary. By using this creek after crossing the Maplins near high water, it is possible for small and shallow craft to reach the Roach without having to sail down the West Swin and up the Whitaker Channel.

At its mouth at high water the Roach is more than a quarter of a mile wide, but mud extends from both banks to reduce the low water channel to half that width. The mud extending from Wallasea Ness is marked by the Branklet Spit buoy (Sph Y). On the eastern side of the entrance a substantial amount of mud extends from Nase Point and many boats have been tripped up here. The best water is to be found close to the Branklet Spit itself. However, once inside the Roach keep to port as shoaling has been reported south of the Branklet, with less than 1m at low water springs.

QUAY REACH

There is not much less than 6m at low water in the middle of the river right along Quay Reach. The direction of this lowest reach of the Roach is roughly north – south, and because of this it often provides a more comfortable berth than any anchorage in the Crouch below Creeksea. Not only is there good protection from westerly and easterly winds, but there is also plenty of room and good holding ground in stiff mud towards either shore.

On the eastern shore there are some landing steps built into a small promontory in the Foulness seawall. It is possible, but not easy, to land here and walk to Church End. The landlord of the weather-boarded George and Dragon pub sadly gave up his struggle with the restrictions imposed by his MOD landlords and closed in 2007. There is a chance, however, that it may re-open in 2009; check by phoning 01702 219460. Meanwhile, you can still visit the church and the Foulness Heritage Centre in the old School House (open in the afternoons on the first Sunday of each month from April to October). St Mary's Church, the spire of which, along with those of nearby Little and Great Wakering and Barling churches, served as a useful landmark for sailors along this low-lying and otherwise featureless coast. Indeed when St Mary's was re-built in the 1850s, Trinity House made a large donation on condition that it had a spire. The walk takes 30 to 40 minutes, but remember that Foulness is MOD property, so you must keep to the track.

It is just over a mile from the entrance up to Horseshoe Corner at the southern end of Quay Reach; then the river turns through more than a right angle to continue westerly into Devil's Reach. The deep water round this bend, known as Whitehouse Hole, is marked by a yellow racing buoy – Roach – in about 6m at low water. The many named yellow buoys in the lower reaches of the Crouch and Roach from March to December are used by the Burnham yacht clubs' racing fleets.

The next racing buoy is Wade (formerly Whitehouse) located further up-river, after which the channel divides just below Potton buoy. The principal arm continues westerly along the northern side of Potton Island, leading to Paglesham Reach, while the other branch turns south, along the eastern side of Potton, into the Yokesfleet.

Just upstream of the second set of cable markers, and between Potton and Wade racing buoys in Devil's Reach, there are oyster crates at low water springs. These extend for about 300 yards and are

The Roach (left), Potton Island (centre) with the Yokesfleet and Foulness beyond. Barlinghall and Little Wakering Creeks (foreground and right)

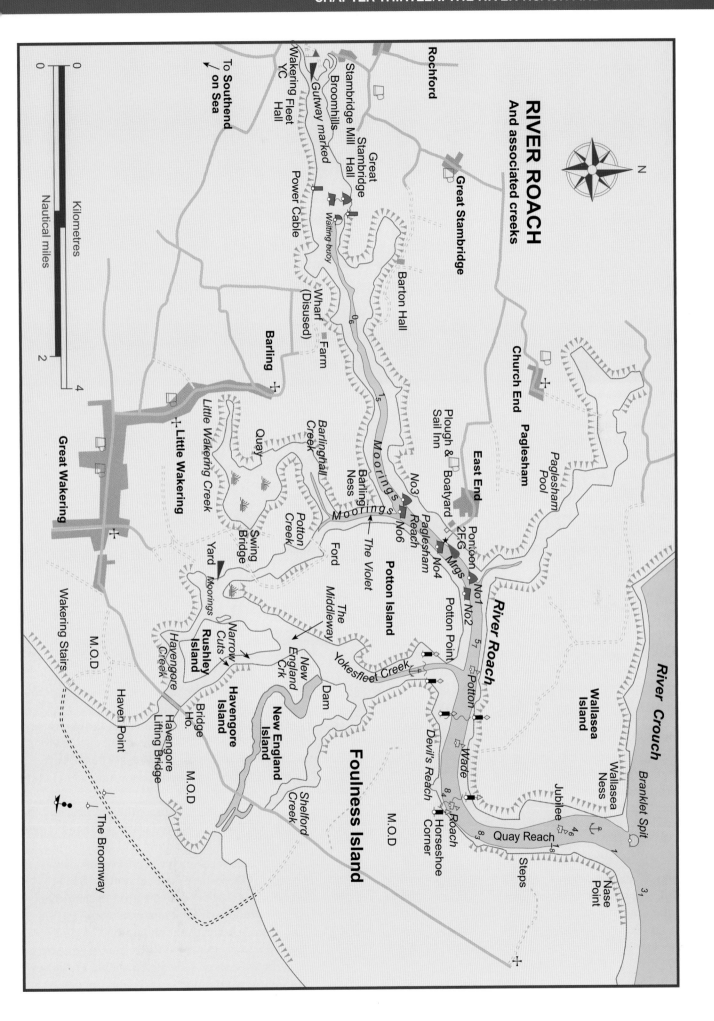

RIVER ROACH
And associated creeks

N

To **Southend**
on Sea

Rochford

Wakering Fleet
YC Hall

Stambridge Mill Hall

Great
Stambridge

Broomhills

Gutway marked

Waiting buoy

Power Cable

Farm
(Disused)
Wharf

Barling

Barton Hall

Great Stambridge

Church End

Pagelsham

Pagelsham
Pool

Plough &
Sail Inn

East End

No3

Pontoon
2FG

No4

Mngs

No6

Pagelsham
Reach

Barling
Ness

The Violet

Potton Island

No1
No2

Potton Point

River Roach

5₁
Potton

No5
Barringhall
Creek

Potton
Creek

Ford

The
Middleway

Yokesfleet Creek

Dam

Devil's Reach
Corner

Wade

8₄
Roach

8₃
Quay Reach

1 8
4 6

Steps

Horseshoe
Corner

Nase
Point

3₁

River Crouch

Branklet Spit

Wallasea
Ness

**Wallasea
Island**

Jubilee

Quay

Little Wakering Creek

Little Wakering

Swing
Bridge

Yard
Moorings

**Rushley
Island**

Narrow
Cuts

New
England
Crk

**Havengore
Island**

**New England
Island**

Shelford
Creek

Foulness Island

M.O.D

Great Wakering

M.O.D

Wakering Stairs

Haven Point

Havengore
Creek

Bridge
Ho.

Havengore
Lifting Bridge

M.O.D

The Broomway

0

Kilometres

2

0

Nautical miles

4

The weatherboarded Punchbowl inn at Church End, Paglesham

marked by a small green buoy on the north shore.

A little further upriver, shortly before the main channel turns south-west along the Potton shore, there are more oyster beds, marked by a pink mooring buoy and withies.

PAGLESHAM

Just before the moorings in Paglesham Reach the main channel turns to the south-west abreast the entrance to Paglesham Pool (or Creek). This narrow creek carries such a small amount of water at low tide as to be of little interest for navigation.

Immediately above the junction of Paglesham Pool with the Roach are the first of the Paglesham moorings, which extend both below and above Shuttlewood's old black shed. In the late 1800s there was a flourishing fleet of oyster smacks on the river, many of which, along with barges, were built in this very shed. A famous ship, HMS *Beagle*, is thought to have finished her life somewhere near here. After many commissions, including the voyage with Charles Darwin, the *Beagle* was sold to the Coastguard in 1845 to be used as a Watch Vessel. She was stationed just inside the mouth of the Roach, and later in Paglesham Reach, watching for smugglers. In those times most people in the surrounding creekside communities, both ashore and afloat, were involved in some way or another with contraband-related activities. At Paglesham, the infamous church warden William 'Hard Apple' Blyth is reputed to have used pages torn from the parish register with which to wrap bottles of illicit liquor before hiding them.

In 1870 the *Beagle* was sold and broken up and it is believed this may have been done on the hard ground

Paglesham Port Guide – Local tel code 01702	
Boatyard	Steve Adams Tel: 07791 549866.
Water	At the yard.
Transport	Buses from East End to Rochford, whence trains to London.
Telephone	Near Plough and Sail at the top of the lane.
Food and drink	Plough and Sail, East End, half a mile up the lane, Tel: 258242. The Punchbowl, Church End, Tel: 258376.
Yacht clubs	Roach Sailing Association, www.paglesham.org.uk. Hostellers Sailing Club.

in front of the shed. Copper, deck beams, grown frames and anything useful would have been salvaged from her hulk and the remains may have been burnt, or possibly they still lie beneath the Essex mud somewhere along the foreshore.

Moorings are laid on both sides of the channel, and the Crouch Harbour Board's port and starboard-hand buoys mark the extent of a fairway within which anchoring is prohibited. Visiting yachtsmen can anchor just below the moorings off Paglesham Pool; or craft with little draught and those that can take the ground can anchor in the Pool (the mouth dries at low water springs). The Crouch Harbour Authority has laid a small landing place inside the Pool, about 100 yards from the concrete pill box on the west shore seawall. This allows (almost) clean landing from a dinghy whence you can walk north to the Punchbowl at Church End or west along the seawall to the boatyard. A riding light is essential when anchored in the Roach overnight – the river is regularly used by fishing vessels both day and night, several have their moorings in and beyond The Violet, which leads to Barlinghall and Potton Creeks.

'Off Paglesham itself the trees in the background, contrasting with the flat land all around, make it a pleasant place at which to lie at anchor, the more so as Mr Shuttlewood has lately made an excellent hard upon which (one) can land cleanly.'

Since Archie White wrote that about the Roach in 1948, the hard has been widened to a slipway and, alongside it, a pontoon has been added. Clean landing is possible at most stages of the tide and you can tie a dinghy to the pontoon, the end of which is marked by two fixed green lights. However, it is not advisable to bring a yacht alongside this pontoon, other than for a short period at the top of the tide, as it dries out. In recent years there have not been many facilities for visiting yachtsmen at the yard except for fresh water. In early 2008 the yard at Paglesham Waterside was for sale, Essex Boatyards Ltd having moved its huge motor-boat sales operation to Essex Marina at Wallasea. It is to be hoped that a new owner might return the yard to the attractive destination it once was.

The boatyard moorings in Paglesham Reach have not been regularly maintained in recent years, so visiting yachtsmen are advised to use those in the two rows of private moorings immediately downstream of the pontoon and slipway. Labelled RS1 – 13, these moorings are run by members of the Roach Sailing Association, who will allow visitors to use vacant buoys. Please take heed of the tonnage details on each mooring. The Roach Sailing Association is based at Paglesham and, although it has no formal clubhouse premises, it runs a series of annual handicap races, cruises and social events. Together with the Roach Area Fairway Conservation Committee, the RSA is a source of local pilotage information, in particular for the Havengore route.

The hamlet of East End, which yachtsmen usually think of as Paglesham, is about half a mile up the lane from the boatyard. Food and drink are available at the Plough and Sail, a traditional, weatherboarded Essex inn with Jamie Oliver connections.

Members of the Hostellers Sailing Club, a dinghy cruising branch of the Youth Hostel Association, sail from Paglesham and keep Wayfarer dinghies on half-tide moorings near the pontoon. Not many people know that Dame Ellen McArthur started sailing at Paglesham on her aunt's cruiser, which was based here, and for a couple of years Ellen kept a little boat of her own on the river.

Above the Paglesham moorings the river forks again at Barling Ness, the main stream continuing westerly towards Rochford and the other arm turning south between Barling Marsh and Potton Island. The continuation of the main channel west of Barling Ness is sometimes referred to as the Broomhill River. There is 1 to 1.5m of water at low water springs up as far as the disused Barling Quay on the south bank, after which the channel narrows rapidly into a gutway that can be navigated only towards high water, and then only with much sounding or local knowledge. At high water boats drawing 1 to 1.5m can continue as far up river as the mill at Stambridge – a mile short of the town of Rochford. On the whole, best water will be found roughly midway between the banks in these upper reaches, but the broad entrance to Bartonhall Creek must be avoided on the north bank. A power cable crosses the river hereabouts and is marked by a green conical and a red can buoy.

STAMBRIDGE

Just below Stambridge Mill the river divides for the last time, the southern arm becoming Fleethall Creek where there is a wharf once used by small freighters. There is a slipway here at Carter and Ward's yard and three travel hoists capable of handling craft up to 50 tons and 80ft LOA, with water and power and all facilities on the quayside. A series of green starboard-hand withies, some with traffic cones atop, leads up to the yard, which a number of boats now use for winter laying-up.

The Wakering Yacht Club has its clubhouse at this yard and a pontoon that extends downriver, but this is only suitable for shoal draught craft as there is very little water even at springs. The club, which has a bar, is open at weekends and serves Sunday lunch.

Bob Roberts' *Cambria* is thought to have been the last barge to trade under sail, bringing grain in the 1960s to the currently disused Stambridge Mill at Broomhills on the north bank near the navigable head of the River Roach.

The boatyard and Wakering Sailing Club at the top of Fleethall Creek can be reached at high water

Stambridge Port Guide – Local tel code 01702

Boatyard	Carter and Ward Tel: 01268 733421 (Graham Carter).
Yacht club	Wakering Yacht Club Tel: 530926; VHF Ch 68.
Food and drink	Bar and Sunday lunch at yacht club.

YOKESFLEET CREEK

Returning now to the south bank of the river, the branch of the Roach, which turns south at Potton Point, is variously known as Yokesfleet Creek and the Gore Channel. The entrance to this creek requires care as a spit of mud stretches out from Potton Point and there is also an extensive mud flat off the opposite point. Best water will be found close under the Potton or western shore for the first few cables inside. There are depths of about 2m at low water for the first quarter of a mile or so inside the creek, and the spot provides a quiet and comfortable anchorage during either westerly or easterly winds.

About a mile within Yokesfleet Creek, two lesser creeks branch out on the eastern side. The first is Shelford Creek, which once reached the sea along the south side of Foulness Island; and the second, New England Creek, has been dammed just within its entrance. This barrier across New England Creek provides a useful reference point as it is at the next division of the main channel that Narrow Cuts leads off south-easterly towards Havengore Bridge.

Shelford Creek is blocked by a fixed road bridge towards its seaward end and is therefore of little use to yachtsmen, but there is enough water for most small boats to lie afloat in Yokesfleet Creek or the Middleway, which it becomes above the junction of Shelford and New England creeks. About half a mile along the Middleway the channel again divides, this time around Rushley Island. Narrow Cuts, the more easterly arm, is used by craft passing to and from Havengore Bridge. Although it all but dries out at low water, there is enough water in the gutway through Narrow Cuts to allow boats drawing up to 1.5m to get through towards high water. But the narrow channel is tortuous and must be followed, even at high water, to avoid grounding.

After leaving Yokesfleet Creek at the junction of the Middleway, keep close to the port-hand sea wall up to a sluice, then begin to alter course towards the starboard bank, using the low roof of a distant barn as a mark. There may be a stake marking a hump on the starboard hand, followed by an even more important red-topped stake to be left to port, after which there may be no more marks. On sighting the bridge from Narrow Cuts, do not be tempted to take a short cut at high water, but remain close to the starboard bank. It is certainly preferable for a stranger – if he can – to make his first acquaintance with Narrow Cuts early on a tide, while the mud is still largely uncovered.

Just before reaching the bridge the channel emerging from Narrow Cuts is joined by Havengore Creek, which winds round the western side of Rushley Island to merge with the Middleway. When bound inward, there is little point in taking the longer route to the Crouch via Havengore Creek.

The saltings at the southernmost tip of Potton Island extend about 100m from the seawall and are covered at high water springs. The best water runs round this point, about 30m from the edge of the saltings; the channel begins to fill at about half tide. When leaving Sutton and Smiths yard at Wakering, bound for the Roach or Crouch via the Yokesfleet, careful sounding will be necessary as the edge of the saltings is unmarked and the leading marks on Rushley Island have gone.

When bound seaward through Havengore Bridge, keep close to the Rushley Island side for about half a mile because the best water will not be found on the outside of the bend, as might be expected. A mud bank extends off Mill Bay at the junction of Potton and Havengore Creeks, so deeper draught boats bound for the Havengore Bridge from Potton Creek may need to use the Narrow Cuts route.

POTTON CREEK

Potton Creek joins the Roach between Potton Island and Barling Ness and runs in a southerly direction to join up with Havengore Creek.

A very long spit extends north-easterly from Barling Ness and it is safest to hold the east shore when entering Barlinghall Creek from the Roach. The first reach in the creek, known locally as The Violet, is largely occupied these days by local fishing boats operating out of Barling.

Barlinghall Creek, leading to Little Wakering Creek, leaves Potton Creek about half a mile south of Barling Ness and winds up to the villages of Barling and Little Wakering. Although barges once visited the quays

The Potton swing bridge will open on request

Looking north-east across Rushley Island to Foulness, the Yokesfleet (left) and Havengore Bridge (right). Potton Bridge and the boatyard at Wakering are to the bottom left

dotted about the upper reaches of these creeks, the landings are mostly disused and, of course, no water remains at low tide.

About a quarter of a mile above the junction of Barlinghall Creek, beware of a concrete ford between Potton Island and the mainland. It is not safe to try to pass this way before half flood. From here, the bridge over Potton Creek will be seen about half a mile ahead. This swing-bridge, used only by the Ministry of Defence, will be opened on request – VHF Ch 16, 72; Tel: 01702 219491; or three toots on a horn, Dutch fashion – at any time of day and night, two hours either side of high water. The MOD requires the bridge keeper to log the names of boats passing through, so if your boat name is not easy to distinguish, it helps if you tell him when you call him up. Keep well over to the east side of the creek when approaching the bridge; members of the Roach Sailing Association have put withies here.

The Sutton and Smith boatyard is situated just south of the bridge where there are permanent and visitors' berths on swinging or pontoon moorings, with the usual facilities including a slipway, repair and engineering services.

Potton Bridge – Local tel code 01702

Bridge keeper	VHF Ch 72; callsign *Potton Bridge*; Tel: 219491. Opens on request, day or night, two hours either side of high water.

Wakering Port Guide – Local tel code 01702

Sutton and Smith Boatyard	
	Tel: 219422; www.suttons boatyard.co.uk.
Water	At yard.
Stores/pubs	Great Wakering (about 1¼ miles away).
Repairs	At yard. Slip and cranes.
Transport	Buses run from Wakering to Southend.
Yacht clubs	Wakering Yacht Club (headquarters at Stambridge), Tel: 530926; VHF Ch 68.

THE HAVENGORE ROUTE

This passage northwards to the River Roach across the Maplin Sands and via the Havengore Bridge, Narrow Cuts, Middleway and Yokesfleet Creeks should only be made during spring tides, and then only by craft drawing no more than 1.5m.

The mouth of Havengore Creek has been silting up in the first years of the 21st century and anyone considering using this route for the first time would be well advised to consult the Roach Sailing Association's website where there are pilotage notes and photographs produced by the Roach Area Fairways and Conservation Committee.

The approach to Havengore Creek over the Maplins crosses the Shoeburyness Gunnery Range, established in the 1850s for use by the British School of Gunnery, which had a major artillery training and experimental

Shoebury Ranges

Range Operations Officer	Tel: 01702 383211; VHF Ch 72 callsign *Shoe Base*.
SHOE RADAR	Tel: 01702 383260 Monday to Friday.

base at Shoebury. The MOD range is still used on weekdays for bomb disposal training and gunnery testing, so it is as well for yachtsmen to understand their rights and responsibilities when intending to use the Havengore route. The complete bye-laws governing firing practice over the Maplin and Foulness sands are to be found in Statutory Rules and Orders No 714 of 1936, obtainable from HMSO. But the section of these bye-laws, which is of greatest importance to yachtsmen, reads: 'Any vessel wishing to enter Havengore Creek during such time or times as the whole of the target area is not closed in accordance with Bye-law No 3 must enter the target area not later than half an hour before high water and proceed by the shortest possible course to the Creek.'

Red flags are hoisted from a number of points along the sea wall, among them Wakering Stairs and Havengore Bridge, an hour before exercises commence and throughout the period of activity (in some places red lights are shown). These flags are often left up all the time. It is, in any case, difficult if not impossible to see these signals before setting course across the Maplins from the West Swin.

Firing does not usually take place at weekends, but it is best to check beforehand. During the week it is dangerous to make the passage without first obtaining permission. Yachtsmen should telephone the Range Operations Officer at Shoeburyness to ask when, if possible, the bridge will be lifted and firing suspended. Every consideration is given to yachtsmen in this respect.

Night firing is normally confined to periods when the Maplins are uncovered, and in any case, as the swing bridge is not manned between sunset and sunrise, the passage cannot be made after dark.

The Maplin sands should not be crossed from the Swin much earlier than three-quarters flood, and it is difficult for any other than light draught boats

to get over the Broomway much before high water. The Broomway is a causeway built long ago along the Maplin Sands to connect Foulness Island, Havengore and New England Islands with the mainland at Wakering, before any bridge was constructed.

The Broomway, its course once marked by withies or brooms, stands proud of the mud and sand in some places, and there is probably about 1.5 to 2m of water over it at high water springs, but often 0.5m or less at high water neaps.

Havengore Creek cannot be distinguished from the West Swin, as any marks off the entrance are too small to be seen over the 2½ miles. See charts on page 138 and 141.

A course of 345°M from the yellow spherical buoy with topmark (Fl (5) Y 20s) which has replaced the East Shoebury beacon will lead towards the entrance to Havengore Creek and passes near a wreck, marked by two spheres on a post, about one mile off. There have been attempts in recent years to establish marks that would assist yachtsmen using the Havengore route, but it is extremely difficult to erect structures strong enough to withstand wind and tide for more than a year or so. Two stayed, metal posts were established in 1995: one 200 yards to seaward of the Broomway and one on the Broomway itself. Just west of the first post is the previously mentioned wreck. The best water is close to these two posts, but although they can be seen easily from the mouth of Havengore Creek they are difficult to make out from seaward against the coastline. There are many other posts and range markers on the sands.

The gutway leading into the creek has a silting bar across it, with best water marked with steel withies – red to port and green to starboard. These sometimes have traffic cones on them which can be confusing.

Looking inland from the Havengore Bridge near low water. Narrow Cuts curving away to the right

The Havengore Bridge is raised for dinghies from the Hostellers Sailing Club, outward bound for the Swale and Medway

Once between the sea walls the deepest water will be found towards the north bank up to the bridge.

It must be realised that depths over the Maplins and the Broomway will vary considerably with the direction and strength of wind as well as with barometric pressure. Northerly winds will raise and southerly winds will lower the tidal levels, while a decrease or increase in barometric pressure equivalent to 25 millibars (one inch) of mercury will respectively raise or lower the depth of water by 0.3m (one foot). Therefore, the more settled the weather, the more likely is the pressure to be high and the tides lower than predicted.

HAVENGORE BRIDGE

The MOD-operated bridge over Havengore Creek has a lifting bascule which allows unrestricted passage for any yacht. The bridge is manned and will be opened as required during the period one to two hours each side of high water during daylight hours – provided the firing range is not being used. Fortunately, firing seldom takes place at weekends, but anyone planning to use the Havengore route is advised to first contact the Range Operations Officer, who will probably be able to give you the time of local high water at the bridge. Before approaching the bridge contact the bridge keeper on VHF or by telephone (see page 136 – if high water is at twilight, warn bridge keeper by calling earlier while it is still manned).

As with Potton swing bridge, the Havengore bridge keeper is instructed to log boat names, so if yours is not easily distinguishable, he likes you to let him know the name when you call him up.

The tidal streams hereabouts are somewhat complicated – largely because of the barrier formed by the Broomway. The flood tide from the Roach and the flood over the Maplins meet and cover the Maplins about two hours before high water, after which the tide runs back into Havengore Creek until high water. Then with virtually no period of slack, the ebb runs out of the creek with great strength until the Broomway is again uncovered. These facts should be remembered when using the Havengore route since, when coming from the Swin, it is important to reach the bridge before the ebb commences. When bound out of the creek it is equally desirable to be at the bridge before the last hour or so of the flood, which runs north into Narrow Cuts.

When bound through the bridge and out of the creek, it helps the bridge-keeper if some kind of signal can be made to indicate that the bridge should be raised. Traffic signals will signify when it is safe to proceed. The port and starboard withies marking the channel upstream from seaward of the bridge continue towards Potton on the landward side, so if you are approaching the bridge from the inside, the marks must be followed in a downstream sequence.

Looking north-west over Havengore Creek. Inside the bridge the creek divides around Rushley Island, left towards Potton Creek and right into Narrow Cuts

Traffic signals are shown from the south bascule of Havengore Bridge

In Conrad's novel *Chance*, the character Powell was in the habit of disappearing mysteriously from the Thames Estuary in his small cutter, but was eventually followed (probably into Havengore) by Marlow, who describes the chase:

'One afternoon, I made Powell's boat out, heading into the shore. By the time I got close to the mud flats his craft had disappeared inland. But I could see the mouth of the creek by then. The tide being on the turn I took the risk of getting stuck in the mud suddenly and headed in. Before I had gone half a mile, I was up with a building I had seen from the river... it looked like a small barn.'

There would have been no bridge over the creek when Conrad wrote *Chance*, but the barn may still exist, for a similar building (at Oxenham Farm) can still be seen over the sea walls in the Havengore area.

Havengore Bridge

Bridge keeper	During daylight high water periods, Tel: 01702 383436; VHF Ch 72 callsign *Shoe Bridge*.

Limehouse Basin Marina provides access to the inland waterways network via the Regents Canal

Chapter fourteen
The River Thames

Tides	Southend Pier – HW Dover +1.20. Range: springs 5.2m; neaps 3.4m (HW Tower Bridge approximately 1hr 20mins after HW Southend)
Charts	Admiralty 1185 (Sea Reach), 2151, 2484, 3337; Imray C1, C2, 2100 series
Waypoints	NE Maplin Buoy 51°37'.46N 01°04'.79E
	Maplin Buoy 51°34'.03N 01°02'.29E
	Blacktail Spit Buoy 51°31'.48N 00°56'.75E
	Southend Pierhead 51°30'.87N 00°43'.41E
	Sea Reach No 1 Buoy 51°29'.45N 00°52'.57E
Hazards	Large ships (steer clear of dredged channel); fast water taxis/ferries in upper reaches

John Evelyn, whose diary is not so often quoted as that of Samuel Pepys, reported on a day on the Thames he had with Charles II in 1661: 'I sailed this morning with His Majesty in one of his pleasure-boats, vessels not known among us till the Dutch East India Company presented that curious piece to the King; being very excellent sailing vessels. It was a wager between his other new pleasure-boat frigate-like, and one of the Duke of York's – the wager 100-1: the race from Greenwich to Gravesend and back. The King lost in going, the wind being contrary, but saved stakes in returning.'

Since then there has never been a time when yachtsmen have not sailed on the Thames – some of them, such as the marine artist Wyllie in his book *London to the Nore,* have tried to capture the spirit of the London River in, as he put it, '... all of its grime and much of its wonder'.

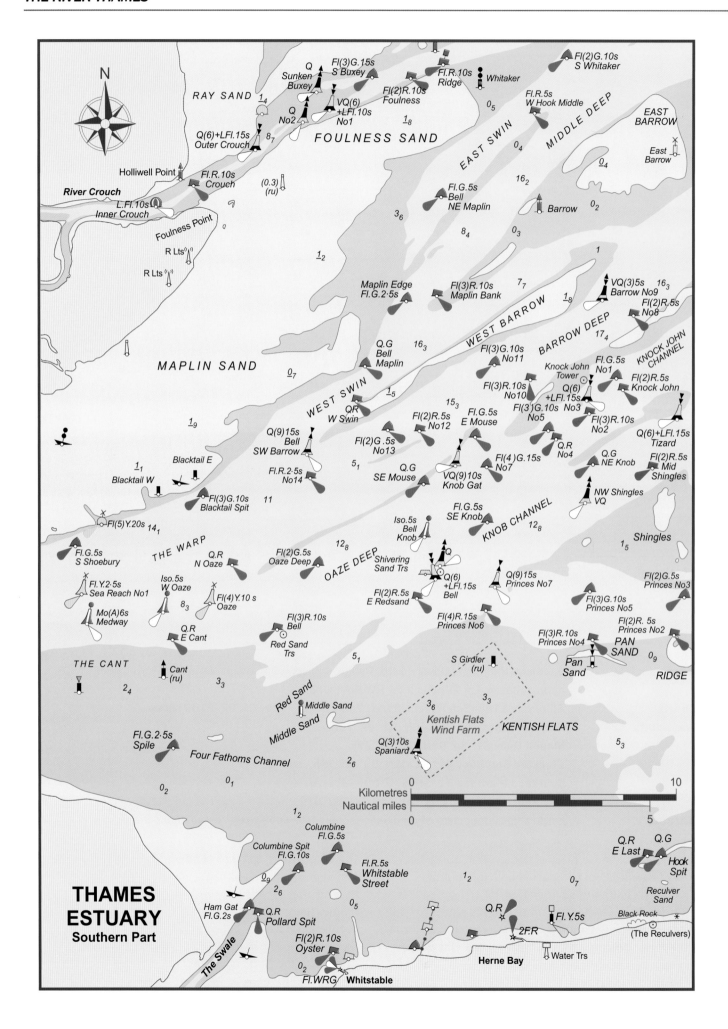

RAY SAND

Q
Sunken
Buxey
Fl(3)G.15s
S Buxey

Q(6)+LFl.15s
Outer Crouch

Q
No2

VQ(6)
+LFl.10s
No1

Fl(2)R.10s
Foulness

Fl.R.10s
Ridge

Whitaker

Fl(2)G.10s
S Whitaker

Fl.R.5s
W Hook Middle

EAST
BARROW

East
Barrow

Holliwell Point

Fl.R.10s
Crouch

River Crouch

L.Fl.10s
Inner Crouch

Foulness Point

R Lts

R Lts

FOULNESS SAND

EAST SWIN

MIDDLE DEEP

Fl.G.5s
Bell
NE Maplin

Barrow

Maplin Edge
Fl.G.2·5s

Fl(3)R.10s
Maplin Bank

WEST BARROW

BARROW DEEP

VQ(3)5s
Barrow No9

Fl(2)R.5s
No8

KNOCK JOHN
CHANNEL

MAPLIN SAND

Q.G
Bell
Maplin

WEST SWIN

Fl(3)G.10s
No11

Fl(3)R.10s
No10

Knock John
Tower

Q(6)
+LFl.15s
No3

Fl.G.5s
No1

Fl(2)R.5s
Knock John

Fl(3)R.10s
No2

Q(6)+LFl.15s
Tizard

QR
W Swin

Q(9)15s
Bell
SW Barrow

Fl.R.2·5s
No14

Fl(2)R.5s
No12

Fl.G.5s
E Mouse

Fl(3)G.10s
No5

Q.R
No4

Q.G
NE Knob

Fl(2)R.5s
Mid
Shingles

Blacktail E

Blacktail W

Fl(2)G.5s
No13

Q.G
SE Mouse

VQ(9)10s
Knob Gat

Fl(4)G.15s
No7

NW Shingles
VQ

Shingles

Fl(3)G.10s
Blacktail Spit

Fl(5)Y.20s

THE WARP

Q.R
N Oaze

Fl(2)G.5s
Oaze Deep

OAZE DEEP

Shivering
Sand Trs

Fl.G.5s
SE Knob

KNOB CHANNEL

Fl(2)G.5s
Princes No3

Fl.G.5s
S Shoebury

Fl.Y.2·5s
Sea Reach No1

Iso.5s
W Oaze

Fl(4)Y.10s
Oaze

Iso.5s
Bell
Knob

Q

Q(6)
+LFl.15s
Bell

Q(9)15s
Princes No7

Fl(3)G.10s
Princes No5

Mo(A)6s
Medway

Q.R
E Cant

Fl(3)R.10s
Bell

Fl(2)R.5s
E Redsand

Fl(4)R.15s
Princes No6

Fl(3)R.10s
Princes No4

Fl(2)R. 5s
Princes No2

PAN
SAND

THE CANT

Cant
(ru)

Red Sand
Trs

S Girdler
(ru)

Pan
Sand

RIDGE

Red Sand

Middle Sand

Kentish Flats
Wind Farm

KENTISH FLATS

Fl.G.2·5s
Spile

Middle Sand

Four Fathoms Channel

Q(3)10s
Spaniard

Kilometres
Nautical miles

Columbine
Fl.G.5s

Columbine Spit
Fl.G.10s

Fl.R.5s
Whitstable
Street

Q.R
E Last

Q.G

Hook
Spit

Reculver
Sand

THAMES
ESTUARY
Southern Part

Ham Gat
Fl.G.2s

Q.R
Pollard Spit

The Swale

Fl(2)R.10s
Oyster

Q.R

2.F.R

Fl.Y.5s

Black Rock

(The Reculvers)

Water Trs

Herne Bay

Fl.WRG **Whitstable**

Despite the fact that nowadays an increasing number of yachtsmen visit London in their boats, there are still very few comfortable or attractive anchorages between Leigh-on-Sea and any of the five marinas in or near London. Therefore a journey up or down the river is best done on one tide when possible.

Before embarking for the first time on a voyage up the London River to Tower Bridge, there are several things to be considered:

1.   By using the tide wisely, the distance (some 40 miles) can usually be covered in seven hours, arriving in London just before high water.

2.   Do not expect to find any easy or undisturbed anchorages en route and be aware that casual mooring is not usually possible.

3.   In the upper reaches, keep a particularly keen look-out for floating or submerged debris that might damage a prop or bend a shaft. A particular danger nowadays are near invisible plastic bags and sacks.

4.   Stow all loose gear. With a fresh wind some reaches of the Thames can be remarkably rough and the wash from fast moving tugs, pilot launches or waterbuses can sometimes come as a surprise.

5.   Make sure you fully understand the procedure for passing through the Thames Barrier in Woolwich Reach.

6.   Be aware that (in 2008) diesel is available from only two places: the Lock at Gravesend Embankment Marina or from the fuel barge at St Katharine Haven near Tower Bridge. Diesel can be obtained from one or two other places but only by prior arrangement and then in cans.

The Thames – Useful Information

Port Control London VHF	*London VTS.* **Ch 12** for The Estuary below Sea Reach No 4 buoy. **Ch 68** for the river above Sea Reach No 4 buoy to Crayfordness. **Ch 14** above Crayfordness. The half-hourly VHF broadcasts are sometimes of interest to yachts, for example, the tidal information.
Port Control London	Seaward to Crayfordness Tel: 01474 560311 (Gravesend). Up river of Crayfordness, Thames Barrier Navigation Centre Tel: 0208 855 0315.
Thames River Police	Wapping Tel: 0207 488 5291; VHF Ch 14 above Crayfordness, callsign *Thames Police Wapping*; 24 hours.
PLA Patrol Launches	VHF callsign *Thames Patrol* on Ch 69, 68 or 14 and 16, according to location.
Emergencies	Call *Thames Patrol* as above.
Port of London Authority/ Harbour Master (Lower District)	London River House, Gravesend DA12 2BG, Tel: 01474 562200.
Port of London Authority/ Harbour Master (Upper District)	Bakers' Hall, 7 Harp Lane, London, EC3R 6LB. Tel: 020 7743 7900; Fax: 020 7743 7999; www.portoflondon.co.uk.

When sailing in the Thames Estuary or further up-river, it should always be remembered that the dredged channel for shipping is not wide enough to allow a deep-draught vessel to alter course. There is plenty of water either side of the channel for yachts, which should of course keep to the correct (starboard) side in the shallower water.

The Port of London Authority (PLA) has Harbour Service patrol launches as do the Thames River Police, and these are an invaluable source of information regarding moorings, safe anchorages, fuel etc. A useful information leaflet, *A Pleasure User's Guide*, for yachtsmen using the tidal Thames is available from the PLA on request or it can be downloaded free from the PLA website.

APPROACHES

Coming into the Thames from the Channel or the North Sea, it is convenient to consider Sea Reach No 1 buoy as marking the seaward limit of the river. At this point the estuary, to the north of which are Shoeburyness and the Maplin Sands and to the south Warden Point and the Isle of Sheppey, is about eight

Sea Reach No 1 buoy is considered to mark the seaward limit of the London River

miles wide. The edge of the Maplins is steep-to, but the water shoals more gradually to the south, over an area known as the Cant.

SEA REACH

From Sea Reach No 1 Buoy to Lower Hope Point, some 15 miles up-river, the general direction of the channel is westerly. As there is no high ground offering shelter on the Kent shore west of the Medway, a fresh south-westerly wind blowing against the flood tide will kick up a short steep sea.

Shipping bound up the Thames follows the well-marked Yantlet dredged channel, which has a least depth of 10m and a width of about two cables up as far as Shellhaven. This channel is marked by a series of seven special centre line buoys, either pillar or spherical, and coloured either yellow or with red and white vertical stripes. Small craft should steer clear of this main channel, and fortunately there is plenty of water on both sides.

When following an inward course to the north of the dredged channel, a watch must be kept for an obstruction to navigation extending offshore to a point about one mile south-east of Shoeburyness. This obstruction – part of a wartime barrier/boom – has a beacon, Inner Shoebury (Fl Y 2.5s), but does not stretch as far as the drying edge of Maplin Sands, although another post, Shoebury (Fl (3) G 10s), does mark the point where the barrier once reached deep water.

If visibility is reasonable, Southend Pier can be seen from abreast the Shoeburyness obstruction, although a direct course between the two is not advisable between half-ebb and half-flood because it leads over the edge of drying flats. Instead, the West Shoebury (G Con Fl G 2.5s) should be left to starboard or close to port.

There is a Coastguard and radio direction finding station at Shoeburyness.

SOUTHEND PIER

This mile-long pier dates from 1829 and seems never to be out of trouble for very long. A fire at the pierhead in 1976 destroyed the Coastguard and Lloyd's stations, a freighter cut clean through the structure and wrecked the RNLI station in 1986, and in 1995 the bowling alley at the landward end was destroyed by fire. Much of the damage has been repaired and the pier is up and running again. It is even possible for a yacht to tie up alongside for a while to take on water or collect stores from the town. The local RNLI lifeboat house and crew quarters are at the head of the pier.

For a mile or more on both sides of the pier are some 3,000 small boat moorings – all of them drying out on to a more or less muddy bottom. At Thorpe Bay Yacht Club there are visitors' drying moorings which can be very handy for anyone caught out on the way to Havengore; these are accessible for about three hours either side of high water and the clubhouse welcomes visiting yachtsmen. It is possible for deeper draught boats to anchor near the Shoebury wreck, although the holding is not particularly good. The Halfway Yacht Club, near the conspicuous Halfway House pub on Eastern Esplanade, about a mile to

At Thorpe Bay Yacht Club there are dryings moorings and the foreshore can be a handy place for a scrub

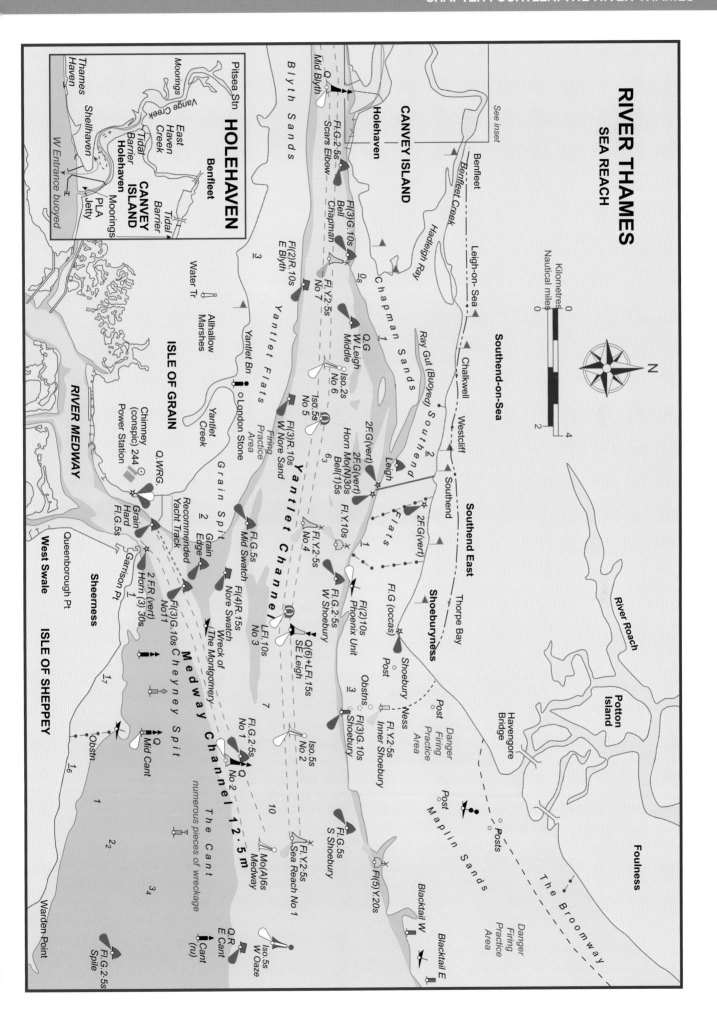

RIVER THAMES
SEA REACH

N

Kilometres
Nautical miles

0
0

2
4

See inset

Benfleet

Benfleet Creek

Leigh-on-Sea

Chalkwell

Westcliff

Southend-on-Sea

Southend

Southend East

Shoeburyness

Thorpe Bay

Shoebury Ness

Danger Firing Practice Area

Post

Havengore Bridge

Potton Island

River Roach

Foulness

Danger Firing Practice Area

Maplin Sands

Post

Posts

Posts

The Broomway

Blacktail W

Blacktail E

CANVEY ISLAND

Hadleigh Ray

Ray Gut (Buoyed)

Southend Flats

Mid Blyth Q

Holehaven

Scars Elbow

Fl.G.2·5s

Bell Fl(3)G.10s

Chapman

E Blyth Fl(2)R.10s

No 7 Fl.Y.2·5s

Blyth Sands

Chapman Sands

Q.G W Leigh
Middle

Iso.2s No 6

Iso.5s No 5

Horn Mo(N)30s
Bell(1)15s 2F.G(vert)

W Nore Sand Fl(3)R.10s

2F.G(vert)

2F.G(vert)

Leigh

Fl.Y.10s

No 4 Fl.Y.2·5s

2F.G(vert)

Fl.G (occas)

Phoenix Unit Fl(2)10s

W Shoebury Fl.G.2·5s

SE Leigh Q(6)+LFl.15s

Shoebury Fl(3)G.10s

Inner Shoebury Fl.Y.2·5s

Shoebury Ness Post

Obstns

Post

3

Sea Reach No 1 Mo(A)6s

S Shoebury Fl.G.5s

Sea Reach No 1 Fl(5)Y.20s

W Oaze Iso.5s

Pitsea Stn

Vange Creek

Moorings

HOLEHAVEN
Benfleet

East Haven Creek

Tidal Barrier Holehaven

CANVEY ISLAND

Moorings

Shellhaven

Thames Haven

W Entrance buoyed

PLA Jetty

3

Water Tr

Allhallow Marshes

ISLE OF GRAIN

Yantlet Bn

London Stone

Yantlet Flats

Yantlet Creek

Grain Spit

Practice Firing Area

Recommended Yacht Track

Chimney (conspic) 244

Power Station

Q.WRG.

Grain Hard

Grain Edge **2**

Fl.G.5s

Garrison Pt

2 F.R (vert) Horn (3) 30s

RIVER MEDWAY

Queenborough Pt

West Swale

Sheerness

ISLE OF SHEPPEY

Yantlet Channel

Mid Swatch Fl.G.5s

Nore Swatch Fl(4)R.15s

No 3 LFl.10s

Wreck of The Montgomery

Medway Channel 12·5m

No 11 Fl(3)G.10s

Cheyney Spit

The Cant

numerous pieces of wreckage

No 1 Fl.G.2·5s

No 2 Q

No 2 Iso.5s

Mid Cant Q

E Cant (ru) Q.R

Cant Fl(5) Spile Fl.G.2·5s

Horn (3) 36s

Obstn

Warden Point

6₃

0₈

1

1

2

3

7

10

1₇

1₆

2₂

3₄

Benfleet Creek looking eastward towards Leigh-on-Sea and Southend Pier

the east of the pier, has one visitor's drying mooring for up to 26ft.

There is plenty of water off the end of the pier (5m or 6m) and an anchorage can usually be found on the edge of the flats on either side. There is little protection except from the north.

During the sailing season spherical red racing buoys are laid on the north side of the Sea Reach Channel off Southend.

From the end of Southend Pier, a course due west (M) will lead to the West Leigh Middle green conical buoy (QG). Leigh Middle is a shoal area that almost dries out along the southern edge of the drying sands extending eastward from Canvey Point.

In order to avoid the busy new freight terminal at Shellhaven, inward-bound craft from the north are advised by the PLA to cross to the south side of the Yantlet Channel at West Leigh Middle, making sure that the fairway is clear, heading for the East Blyth buoy before turning onto the inward track. Remember that outward-bound ships will pass close to the port-hand fairway buoys. The Mid Blyth, West Blyth and Lower Hope buoys can then be safely passed to the south. Once in Lower Hope Reach, you should cross back to the correct side as soon as it is safe to do so.

Outward-bound to the north, yachts should reverse

the above route, but cross back to the north between Sea Reach Nos 4 and 5 buoys.

If you are coming in from the south, keep clear to the south of Sea Reach fairway and cross to the north side in Lower Hope as previously described.

A spoil ground buoy is usually located somewhere to the east of West Leigh Middle buoy and is often in little more than 2m at low water springs. A green conical bell buoy (Fl (3) G 10s) – Chapman – is established close to the old lighthouse position, about a quarter of a mile south of the drying edge of the Chapman Sands half a mile off the Canvey Island shore. The edge of the sand near here is steep-to, there being depths of 20m within half a cable of the buoy.

About a mile west of Scars Elbow buoy (Fl G 2.5s) is the entrance to Holehaven Creek – a favourite anchorage with earlier generations of Thames yachtsmen, but becoming less attractive as each year passes.

After Scars Elbow, there are no further marks on the north side of Sea Reach, but there is deep water right up to the numerous jetties, dolphins and mooring buoys which once served the Shellhaven oil refineries and storage depots. This area is being redeveloped (2008) as a freight terminal which involves major berth construction work and an increase in shipping in Sea Reach.

LEIGH-ON-SEA

Almost the whole of the foreshore of the adjoining towns of Leigh, Westcliff and Southend dries out soon after half-ebb, so yachts drawing more than 1m should not expect to cross Canvey Point Shoals or Marsh End sands at less than three hours before or after high water.

Leigh Creek, however, does enable craft of moderate draught to reach the quays at Old Leigh, where there are a couple of boatyards and several pubs including the Crooked Billet, The Old Smack and The Peterboat and a glamorous restaurant, The Boatyard, on the site of the former Sea King Boatbuilders. At the quaint collection of weather-boarded shellfish sheds alongside the railway line you can buy Leigh cockles, brought back by a motorised and much reduced version of the bawley fleet that used to fish under sail for shrimps and whitebait as well as for cockles – a famous local speciality much loved by day trippers.

In *London to the Nore* (1905) WL Wyllie describes the Thames shrimpers of those days 'Down they come, bawley after bawley, some with red sails, some with grey… The smell of a fleet of shrimpers is quite unlike that of any other fishing craft. It is distinctly a good smell. The craft work right in the middle of the traffic, all among the liners, tramps, tugs and barges…The shrimp go straight into a cauldron of boiling water in the middle of the boat.'

Except at or near to high water, an approach to Leigh should be made from a position close to the Leigh buoy – Low-Way – located about half a mile west of Southend Pier. Although the Leigh buoy is conical and green, it must be considered a port-hand mark when entering the Ray Gut. A survey carried out by members of the

Leigh-on-Sea and Southend Port Guide Local tel code 01702	
Southend Pier	Tel: 215620.
Water	From Pier, Bell Wharf Leigh, boatyards or yacht clubs.
Stores	From shops in Leigh. Early closing on Wednesdays.
Chandlery	A small chandlery can be found at Mike's Boatyard.
Repairs	Lower Thames Marine (previously Johnson & Jago) Tel: 479009 (near Leigh station beyond the cockle sheds) slip, hoist and crane; Mike's Boatyard Tel: 713151 (on the wharf in Leigh Old Town) cranage, wharfage.
Fuel	Diesel and gas from Mike's Boatyard.
Transport	Good train service Leigh to London (Fenchurch Street).
Telephone	Outside The Smack.
Yacht clubs	Leigh-on-Sea Sailing Club Tel: 476788, bar; Essex Yacht Club Tel: 478404; Alexandra Yacht Club (Southend) Tel: 340363, bar; Thames Estuary Yacht Club (Westcliff) Tel: 345967; Halfway Yacht Club (Thorpe Bay) Tel: 582025; Thorpe Bay Yacht Club Tel: 587563, slip, bar, restaurant.
Food and drink	Peter Boat Inn Tel: 475666; The Old Smack Tel: 476765; Crooked Billet Tel: 714854; The Boatyard Restaurant Tel: 475588.

Looking up Leigh Creek towards the shellfish sheds in Old Leigh near high water

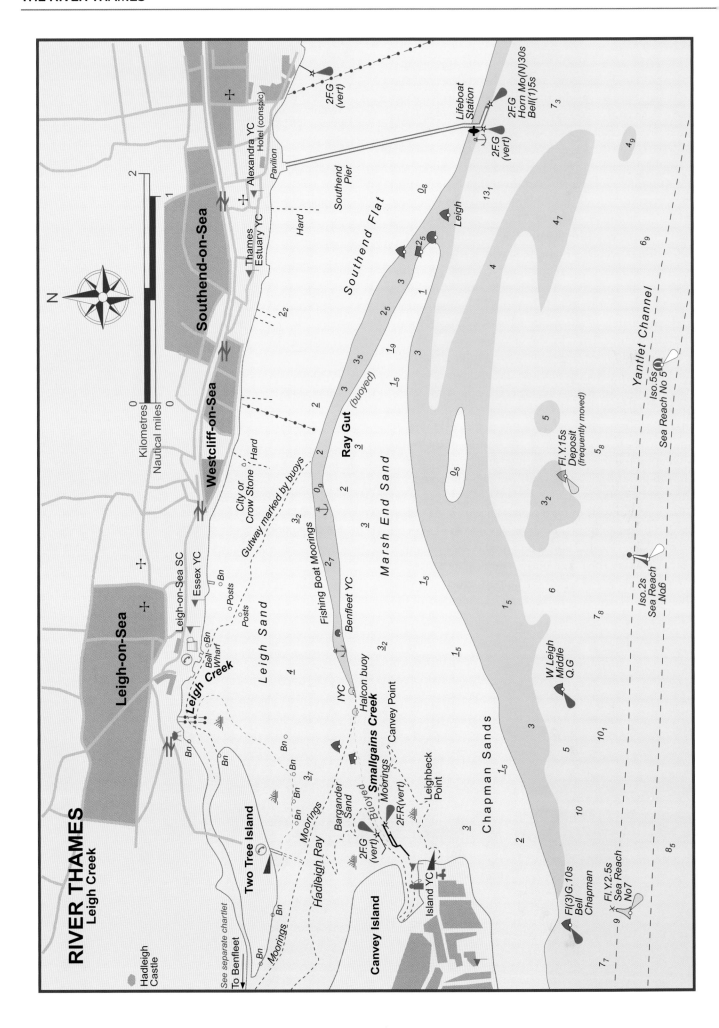

RIVER THAMES
Leigh Creek

Hadleigh Castle

See separate chartlet
To Benfleet

Leigh-on-Sea

Two Tree Island

Canvey Island

Westcliff-on-Sea

Southend-on-Sea

Leigh-on-Sea SC

Essex YC

Leigh Creek

Bell Wharf

Leigh Sand

Fishing Boat Moorings

Benfleet YC

IYC

Halcon buoy

Smallgains Creek

Canvey Point

Leighbeck Point

Island YC

Bargander Sand

Hadleigh Ray

Moorings

Buoyed

2.F.G (vert)

2.F.R (vert)

Fl(3)G.10s
Bell
Chapman

Fl.Y.2.5s
Sea Reach
No7

Thames Estuary YC

Alexandra YC

Hotel (conspic)

Pavilion

Hard

Hard

City or
Crow Stone

Gutway marked by buoys

Posts

Posts

Ray Gut
(buoyed)

Marsh End Sand

Southend Flat

Southend Pier

Leigh

Lifeboat Station

2.F.G (vert)

2.F.G
Horn Mo(N)30s
Bell(1)5s

2.F.G (vert)

Chapman Sands

W Leigh Middle
Q.G

Fl.Y.15s
Deposit
(frequently moved)

Yantlet Channel

Iso.5s
Sea Reach No 5

Iso.2s
Sea Reach
No6

N

Kilometres
Nautical miles

The Essex Yacht Club has its clubhouse on HMS *Wilton*, an ex-minesweeper

Leigh Sailing Club showed that there is practically no water to the west of it at low water springs. The Gut is just over a cable wide between its steep-to banks, and it carries some 3m at low water for a distance of nearly a mile in a generally north-westerly direction. A little way in from the entrance, deep water in the Ray is indicated by permanent moorings and fishing craft.

The channel leading to Leigh Creek and the Creek itself was re-marked as the result of co-operation between Southend Council and local fishermen. But unless a craft is able to take the ground without much inconvenience, it will be preferable to bring up in Hadleigh Ray, where several of the local bawleys are usually moored. There is enough water to stay afloat in Hadleigh Ray almost as far west as Canvey Point, but there is little protection except from the north.

At or near high water, a cross-sand route may be taken direct from West Leigh Middle Buoy to Bell Wharf on a bearing of 005°M.

It is sometimes possible for a deeper draught boat to find a berth alongside Bell Wharf, where Leigh Creek closely approaches the old town of Leigh. There is a landing place – a narrow strip of beach – just west of Bell Wharf, and it is also possible towards high water to land on the groynes further east, close to the Essex Yacht Club. This thriving family-oriented sailing club has an ex-minesweeper, the Hunt class HMS *Wilton*, berthed on the foreshore for its clubhouse.

From Leigh it is approximately two miles to Hadleigh Castle from where there are striking views of the estuary – just as there were in Constable's day.

HADLEIGH RAY AND BENFLEET CREEK
The deep-water moorings in Ray Gut extend westward almost to Canvey Point, but thereafter only the shallowest of craft can remain afloat throughout even a

neap tide. However, there are hundreds of small craft moored between Canvey Point and the causeway at Two-Tree Island and in Smallgains Creek.

At the western end of Ray Gut, near the Leigh Sands beacon, Island Yacht Club and Benfleet Yacht Club have established a couple of mooring buoys which can be used when waiting for the tide.

The landing and launching place on Two-Tree Island is approached via the Hadleigh Ray over a shoal patch, which may easily stop a yacht around low water. The outer end of Hadleigh Ray is marked by a pair of port and starboard-hand buoys situated just north of the Halcon 'mooring-type' buoy that indicates the entrance to Smallgains Creek. Otherwise, a course through Hadleigh Ray from one moored yacht to the next, following the larger craft, will lead to the causeway, which extends to the low water mark.

There is a car park and a road to Leigh Station. A hard-master is present during the day and water is available while he is there, together with an emergency telephone.

Benfleet Bridge and tidal barrier are about two miles upstream of the causeway at Two-Tree Island. The channel of Benfleet Creek, which dries out two hours either side of low water, is best learned by sailing up early on the tide. The gutway is marked by a series of numbered red port-hand buoys and green starboard-hand marks. Beware the mud horse in mid-channel at the eastern end. There is a beacon with a conical topmark on the north shore near No 5 buoy, and at this point your course must be changed to bring a pair of leading marks in line on the opposite (south) bank. The front one of these two beacons has a triangle topmark

Benfleet Port Guide – Local tel code 01268	
Water	From yacht club or yard.
Chandlery	At Dauntless Boatyard.
Stores	Shops in Benfleet.
Repairs	Dauntless Boatyard Tel: 07833 562563 or 07771 944288.
Fuel	Diesel at club – daytime hours.
Transport	Trains to London (Fenchurch Street).
Yacht club	Benfleet Yacht Club, Tel: 792278. Showers are available here.

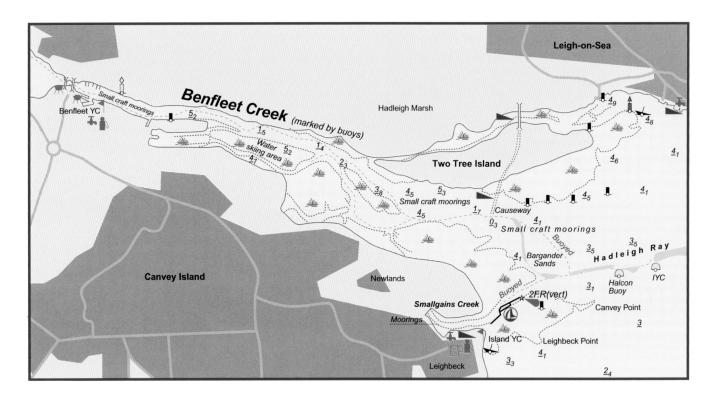

and the other a diamond-shaped topmark. Moorings are then continuous up to the tidal barrier and road bridge just above the yacht club, and help to indicate the channel.

Benfleet Yacht Club produces a chart of Benfleet Creek, copies of which can be obtained by visiting yachtsmen. Visitors are welcome at the fine clubhouse, situated alongside one of the best slipways in the Thames Estuary. This spotless slip is flushed each tide with an automatic pump which continues for hours and may keep you awake. Some visitors' moorings are available for yachts up to 45ft. In 1967 Robin Knox-Johnston joined Benfleet Yacht Club, which he describes in his book *Force of Nature* as '…a nice friendly club that has stayed that way, so I'm still a member there.' *Suhaili* was laid up in the creek while Knox-Johnston

was away at sea, before his first single-handed non-stop circumnavigation in her.

SMALLGAINS CREEK

This little creek off the eastern tip of Canvey Island is hardly more than a mile long, but is packed with drying moorings and stagings on both sides for most of its length. Fishing vessels regularly use it by night and day.

From the Smallgains (Halcon) yellow spherical buoy at the entrance, the creek is identified by a series of three green starboard-hand and four red port-hand buoys (lit with flashing lights) up to the Island Yacht Club's outer mooring jetties, which are marked on either hand by 2FG and 2FR lights. The buoys are sponsored by Island Yacht Club and Smallgains Marina. Approaching the Island Yacht Club, the channel turns to port and best water is indicated by sets of leading marks on the north bank and on the Island Yacht Club staging on the southern shore. A chartlet of the creek is downloadable from the Island Yacht Club website.

Island Yacht Club is on the Canvey shore about half a mile inside the creek. Provided they are prepared to dry out, visiting yachtsmen can be accommodated on request and food is available from the modern clubhouse at weekends. Moorings and stagings at the lower end of the creek belong to the club, which also has a wide concrete slipway.

Further upstream is Smallgains Marina (formerly Halcon Marine), with moorings on both sides of the creek, slipway, fuel and water pontoon, drydock and lifting facilities.

The marina fuel pontoon can be reached by craft with a metre draught approximately one hour before high water neaps.

Alongside at the Benfleet Yacht Club

Canvey Island (Eastern End) Port Guide
Local tel code 01268

Water	From wharf downstream of Island Yacht Club, or Smallgains Marina.
Fuel	Diesel is available at Smallgains Marina pontoon.
Stores	All kinds.
Repairs	Smallgains Marina Tel: 5116111. Dry dock, slip and lifting facilities.
Transport	From Benfleet Station (two miles away).
Yacht clubs	Island Yacht Club Tel: 510360; www.islandyachtclub.co.uk; Chapman Sands Sailing Club.
Food and drink	Island Yacht Club at weekends.

THE KENT SHORE

If the course in from the Estuary has been along the Kent coast, south of the dredged channel and north of the Medway channel, then a course keeping about half a mile south of the Yantlet dredged channel will serve as far as the East Blyth buoy, some five miles away.

The Nore Sand (the first shoal ever to be marked with a light in the Thames Estuary in 1732) used to dry out, but now has nowhere less than 2m over it.

When passing south of the Nore Sand, as from the Medway, an entrance to the Nore Swatchway should be shaped from a position close to the Nore Swatch buoy (R Can Fl (4) R 15s). From this mark, a course approximately 300°M will lead close to the Mid Swatch buoy (G Con Fl G 5s) guarding the south side of the shoal. Close south of the Mid Swatch buoy there is 8-9m, but there is little more than two cables between the buoy and the very steep edge of Grain Sands to the south. The same course (300°M) continued from the Mid Swatch buoy will lead out of the swatchway and up to the West Nore Sand (R Can Fl (3) R 10s).

YANTLET CREEK

There are not many landmarks along the south shore of Sea Reach, but the Yantlet Beacon (black with ball topmark), marking the west side of the entrance to Yantlet Creek, is visible from the West Nore Sand buoy. Small craft can reach this creek via a gutway running roughly south-westerly through the Yantlet Flats, and there is a pool carrying about a metre of water approximately a cable south-west of the beacon. Near the beacon on the Isle of Grain shore stands the London Stone that used to mark the downstream jurisdiction limit of the City of London Corporation. Its opposite number, the Crowstone, stands on the foreshore across the river at Westcliff-on-Sea.

The place is still used by yachtsmen in search of a remote and secluded anchorage, although the whole area is close to the MOD Yantlet firing ranges that lie to the east off the Grain marshes. A useful temporary anchorage can also be found along the edge of Yantlet Flats in about 4m.

The next light buoy is the East Blyth (R Can Fl (2) R 10s), located about a quarter of a mile off the edge of the flats, which at this point extend for almost a mile from the Kent shore. The drying edge is particularly steep-to abreast the East Blyth buoy, but shelves more gradually further west and changes from sand to sand and mud and then mud alone at the western end of the Sea Reach. The next buoy is the Mid Blyth.

The Port of London Authority (PLA) recommends that yachts should stay south of a line from East Blyth through Mid Blyth to West Blyth to keep clear of the freight terminal at Canvey, Shellhaven and Coryton. You should then cross to the correct side in Lower Hope Reach as rapidly as possible when it is safe to do so.

HOLEHAVEN

Owing to first the oil refineries and now the major development of a new freighter terminal at Shellhaven, Holehaven is not the useful anchorage it once was, but if it blows hard from the east, it might prove a worthwhile bolt hole.

At high water the entrance to Holehaven appears easy because of its apparent width, but in fact the only deep water runs about half a cable from the Canvey or the east side of the inlet. To the west the PLA has buoyed an entrance to be used by rubbish lighters. Drying mud with a steep-to edge stretches for nearly half a mile from Shellhaven Point. There is only about 1.5m of water in the entrance at low water springs, but once over this bar, depths increase to more than 2m, and about a quarter of a mile inside, soundings deepen to more than 5m in a hole (pool), which no doubt gave the creek its name.

After entering, a useful leading line is usually provided by the many fishing craft already moored in the creek, all of which should be left close to port.

There is no longer a PLA office at Holehaven and the long PLA pier is disused. However, the landing slipway just to the south of the pier has been renovated, and once over the sea wall, the Lobster Smack will be there waiting for you as it has for generations of sailing men before.

Holehaven was one of the most popular anchorages on the London River when the Wyllies' *London to the Nore* was published in 1905. If it was 'dark or rough' after a day's racing at Erith, rather than sail home to the Medway they '...used to run into the haven, anchor up, and crave a bed at the Lobster Smack' where the proprietress 'would give us a huge meal, a comfortable bed, and dry our clothes.' In the creek lie 'eel schuits

laden with fish from Holland for the London market…
and boats of all kinds, small yachts full of young
fellows…old yachts and barges…moored hulks full of
explosives, a steam ship…'

About half a mile within the entrance an overhead
pipe line crosses the creek from the new jetty to Canvey
Island. This structure gives a clearance of 30ft (9.2m) at
high water springs so some boats can pass under and
proceed with the tide towards Pitsea up Vange Creek.
A couple of miles upstream on the eastern bank is East
Haven Creek, which runs behind Canvey Island up to
Benfleet. This is closed to navigation, except possibly to
very small craft, by a tidal barrier at its mouth.

Consult the PLA harbour master by phone concerning
moorings in Holehaven. The PLA advises that a
temporary semi-sheltered anchorage can be found in
the lee of Chain Rock Jetty, above the entrance to the
creek; but beware of drying out.

Holehaven Port Guide – Local tel code 01474

PLA Harbour Master   Tel: 562462 (weekdays).

VANGE CREEK

There are many small boat moorings in this creek,
which leads up to the Watt Tyler Country Park where
there is a Motorboat Museum. A slipway, a workshop
and telephone are all situated nearby. The marshlands
fringing Vange and Pitsea were once used for explosives
manufacture and storage and the wharves along Vange
Creek were busy with shipping this dangerous cargo.

THE LONDON RIVER
Lower Hope

Above Thames Haven, the river turns south round
Lower Hope Point into Lower Hope Reach, the width of
which diminishes quite quickly from about two miles
down to less than a mile off Coalhouse Point. There
is room to anchor on Mucking Flats well out of the
channel near to Mucking No 5 buoy (G Con Fl (3)
G 10s). This can be a useful place to be in a strong
south-westerly. The Tilbury buoy (S Card YB Q (6) &
L Fl 15s) off Coalhouse Point and Diver (G Con L Fl
G 10s) on the Tilbury side lead into Gravesend Reach.

GRAVESEND

'Gravesend is a wonderful sight …alive with craft of
every type and tonnage …a strong smell of shrimps
impregnates the air,' wrote Francis B Cooke in
Coastwise Cruising from Erith to Lowestoft (1929). Alas,
although fleets of tugs and pilot boats still operate from
here, the bawley boats are long gone and the '..tea and
shrimps, oilskins, sea-boots and bloaters' with them.

Gravesend Reach runs for about four miles in an
east–west direction, with Tilbury Docks to the north
and Gravesend to the south of the river. To help scour
the Diver shoal, the PLA has built six groynes, exposed
at low water, on the north side of the reach, marked
by lit (Fl G 2.5s) beacons at their southern ends. The
beacons are difficult to see coming up river by day
and no better at night when the shore lights mask the
beacon lights. There are five unlit yellow buoys just
downstream of the first groyne off Coalhouse Point

The Ovens buoy, looking upriver to Gravesend Reach, with the Tilbury coal-fired power station on the Essex shore

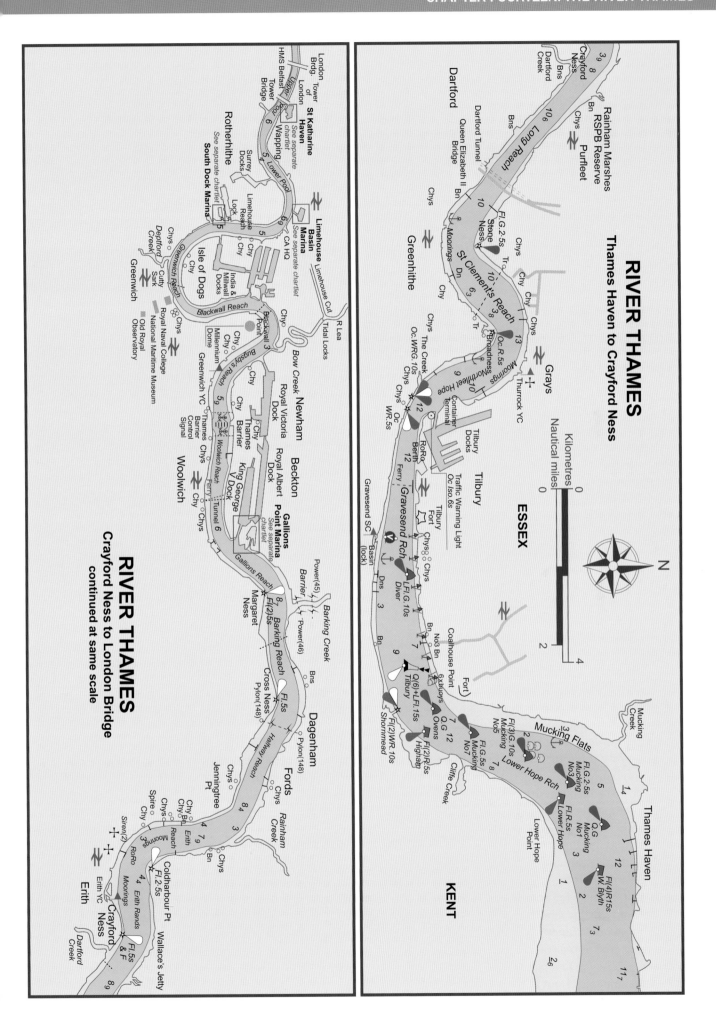

RIVER THAMES
Thames Haven to Crayford Ness

RIVER THAMES
Crayford Ness to London Bridge
continued at same scale

The Embankment Marina at Gravesend is entered via a lock

and there is no passage inshore of these or the beacons. The best course is from north of the Ovens buoy to Tilbury south cardinal, after which leave Diver buoy close to starboard; bear in mind that inbound ships pass close to the Tilbury buoy, so a good lookout astern is recommended.

On the north shore, the Gravesend ferry and cruise liners use the Tilbury landing stage, at the upper end of which there is a RO-RO berth for very large ships transporting cars for Hyundai.

At night piers and stagings of the north bank are marked by two fixed green lights (vert) and those on the south side by vertical pairs of red lights.

The Gravesend Canal Basin bears a large sign – Embankment Marina. Entry and departure through the lock gates are controlled either by traffic lights or by hand signals. The lock-keeper (Tel: 01474 535700) is in attendance at each high water between the hours of 0800 to 2000 April to October (1000 to 1600 winter months) and the gates can be opened from 1½hrs before high water until high water.

A temporary mooring can sometimes be found off the Gravesend Sailing Club, where there are two visitors' buoys, one of which can dry out at low water springs, but the other, at the east end of the club moorings and marked *Visitors*, gives a clear depth of 2m at all times. In addition to the club's moorings, the PLA provides circular yellow 'seaplane' buoys off the promenade, which are intended for larger yachts. Call *Port Control London* VHF Ch 68 for advice on which one to use.

There are steps for landing at the lockside near high water, but at other times use the PLA slipway opposite the rowing club at the west end of the promenade, where it is possible to anchor.

You are able to dry out in the lock cut after high water; the bottom has around 0.5m of soft mud

over concrete; consult the lock-keeper or sailing club members for advice. Assistance is always available from members of the Gravesend Sailing Club (adjacent to the marina) at weekends. The club has scrubbing posts near the promenade wall, but these can be exposed to washes; masts can be stepped or unstepped by prior arrangement. Craft should not be left unattended in the Gravesend anchorage, but arrangements can usually be made with the lock-master to leave a boat in the Embankment Marina.

Gravesend Embankment Marina Port Guide
Local tel code 01474

The Embankment Marina	
Lock-keeper	Tel: 535700; VHF Ch 80; www. theembankmentmarina.com.
Water	From standpipe near entrance to lock.
Stores	From shops in town, short walk.
Chandler	In town – a 10-minute walk, Tel: 350671.
Fuel	Diesel and Calor Gas from lock office, petrol from garage in town, half a mile away.
Crane	Inside the basin, can be used with permission from Gravesend Sailing Club (see below).
Yacht club	Gravesend Sailing Club, Promenade East, Gravesend, Kent DA12 2RN, Clubhouse Tel: 533974.
Facilities	Showers and usual services available at weekends during the season.
Food and drink	The Canal Tavern Tel: 535691; other restaurants in Gravesend.
Transport	Ebbsfleet station is three miles away, from where there are high speed trains to London.

GRAYS THURROCK
Northfleet Hope adjoins Gravesend Reach and runs south-east–north-west for just over a mile to Broadness on the south bank and Grays Thurrock on the north bank. After two channel buoys near Broadness Point, for the rest of the way up-river shore marks are used to navigate from reach to reach.

Moorings belonging to members of the Thurrock Yacht Club, on the north shore upstream of the Port of Tilbury Grain Terminal, are located just below the town causeway and abreast the wreck of the old lightship that once served as the club's headquarters. The club now has a new building and workshop on Kilverts Wharf, where visiting yachtsmen are welcomed and sometimes a mooring can be arranged. All kinds of supplies can be had from the town nearby.

Thurrock Yacht Club – Local tel code 01375	
Thurrock Yacht Club	Kilverts Wharf, Argent Street, Grays, Essex, Tel: 373720; www.thurrockyachtclub.org.
Opening times	Saturday and Sunday all day; weekdays 1000-1500; Thursday evenings 2000-2300.
Fuel	Diesel during opening hours; petrol two miles away.
Visitor's mooring	By arrangement.
Facilities	Showers, toilets, telephone, cooking facilities during opening hours.

GREENHITHE

There are some small boat moorings and a causeway on the foreshore at Greenhithe, opposite Stone Ness (Fl 2.5s), at the southern end of St Clement's Reach.

Close to the shore here is a housing development on the site of a merchant navy training college, which had replaced the earlier training ships, such as the *Worcester* and the *Warspite*, that used to lie off Greenhithe. In 1905 Wyllie recorded that the National Refuge for Homeless and Destitute Children, whose school ship was the old, 50-gun frigate *Arethusa*, had been the means of rescuing some 17,000 lads whose '... only recommendation was that they be good, fatherless and poor.' In the 19th century there were ex-men of war hulks moored up and down the river, used variously as hospitals, reformatories, nautical colleges, powder stores or convict hulks.

QUEEN ELIZABETH II BRIDGE

This impressive bridge between Dartford in Kent and Thurrock in Essex, with its 54m vertical clearance, presents no problem to the yachtsman who passes way below the six lanes of traffic thundering on its way around the M25 overhead.

There are Ro-Ro berths on both banks in Long Reach,

up and downstream of the bridge, and a good look-out should be kept on the ships manoeuvring hereabouts. Legend has it that nearby, where the Mardyke flows into the Thames at Purfleet, is the spot where the first Queen Elizabeth stood to view her fleet at anchor.

There are Ro-Ro berths on both banks up and downstream of the bridge

ERITH RANDS

This short reach between Crayford Ness and the town of Erith runs for about a mile in an east–west direction.

Frank Cowper in his *Sailing Tours* (1892) declared Erith to be '...a capital place to lie off, as it is well sheltered and we can lie out of the way of the traffic; but it is very crowded in the season.'

The Erith Yacht Club, founded in 1900 when the Royal Corinthian Yacht Club moved from Erith to Port Victoria in the Medway, has its headquarters in the old Norwegian car ferry *Folgefonn* on the south shore in Anchor Bay. The club has moorings abreast the clubship for yachts up to 35ft LOA and a buoy can usually be found for a visitor – this can be a useful stop-off for anyone running out of tide on a trip upriver. Larger

The Queen Elizabeth II Bridge spans the Thames between Dartford in Kent and Thurrock in Essex

yachts should anchor above the moorings where there is good holding in mud; shallower draught yachts are able to anchor below the moorings. It is possible to land at the club slipway, where there is a standpipe, or at the nearby Erith town causeway.

At Erith Wharf you will come across yet another busy Ro-Ro terminal.

Much of the London River traffic comprises tugs taking endless tows of rubbish barges to disgorge their contents onto various infill sites, including a monstrous one on the Rainham shore. Also on the north bank, Rainham Marshes, formerly used by the MOD for firing ranges, is now an RSPB reserve.

In Halfway Reach on the north bank is Ford's Dagenham factory where the Fords wharf has ships coming and going most of the time. On the opposite bank is a strikingly modern sewage processing plant. This building is reminiscent of an ocean-going liner or perhaps a whale, as it stands out against the tower blocks of Plumstead and the high ground at Greenwich in the distance.

GALLIONS REACH

Gallions Point Marina, entered via a lock (five hours either side of high water), is situated at the old entrance to the Royal Albert Basin on the north bank. With over 100 berths, it provides a useful stop-over down river of the Thames Barrier.

Erith Yacht Club – Local tel code 01322	
Erith Yacht Club	Tel: 01322 332943; email: secretary@erithyachtclub.org; www.erithyachtclub.org.uk.
Water	Standpipe near club slipway; from clubship at high water by arrangement.
Fuel	Diesel (cans) from club by arrangement, petrol (cans) from Morrisons in Erith.
Stores	Morrisons two minutes walk from Town Causeway.

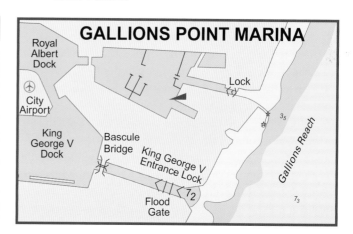

The Gallions Point Marina is very close to the City Airport, which can just be seen in the top left of the photograph

Gallions Point Port Guide

Marina	Gate 14, Royal Albert Basin, Woolwich Manor Way, North Woolwich, London E16 2PU, Tel: 0207 476 7054; VHF Ch 13. Accessible five hours either side of high water.
Facilities	Toilets and showers, pump-out ashore.
Stores	Locally or in Woolwich on the south bank; it's a 15-minute walk to Woolwich Ferry and foot tunnel.
Transport	Docklands Light Railway from North Woolwich to Central London. London City Airport is nearby.

In Woolwich Reach the Woolwich Free Ferries cross the tideway every few minutes

WOOLWICH REACH

When passing through Woolwich Reach, there are two hazards to contend with – the ferries which ply between North and South Woolwich, and the Thames Barrier about halfway along the reach. The pair of Woolwich Free Ferries change places across the tideway every few minutes, laden with lorries on each trip.

The Royal Arsenal, on the south bank, was originally established as an ordnance storage depot in 1671 and has now been regenerated into luxury riverside apartments. Just downstream, the Royal Artillery Quays has a series of eight designer tower blocks rising from them. Things have not always been so thriving in this part of Docklands – during the hard times of the 1930s dozens of sprits'l barges, awaiting work, lay on the 'starvation buoys' in Woolwich Reach.

THE THAMES BARRIER

At the tidal-surge barrier across the Thames in Woolwich Reach a system of extremely powerful light signals is used by day and night to indicate which spans are to be used and which are barred to traffic. Two green arrows (lit) pointing inwards will be displayed from each side of a span that is open to oncoming traffic, while red St Andrew's crosses (lit) shown from each side of a span will mean that no traffic must pass through the span in that direction. Anchoring is prohibited in the vicinity of the barrier.

Large illuminated noticeboards are in position on both banks upstream near Blackwall Point and Blackwall Stairs; and downstream near Thamesmead and Barking Power Station. Flashing amber lights shown at these boards warn ships to proceed with caution while red lights require them to stop. Audible warnings can also be issued from these stations.

The Thames Barrier at Woolwich light signals are used by day and night to indicate which span is open

Whenever possible, vessels should take in their sails and use motor power to navigate through the Barrier. Port Control London advises yachtsmen to talk to traffic control on VHF Channel 14, callsign *London VTS*, or on Tel: 0208 855 0315.

BARRIER CLOSURES

From time to time the Barrier is closed for testing purposes, usually only one gate at any one time but occasionally all gates at the same time. Information regarding the dates and times of closures are given by Woolwich Radio on Ch 14 and in Port Control London's Notice to Mariners.

BUGSBY'S REACH

The Greenwich Yacht Club is situated on the south side of the river in the bight between Woolwich and Bugsby's reaches. Part of the Tideway Sailing Centre, the club has extensive modern premises comprising a clubhouse on a pier with fine views of the city and the river. Facilities incorporate an all-tide pontoon, slipway, boatlift and many moorings, including one swinging mooring for visiting yachts up to 30ft, by prior arrangement. Vacant members' moorings can also be made available; contact the Greenwich Yacht Club harbour master to reserve a place on the pontoon. Anchoring is not allowed because of the considerable commercial traffic in the vicinity, particularly barge trains moored nearby which swing with the tide.

In Bugsby's Reach the Canary Wharf Tower can be seen over the top of the Dome

BLACKWALL

Blackwall Point, on the south bank, is easily identified by the conspicuous Millennium Dome, and the adjacent Dome Pier with its 85m connecting bridge. Opposite, on the north bank, is the entrance to Bow Creek and the River Lea, followed by the India and Millwall Docks just east of Canary Wharf Tower.

The Poplar Dock Marina in Blackwall Basin no longer has visitors' berths.

Bugsby's Reach

The Old Naval College stands on the banks of the river at Greenwich

GREENWICH REACH

This short east-west reach links Blackwall and Limehouse Reaches, round the Isle of Dogs.

Here on the south bank is the Royal Naval College '...standing like a thing of dignity amid the grime of commerce' – as J Wentworth Day described it in *Coastal Adventure* (1949). Nearby is the National Maritime Museum, and the charred hull of the once proud clipper ship the *Cutty Sark* facing an uncertain future following the disastrous fire of 2007. The more fortunate hull of Sir Francis Chichester's *Gypsy Moth IV* has been rescued from her shoreside berth alongside the *Cutty Sark* and taken back to sea. Not far away at Deptford, the Tudor warship the *Mary Rose* was built in the first year of the reign of Henry VIII.

Greenwich Yacht Club	
Greenwich Yacht Club	Peartree Wharf, Peartree Way, London SE10 0BW; www. greenwich yachtclub.co.uk.
Harbour master	Tel: 0208 8587339; VHF Ch M (opening hours)
Visitors' moorings	By prior arrangement.
Water	At clubhouse.
Facilities	Repairs, showers and usual clubhouse facilities.
Bar	Tuesday and Friday evenings and weekends.

The Meridian is crossed three times on the upstream approach to Greenwich.

It is possible for small craft to anchor just below and in line with Greenwich Pier, which is much used by water buses and pleasure steamers.

SOUTH DOCK MARINA

The South Dock Marina is in part of the old Surrey Dock complex on the south bank of the river. The locked entrance, in the southern end of Limehouse Reach, is just over one mile above Greenwich and about 2½ miles down river from Tower Bridge. The conspicuous Baltic Quay building, with its five arched rooftops, is situated at the south-west end of the marina. Call the marina after passing Deptford Creek to be advised what depth there is over the sill and to allow time for the lock to be prepared.

The lock entrance is inside and immediately downstream of Greenland Pier, which is used by large,

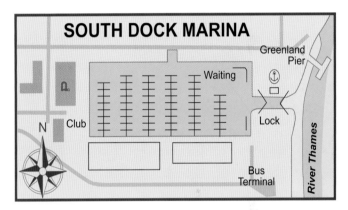

South Dock Marina	
South Dock Marina	Lock Office, Rope Street, Plough Way, London, SE16 1TX, Tel: 0207 252 2244; Fax: 020 7237 3806; VHF Ch 37.
Entrance lock	Three hours either side of high water (1m draught); one hour either side of high water (2m draught).
Berths	350.
Fuel	Diesel and petrol (cans) locally (ask at lock office).
Security	24-hour CCTV.
Facilities	Showers, water, telephone on site; repairs (crane up to 20 tons) – ask at lock office.
Stores	Surrey Quays Shopping Centre, including Tesco, is a few minutes walk away.
Food and drink	Pubs nearby in Greenland Dock.
Transport	Surrey Quays tube for Tower Hill, Canada Water Jubilee line; riverbus from pier; bus service to Greenwich.

The South Dock Marina is in part of the old Surrey Dock complex on the south bank

fast riverbus catamarans. Beware of strong cross tides until you are inside the knuckles. The lock will open for yachts of approximately 1m draught for about three hours either side of high water; about one hour either side of high water for a 2m draught. There is a holding pontoon on the upstream side of Greenland Pier, but there is considerable wash from passing craft so have plenty of fenders ready and do not leave the yacht unattended here.

LIMEHOUSE REACH

The river takes a turn to the north into Limehouse Reach, where to starboard the Canary Wharf Tower and its surrounding buildings on the Isle of Dogs seem to dwarf all else along the river banks. Here and there are glimpses of the old London waterfront left behind, but most of the banksides from Woolwich to Tower Bridge have been extensively developed.

LIMEHOUSE BASIN MARINA

On the north bank, just before the river begins its turn to the south-west into the Lower Pool, the former Regents Canal Dock (built in 1820) contains

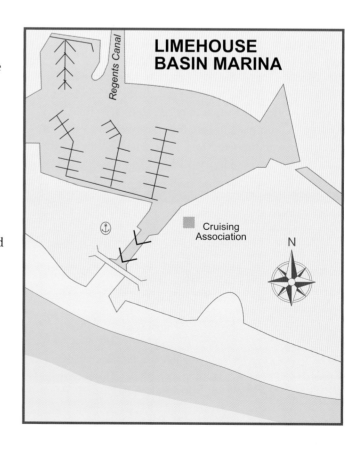

the 90-berth Limehouse Basin Marina and still provides access to the inland waterways network. The swing bridge and lock entrance operate all week, 0800-1800 April to September and 0800-1600 October to March (other times with 24-hour prior notice). There is one metre over the sill at low water neaps and access is possible for about four hours either side of high water. A towering apartment block on the east side of the entrance makes it difficult to identify the swing bridge and lock gates as you approach from downstream. The Barley Mow pub on the waterfront to the west of the bridge has a distinctive white flag pole in front of it. The black swing bridge has Limehouse Marina unmistakably painted in white across its span and this can be picked out when you are abeam of the entrance, where there is a waiting pontoon accessible about 1½ hours either side of low water. Beware of a cross tide in the lock cut at mid-flood and mid-ebb.

Once through the lock, the pontoon berths are to port; the showers, toilets and laundry facilities are beneath the lock-keeper's office, an octagonal building on the port-hand lock corner. There are waste disposal and pump-out facilities, but no fuelling. The basin also houses the headquarters of the Cruising Association (CA).

If you have not been allocated a berth, moor on the walkway to starboard and enquire at the office. The CA bar and restaurant are open on a temporary membership basis to all visiting yachtsmen; food is served every day, with a carvery or barbecue on Sundays in summer.

At Limehouse Basin, where the Regents Canal meets the Thames, east of the London bridges, there is access to 2,000 miles of inland waterways so, not surprisingly, a number of narrowboats and river cruisers are moored in the marina, which is also a regular venue for waterways rallies.

The entrance to the lock at Limehouse Basin Marina

Limehouse Basin Marina

British Waterways	www.bwml.co.uk.
British Waterways Lock Office	
To book berth	Tel: 0207 308 9930 (24-hour answer phone); VHF Ch 80.
Entrance swing bridge/lock	Four hours either side of high water.
Berths	90.
Security	Swipe card for access to pontoon and facilities.
Water	On pontoons.
Electricity	By arrangement.
Showers, toilets, laundry	Beneath lock-keeper's building.
Fuel	Petrol and diesel at Esso garage on Commercial Road (take your own cans).
Gas	Docklands Garden Centre near Limehouse Station.
Chandlery	Limited, at office.
Cruising Association	1 Northey Street, Limehouse Basin, London E14 8BT. Tel: 0207 537 2828; Fax: 0207 537 2266; www.cruising.org.uk.
Food and drink	Three waterside pubs within easy walking; CA bar and catering; many restaurants at Canary Wharf, a 15-minute walk away.
Stores	Limited from small shop in Narrow Street; more small shops in Salmon Lane (round low level walkway and across Commercial Road); supermarkets at Canary Wharf.
Banks and cashpoints	Banks on South Quay on Docklands Light Railway; cashpoint at Texaco garage near Pumpkin Marine.
Transport	Docklands Light Railway from Limehouse to Bank or Tower Gateway; British Rail from Limehouse to Fenchurch Street or Southend; No 15 bus from Commercial Road to West End.

Limehouse Basin Marina is home to the Cruising Association

ST KATHARINE HAVEN

St Katharine Haven is close to the Tower of London and immediately below Tower Bridge on the north bank of the river. This marina, with berthing facilities for more than 100 craft, must surely be one of the most superbly sited yacht harbours in the world.

Entry to the harbour is by way of a tidal lock (30ft x 100ft), which can be accessed from about 2 hours before high water to 1½ hours after (0600-2030 in summer; 0800-1800 in winter). Precise details of monthly lock opening times can be found on the St Katharine Haven website.

The lock leads into the Central Basin with further access via small lifting bridges to the West or East Docks on either hand. Visiting yachts are usually berthed in

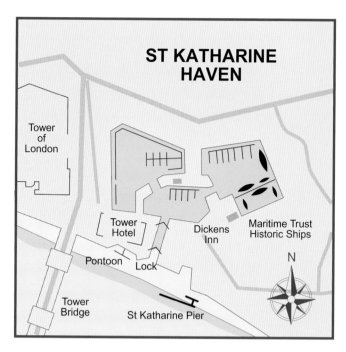

Yachts and a sailing barge locking out of St Katharine Yacht Haven

the Central Basin or East Dock and a week's notice is required during the summer.

Diesel fuel is available from the *Thames Refueller*, moored 400m downstream of the lock entrance (operates 0900-1600 weekdays; 0900-1300 Saturday and Sunday).

There are some visitors' moorings laid east of the lock entrance next to Devon House, and the inside of St Katharine Pier can be used by shoal draught yachts while awaiting entry to the marina. The outside of this pier is heavily used by riverbuses between 0600-1830 when mooring is strictly prohibited.

The Tower of London is just across the road from St Katharine Yacht Haven

Upnor Castle was built in 1559 orginally to defend Elizabeth I's warships

Chapter fifteen
The Medway

Tides	Queenborough – HW Dover +1.35. Range: springs 5.1m; neaps 3.3m
Charts	Admiralty 1185, 1834, 3683, SC5606; Imray Y18, 2000 series; OS map 178
Waypoints	**Medway Lt Buoy 51°28'.83N 00°52'.81E**
	No 11 buoy 51°27'.51N 00°45'.80E
	Grain Hard Buoy 51°26'.98N 00°44'.16E
	Queenborough Spit Buoy 51°25'.81N 00°43'.93E
Hazards	Wreck of the *Richard Montgomery*. Overfalls near Sheerness Fort on ebb
Medway Ports	VHF Ch 74 and 16 (24 hour); callsign *Medway VTS*
Harbour master	Tel: 01795 663025
Medway Yachting Association	
	www.medwayya.co.uk

For centuries the Medway was the Navy's river, with dockyard bases at Sheerness and Chatham, and the even older forts at Folly Point and Darnet Ness. The first warship built at Chatham was launched in 1586, and at Chatham's World Naval Base, formerly the Historic Dockyard and Museum, you can see the most complete Georgian/early Victorian dockyard in the world.

For the yachtsman, the Medway offers very good sailing in the lower reaches, where on the south side there are some quiet anchorages in settings that can have changed little since the Romans established their potteries and even less since the prison-hulks were moored in the area during the Revolutionary and Napoleonic wars. Those who are not afraid of mud can still find relics of both these periods, even though they were separated by thousands of years.

The entrance to the Medway between Sheerness, bottom left, and the Isle of Grain (right). The Grain Tower Battery can be seen on the tideline bottom right

By contrast, the north shore of the river is now almost entirely given over to the Grain oil-fired power station, the Thamesport container terminal, a British Gas LNG terminal, and an aggregates wharf – all on the Isle of Grain – plus the coal-fired power station at Kingsnorth with its associated coal jetties at the western end of Long Reach.

The river is navigable by quite large vessels for some 13 miles from its mouth at Sheerness to Rochester, where the headroom under the bridge is 30ft at low water springs. The tide flows for a further 12 miles to Allington Lock, one mile above the lower arched bridge at Aylsford. Then, for a further 17 miles, the river winds through pleasant country to Maidstone and Tonbridge, with eleven locks. Craft drawing 2m can get as far as Maidstone, while those drawing 1.2m can reach Tonbridge. Maximum length 18m, beam 4.5m.

The Port of Sheerness is responsible for the ports at Sheerness, Isle of Grain, Faversham and Rochester. There is considerable commercial traffic in both the Medway and the Swale, and Sheerness itself is solely a commercial harbour handling chilled fresh produce, trade cars, steel and forest products.

LANDMARKS

From the Thames Estuary the tree-covered cliffs of Warden Point on the Isle of Sheppey, some six miles east of the Medway entrance, are conspicuous. On the west side is the 800ft chimney of the Grain Power Station, the most prominent daylight mark in the whole of the Thames Estuary, sometimes visible from as far north as the Wallet. The chimney displays four sets of four vertical red lights, the top ones of which are flashing. At a lower level on the Grain flats is the Grain Tower Battery connected to the shore at low water by a causeway.

On the east side of the entrance is Sheerness Port and the fort at Garrison Point (now used by Medway Ports) from which a powerful flashing light is shown by day or night when large ships are under way.

APPROACHES

There are three main approaches to the Medway (see River Thames Sea Reach chart on page 141):

(i) The main deep water route. From the Medway Pillar Lt Buoy (RWVS Mo (A) 6s Sph topmark) some three-quarters of a mile south of Sea Reach No 1 Buoy, the channel runs in a west by southerly direction between Sheerness Middle Sand and Grain Spit to the west, and the flats of the Cant to the east. It is wide and well lit, with all the starboard-hand buoys having green lights and the port having red. The stranded wreck of the ammunition ship *Richard Montgomery* lies on Sheerness Middle Sand, very near No 7 and No 9 buoys. It is dangerous but clearly marked by special buoys (yellow) on all sides.

The tidal stream off the approach sets west by north and east by south at a maximum rate of 2½ and

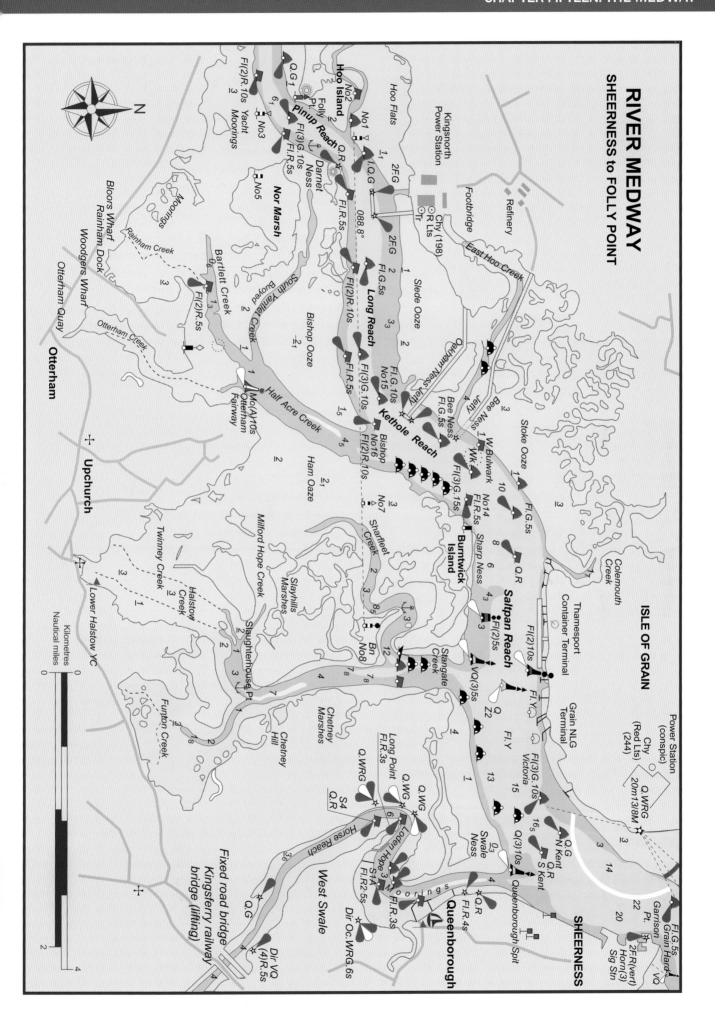

RIVER MEDWAY
SHEERNESS to FOLLY POINT

The wreck of the ammunition ship *Richard Montgomery* is marked by special buoys

3 knots respectively, slightly across the channel, but as Garrison Point is neared they run fairly up and down the channel.

(ii) The Nore Swatch, formerly known as the Jenkin Swatch, is not quite so important now that the Nore Sand has 2m or more over it at low water springs. From the west the Swatch can be located by the West Nore Sand Lt Buoy (R Can Fl (3) R 10s), which lies on the south side of Sea Reach almost opposite Southend Pier. A course of 120°M leads to pass the Mid Swatch light buoy (G Con Fl G 5s) close to port and, continued, reaches the Nore Swatch light buoy (R Can Fl (4) R 15s). From here a southerly course leaving the green conical Grain Edge Buoy to starboard leads into the main channel.

(iii) Across the Cant. Vessels making from the eastward via the Four Fathom Channel or out of the West Swale can carry about 3m least water on a course 300°M from the Spile Buoy (G Con Fl G 2.5s), keeping about two miles from the Sheppey shore. Several unlit beacons and Cheney Spit, a shingle bank with about 1m least water, extend eastwards from Garrison Point. These hazards make it inadvisable to get much closer than a mile offshore. Cheney Rocks, an unmarked drying patch of stones, lies half a mile off the eastern end of Sheerness town. A north cardinal buoy (VQ) marks the seaward end of the Jacob's Bank obstruction extending from the shore just east of Garrison Point. Tides over the Cant are slacker than those in the channels. The Medway may also be entered through the Swale (see Chapter 16 page 173).

ENTRANCE

Medway Ports have allocated a recommended yacht track, in the vicinity of the Little Nore Anchorage, for both inward and outward bound leisure craft. The track is from a position near the No 11 starboard-hand buoy to near the Grain Hard starboard-hand buoy and keeps small craft to the north of the shipping channel past Garrison Point and Sheerness.

The entrance to the Medway is between Garrison Point to port and Grain Hard buoy (G Con Fl G 5s) to starboard.

Garrison Point is steep-to, and on the first of the ebb during spring tides there are considerable overfalls on the east side of the entrance. The flood runs at 2½ knots at springs, setting sharply on to Garrison Point and causing a pronounced north-going eddy along the Sheppey shore. However, the ebb is much weaker on the Grain side of the river, so a yacht entering against the stream should seek this shore, as per the recommended yacht track. But bear in mind that the edge of the mud is quite steep.

A powerful white light (Fl 7s) shown to seaward from Garrison Point means that a large ship is under way outbound and small craft must keep clear; if the light is shown upriver then a large ship is inbound.

On the Grain shore the flats run out for half a mile almost to the Grain Hard buoy. No attempt should be made to pass to the west of this buoy as there are the remains of an obstruction running out from the Grain Tower Battery.

Once inside, the river broadens out and the busy commercial harbour of Sheerness will be seen to port. On the east shore the infilled Lappel, once an anchorage, is used as a container/car park, which is often brilliantly illuminated at night.

QUEENBOROUGH

A sheltered mooring will be found at Queenborough, 1½ miles further south and just inside the West Swale. The entrance is narrow and is marked by Queenborough Spit Pillar buoy (E Card BYB Q (3) 10s), which should

There is a scrubbing berth alongside the quay in Queenborough Creek

The Queenborough all tide landing (ATL) pontoon near low water; the Grain Power Station chimney can be seen across the river

be left close to starboard. After this, two dolphins with flashing red lights, marking the remains of the old packet pier, in regular use by the Flushing paddle boat ferries 100 years ago, should be left strictly to port because of the extremely foul ground inside them.

For the next mile or so the river is lined on both sides by more than 100 moorings that are controlled by the Swale Borough Council. There are several visitors' moorings (yellow) on the east side, north of the all-tide landing (ATL) pontoon; a pair of large buoys north of the ATL can be used by up to six yachts on the larger and up to four on the smaller. The two large buoys south of the Hard are used by fishing boats.

The ATL, which is owned by the local Queenborough Yacht Club, is marked by two fixed red vertical lights and extends from the former Crundells Wharf, just down-river from the original town hard. Going ashore via the hammerhead pontoon is easy, but remember that to get back onto the pontoon via the heavily fortified (anti-vandal and trespasser) turnstile gate, you need to purchase a token (50p per person in 2008) from the Queenborough Yacht Club, any of the pubs or town traders. A stay alongside is limited to 15 minutes. However, prior arrangement can usually be made with the yacht club for an overnight (after 1600) stay.

Swale Borough Council trot boat has not been operating recently. The overstretched Queenborough Yacht Club trot boat service, run by club volunteers, operates on Friday evenings and Saturdays from 1600 to 2300; see details in the Port Guide opposite. There is a restaurant and bar at the yacht club's

clubhouse, situated in an old pub. Good value meals are served here on Friday and Saturday evenings and visiting yachtsmen will be made welcome.

Queenborough Port Guide
Local tel code 01795

Supervisor Harbour Master	
Swale Borough Council	On Town Quay, Tel: 662051; VHF Ch 74 callsign *Sheppey One*.
ATL Queenborough Yacht Club	
QYC Bosun	Tel: 07957 180373.
QYC Trot Boat	Tel: 07958 454742; VHF Ch 08 callsign *QYC Trotboat* (1600-2300 Saturday).
Water	On ATL pontoon head.
Stores	Queenborough Stores nearby, shops in town. Early closing on Wednesdays.
Repairs	Jim Brett Marine, Tel: 668263. Yard with slip at Town Quay.
Fuel	Garage in town.
Transport	Train service to London via Sittingbourne, station ½ mile.
Yacht clubs	Queenborough Yacht Club, High Street, Tel: 663955, equipped with bar, restaurant and showers; Sheppey Yacht Club (Cruiser Section).
Food and drink	Queenborough Yacht Club (meals Fridays and Saturdays), the pub The Old House at Home at top of hard, Tel: 662463; Captain Crimps Seafood Shop, Town Quay Tel: 664209.

The Guildhall Museum in Queenborough tells the story of the industrial and naval history of the town

A concrete barge, which can be booked from Swale Borough Council for barbecues, is situated on the west side of the river, opposite the hard, upstream of the ATL. It should be noted that the hard extends a long way and care must be taken to avoid its submerged end. The hard gives direct access to the top of the High Street, but unattended dinghies left on the hard might be vulnerable.

Queenborough Creek is a narrow gut that leads in behind the town to Queenborough Quay; it is used by fairly large fishing vessels, motor boats and other small craft which dry out alongside or in mud berths on the opposite bank. The entrance is just upriver from the Hard and the creek's course is marked by half a dozen red can and green conical buoys. The Town Quay, which is administered by Swale District Council, can be reached around high water. There is a scrubbing berth alongside which can be pre-booked at the harbour master's office on the quayside.

The east side of the channel is marked by a red can (Fl R 3s). Anchorage is forbidden in the fairway because of the large vessels that come by on their way to and from Ridham Dock and Grovehurst Coal Jetty. A series of lit beacons on the mainland shore are used by the commercial shipping navigating Loden Hope

and around Long Point into the West Swale.

The tide runs south past Queenborough for the first hour after high water.

SHEERNESS TO ROCHESTER

Standing on up the Medway through Saltpan Reach the river widens and tidal streams are less strong. Almost the whole of the north shore is occupied by tanker and container ship berths and jetties. The tankship jetties at the British Gas LNG (liquefied natural gas) terminal are marked by spherical yellow buoys (Fl Y) and this potentially dangerous area must be given a wide berth. At the western end of all these jetties is Colemouth Creek, which formerly joined the Yantlet Creek in the Thames to form the Isle of Grain. This carries 2m at low water for half a mile, but is of little interest because of its environment.

Very few yachtsmen sailing through Saltpan Reach will know that, in 1897, the Royal Corinthian Yacht Club made a deal with the South Eastern Railway Company to move its headquarters from Erith to Port Victoria, today the site of the Thamesport container terminal with its busy jetties. A splendid clubhouse was erected and members came down from London by train to join their yachts on moorings opposite Stangate Creek. In *London to the Nore* (1905) Wyllie painted a watercolour of the scene and described sailing past 'the Royal Corinthian clubhouse, a blaze of light reflected in the placid water studded with racing boats and cruisers, the large yachts outside, and beyond them the mass of great coal hulks…' The coal was for the battleships and cruisers that were in the Medway in the days when Sheerness was an important naval base.

A line of large, unlit tugboat mooring buoys extends along the south side of Saltpan Reach about a half mile east of the entrance to Stangate Creek. Other mooring buoys are located in mid-channel, the first and last of which are lit (QR).

STANGATE CREEK

This creek, running south of Saltpan Reach, provides perhaps the most useful anchorage in the Medway. A spit extends from the western side of Stangate Creek and this is marked by an east cardinal pillar buoy (BYB VQ (3) 5s). The eastern side of the entrance is fairly steep-to.

Half a mile into the creek, wreckage on the starboard hand is marked by a green conical buoy and just beyond, opposite a red can buoy, is the entrance to Sharfleet Creek.

The creeks hereabouts have a remote and ghostly feel to them. Perhaps this is not surprising as at low tide Roman pottery can sometimes be found, although there are no longer coffins in the saltings as described in *London to the Nore* – 'Doubtless the poor fellows died on the hulks that during the wars of a hundred years ago were here moored as prison-ships.'

For a further mile to the south, the depths in Stangate Creek decrease gradually from some 10m to about 4m low water springs at Slaughterhouse Point, where the creek divides. Funton Creek to port holds water for only a little way, but can provide a quiet berth. To starboard, the main channel carries 2m for a quarter of a mile or so and then divides again into Halstow, Twinney and Milford Hope Creeks, all of which dry out. For about 1½ hours either side of high water it is possible for shoal draught craft to reach the wharf at the head of Halstow Creek, where there is a Saxon church, The Three Tuns Inn, Tel: 01795 842840, and the Lower Halstow Sailing Club, www.lhyc.org.uk; Hon Sec Tel: 01634 324517. There is water at the club and provisions are available from nearby Upchurch where you will find a Co-op. Visitors are welcome to use the club jetty, by prior arrangement, to get ashore; mud berth moorings are made available for those staying overnight. The barge *Edith May* has recently been undergoing restoration in the former Eastwoods brick dock here.

SHARFLEET CREEK

A sheltered anchorage lies in relatively deep pools within Sharfleet Creek, but at weekends there is often not very much room! From about four hours flood it is possible to wriggle right through the creek and out into Half Acre, passing just south of Beacon No 7 (BW triangle topmark). The whole area is a maze of creeks and saltings and for the first time passages over drying areas should only be attempted on a flood with frequent soundings.

MIDDLE REACHES

Leaving Stangate for the main river, it is desirable to stand well out before turning west in order to pass round the east cardinal buoy marking the spit at the entrance. Once clear of this, all is plain sailing until the river takes its south-westerly turn at Sharp Ness.

The passage is well marked with fairway buoys, which are all lit, but a good look-out must be kept, especially at night, for any unlit mooring buoys on the east side of the channel opposite Bee Ness Jetty.

There are two conspicuous jetties in Kethole Reach, the dilapidated Bee Ness and Oakham Ness, used for unloading coal from tankers. The pipeline and walkway on the Bee Ness Jetty have been removed but the support trestles remain, sometimes covered at high water. Close to the west of the Bee Ness Jetty is East Hoo Creek which, although uniformly narrow, carries a useful depth of water for about half a mile within its entrance and therefore offers a quiet anchorage except in easterly or south-easterly winds.

In the upper reaches of the creek lies the paddle steamer *Medway Queen*, which went to the evacuation of Dunkirk but is now sadly a rotting hulk, various restoration plans having failed to come to pass. Other maritime remains can sometimes be seen in the mud of Stoke Ooze at low water, including several surrendered Word War I German U boats which were probably broken up at Rochester in the 1920s.

No more than two cables north-east of the end of Bee Ness Jetty lies the wreck of *Bulwark*, marked with one green conical buoy (Fl (3) 15s) and one unlit red

The Medway looking north-east towards Sheeerness, showing the forts at Folly Point and Darnet Ness with Kingsnorth Power Station beyond

can. HMS *Bulwark* was a World War I cruiser which blew up while being re-fuelled in 1915.

HALF ACRE CREEK

Towards the south end of the Kethole Reach, opposite Oakham Ness Jetty, is the entrance to Half Acre Creek. This broad creek carries 4 to 6m at low water for about a mile where it then splits into Otterham, Rainham and South Yantlet creeks, the junction being marked by a red and white Otterham Fairway light buoy flashing the Morse 'A' 10s. Otterham and Rainham creeks both lead south towards the shore before drying out, but South Yantlet Creek, marked by four unlit spherical buoys (RWVS), joins the main river just south of Darnet Fort, where it dries 0.7m at low water springs, although at half tide there will be some 2m over the bar. The best water can be found on a westerly (°M) course from No 4 buoy (RWVS) with a spherical topmark.

OTTERHAM CREEK

The buoys marking the gutway into Otterham Creek are unlit because this narrow channel is no longer frequented by commercial vessels. The quay at the head of the creek was once used by sailing barges to load cement. The Three Sisters pub is up the lane and at the nearby Woodgers Wharf, the Otterham Creek Boatyard (Tel: 01634 260250) has a dry dock. The village of Upchurch, where there is a Co-op shop, is about one mile away.

RAINHAM CREEK

At high water it is possible to get to the head of Rainham Creek and reach Bloors Wharf, where the scrap/breakers yard has gone and the area has been tidied up. Nearby is a riverside country park and another little quay, the site of Goldsmith's old cement works, the mud for which was dug from the neighbouring marshes and brought to the dock in spritsailed 'muddies'. The Saxon Shore long distance footpath follows the shoreline along the head of the creek.

The entrance to the creek is marked by a red can light buoy (Fl R (2) 5s), while a couple of unlit red buoys mark the gutway further in.

LONG REACH

The main river from the entrance to Half Acre Creek bends westward along Long Reach, where the deep water is hardly more than a quarter of a mile wide. Long Reach is dominated by the buildings and chimneys of Kingsnorth Power Station on the north shore. Three port hand buoys (Nos 18, 20 & 22) mark the south side of the channel along this reach.

HOO MARSH PASSAGE

Middle Creek, which near its entrance provides a useful anchorage, leads through Hoo Flats towards the old wharves near the village of Hoo. The creek is tortuous, but quite well buoyed.

The entrance to the creek is marked with a conical green buoy to be left close to starboard, after which a red can must be left to port. Then, turning south-west with Gillingham gas holder ahead, another conical green buoy is left to starboard. Having turned sharply to the north with Hoo Church ahead, the fourth mark, a yellow and black south cardinal buoy, is passed on its south side, after which the remaining buoy, a red can, is left to port before reaching either the quays or the marina at Hoo.

This passage should only be attempted on the last hour or so of the flood, until it is known, as the gutways are narrow and very tortuous.

MIDDLE CREEK TO GILLINGHAM

At the western end of Long Reach, opposite the entrance to Middle Creek, the main river bends to the south to round Darnet Ness into Pinup Reach. Darnet Ness, on which stands a fort, is marked by a

The Fort at Darnet Ness is marked by a port-hand beacon and here the river swings to the south into Pinup Reach

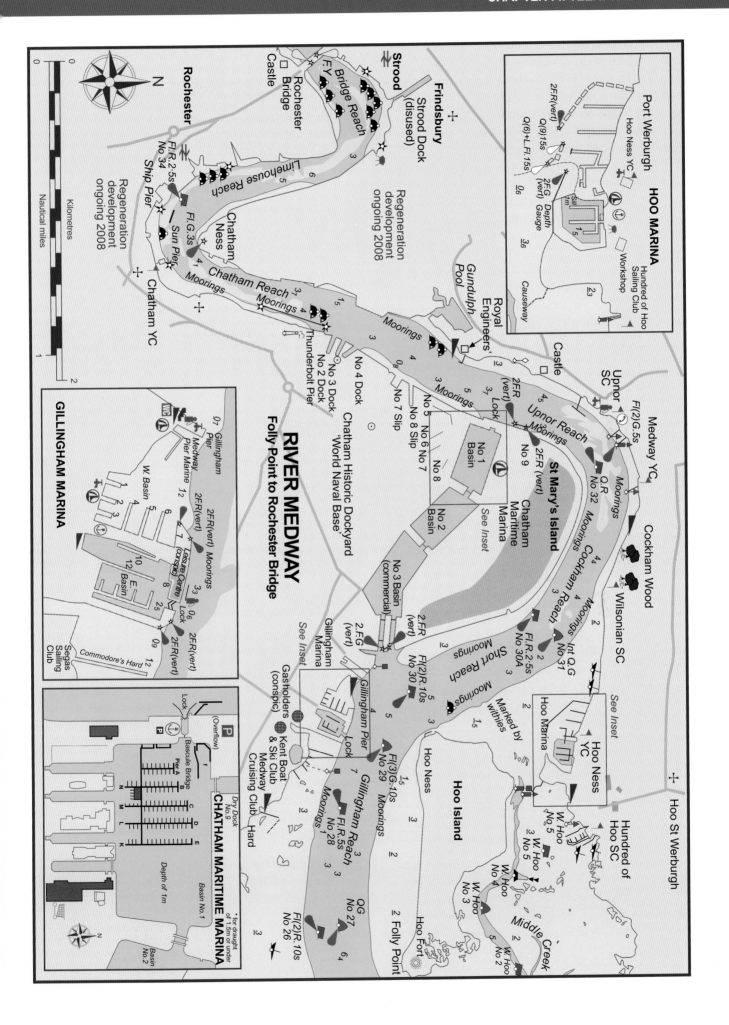

HOO MARINA

Port Werburgh

Hundred of Hoo Sailing Club

Hoo Ness YC

Workshop

2F.R(vert)

Q(9)15s

Q(6)+L.Fl.15s

2F.G (vert)

Depth Gauge

Sill 1m

Causeway

RIVER MEDWAY

Folly Point to Rochester Bridge

Strood

Frindsbury

Strood Dock (disused)

Regeneration development ongoing 2008

Bridge Reach

F.Y

Rochester Bridge

Castle

Rochester

F.Y

Fl.R.2·5s No 34

Ship Pier

Sun Pier

Fl.G.3s

Chatham YC

Chatham Ness

Limehouse Reach

Chatham Reach

Moorings

Moorings

Moorings

Regeneration development ongoing 2008

Gundulph Pool

Royal Engineers'

Thunderbolt Pier

No 2 Dock

No 3 Dock

No 4 Dock

No 7 Slip

No 8 Slip

No 6 No 7

No 5

Chatham Historic Dockyard 'World Naval Base'

Castle

Upnor SC

Upnor Reach

Medway YC

Fl(2)G.5s

Cockham Wood

Wilsonian SC

Moorings

2F.R (vert)

2F.R (vert)

No 9

No 32

Q.R

St Mary's Island

No 1 Basin

No 2 Basin

Lock

Chatham Maritime Marina

See Inset

No 3 Basin (commercial)

2F.R (vert)

Cockham Reach

Fl.R.2·5s No 30A

Int Q.G No 31

Short Reach

Moorings

2.F.G (vert)

2.F.R (vert)

Gillingham Marina

Fl(2)R.10s No 30

Fl(3)G.10s No 29

Hoo Marina

Hoo Ness YC

Marked by withies

Hoo Ness

Hoo Island

Gillingham Pier

Lock

Gas holders (conspic)

Kent Boat & Ski Club

Medway Cruising Club Hard

Gillingham Reach

Fl.R.5s No 28

Moorings

Fl(2)R.10s No 26

Q.G No 27

Hoo Fort

Folly Point

Middle Creek

W. Hoo No 2

W. Hoo No 3

W. Hoo No 4

W. Hoo No 5

Hundred of Hoo SC

Hoo St Werburgh

See Inset

GILLINGHAM MARINA

Gillingham Pier

Medway Pier Marine

W. Basin

E. Basin

Leisure Centre (conspic)

Lock

2F.R(vert)

2F.R(vert)

2F.R(vert)

Moorings

Commodore's Hard

Segas Sailing Club

CHATHAM MARITIME MARINA

Lock

(Overflow)

Bascule Bridge

Pier A

Dry Dock No.9

Depth of 1m

Basin No.1

Basin No.2

* for draught of 1.5m or under

0 Nautical miles 1 2

0 Kilometres 1 2

N

red beacon (QR) and is steep on its northern face, but should not be approached too closely on its western side because of a causeway projecting from it. South of this causeway there is anchorage with shelter from easterly winds, near the entrance to South Yantlet Creek.

In Pinup Reach the flood sets sharply towards Folly Point on the starboard hand, on which stands another fort. A rocky spit projecting some 200m from this point is marked by Folly Beacon (BW Con topmark) and no attempt should be made to pass between it and the shore – in fact this corner should be given a wide berth because a spit of mud seems to be extending ever further from it.

Rounding Folly Point into Gillingham Reach, the mud stretches some 300 yards from the north shore and the course should be set for the left-hand side of the large gas holder at Gillingham until out in mid-stream.

Approaching Gillingham Reach. The conspicuous building is the leisure centre adjacent to Gillingham Marina

The south side of this reach is lined with the moorings of the Medway Cruising Club, many of whose members build and restore traditional craft, gaffers and smacks – there are usually some on the moorings – and in recent years the half-size barge *Seagull II* could be seen in the dry dock. The clubhouse, established in 1895, stands on Gillingham Strand, just east of the gasworks. Landing is possible at the causeway at all states of the tide. Once abeam of the gas holders, the entrance to Gillingham Marina becomes apparent. A conspicuous waterside leisure centre building is immediately upstream of the lock gates.

GILLINGHAM MARINA

The locked basin section of Gillingham Marina can accommodate 250 craft and is accessible through a lock for about four hours each side of high water during daylight hours. Bear in mind that tides run hard across the entrance. Yachts in the tidal basin section of the marina, upstream of the lock entrance, can arrive or leave for about two hours before or after each high tide. There are deep-water moorings in the river for arrival

or departure at other times. Fuel can be obtained from the upstream side of the lead-in pontoon (angled across the run of the tide to deflect the stream) on the west side of the lock entrance. Visiting yachts can usually be accommodated in the locked basin, but it is preferable to book at least 24 hours in advance. Hoists and extensive repair facilities are available at the marina, and a well-stocked chandlery is a short walk away on Pier Road with a mini-store next door.

A small marina (Medway Pier Marine Tel: 01634 851113) is situated off the end of Gillingham Pier, with pontoon berths for about 35 boats. As part of the Medway regeneration scheme an 800-property development and a hotel are scheduled to be built near Gillingham Pier in the not too distant future.

At the western end of Gillingham Reach is the locked entrance to the commercial quays of Chatham Docks in Basin 3, while Basin 2 contains the Arethusa watersports centre.

The river now turns north-west round Hoo Ness into Short Reach, with the high, wooded bank of Cockham Reach ahead and the prominent housing development on St Mary's Island lining the riverside to port from Finborough Ness to Upper Reach.

Hoo Ness, with a small jetty (two pairs vertical fixed green lights), is steep-to, but to the north-west of it a large expanse of mud, covered at half-tide, must be crossed to reach the marina at Hoo.

Gillingham Port Guide – Local tel code 01634

Gillingham Marina	Tel: 280022; Fax 280164; www.gillinghammarina.co.uk.
VHF	Ch 80 callsign *Gillingham Marina Lock*.
Lock access	Four hours either side of high water during daylight hours.
Water and electricity	All berths.
Fuel	Diesel, petrol and gas from lead-in pontoon upstream side of lock entrance.
Showers	Two unmetered shower blocks and launderette.
Stores	Mini-market and off-licence, Pier Road.
Chandlery	Pier Road, Tel: 283008.
Repairs	Autoyachts, Tel: 281333; slipway, 20 ton straddle lift.
Security	24-hour.
Leisure centre	On site.
Food and drink	Bar and club temporary membership available at marina.
Transport	Gillingham main line station three minutes taxi ride. Helicopter landing pad on site.
Yacht clubs	Medway Cruising Club; www.medwaycruisingclub.co.uk.

Gillingham Marina has a locked basin section and a tidal basin section upstream of the lock entrance

HOO

Hoo Marina, constructed adjacent to the old harbour, was the first marina to be established on the East Coast. Its new basin is protected by a sill so that there is a depth of about 1.5m of water inside. Usual services are supplied to the finger berths, with toilets and showers ashore.

The marina can be approached across the mud flats near high water, but is accessible three hours either side of high water (5ft draught) via a creek or gully known locally as the Orinoco. Entrance to this gully is almost a mile from the yacht harbour and about half a mile north-west of Hoo Ness. The creek mouth is usually marked by a west cardinal pillar buoy to starboard, to be found just inside a line of large Medway Port Authority mooring buoys and about five orange buoys which are connected to assist fore and aft mooring. The latter can be used while waiting for the tide to make.

The Orinoco is identified by posts to be left to port. But the final mark, a small yellow buoy, must be left close to starboard immediately before crossing the sill.

The Hoo Ness Yacht Club is nicely situated on the shore overlooking the old harbour, slipway and mud berths. It has a bar and restaurant and visitors are welcome. A walk through the chalet park to the nearby village of Hoo St Werburgh will bring you to the churchyard where it is thought that Dickens based the meeting of Pip with the escaped convict in *Great Expectations* – the prison hulks used to lie in the river

nearby. Along the shore to the east of the marina are some wharves, yards and old craft in mud berths overlooking Hoo Flats. At Stargate Marine,

Hoo Port Guide – Local tel code 01634	
Hoo Marina	Tel: 250311; Fax 251761; VHF Ch 80.
Water	At marina and Hundred of Hoo Sailing Club.
Facilities	Toilet, shower and laundry block.
Fuel	Diesel (own cans) from marina, gas from hardware shop in village.
Repairs	Chandlery and 16 ton crane at marina. Slip and crane in West Hoo Creek.
Stores	Well-stocked general store in adjacent chalet park. Shops at Hoo village. Early closing on Tuesdays.
Transport	Buses to Rochester.
Telephone	At chalet park.
Yacht clubs	Hoo Ness Yacht Club Tel: 250052; www.hooness.org.uk; Hundred of Hoo Sailing Club Tel: 250102 (mooring sometimes available for visitors); www.hundredofhoosc.org.uk.
Food and drink	Café at marina open seven days; bar and restaurant at Hoo Ness Yacht Club – meals at weekends.

Robert Deard and his son Luke restore Thames sailing barges including *Ena, Montreal, Felix, Kitty* and *Marjorie,* which is skippered by Robert.

There is a pleasant walk from Hoo Marina to Upnor along part of the Saxon Shore Way that runs below Cockham Woods – to remain dry shod it is best undertaken before or after high water.

Hoo Marina and Hoo Ness Yacht Club

COCKHAM REACH & UPNOR

The Medway Yacht Club at Lower Upnor is situated in Cockham Reach, the prettiest reach on the tidal Medway. The river here is thick with yacht moorings (many fore-and-aft) on both sides, three lines on the north shore and a single trot round the bend on the south side. If a mooring cannot be found, a brief stay can be made at the hammerhead pontoon off the

Medway Yacht Club. A trot-boat is operated and there are two slipways at the club.

Upnor Sailing Club is on the waterfront at Upnor between The Pier Inn, which usually has a barge or two moored nearby, and The Ship. The club has an all-tide landing and its own fore-and-aft moorings opposite the clubhouse; visitors' moorings can be made available.

Beyond the clubs and Upnor Pier is Upnor Castle, which once guarded the river against the marauding Dutch fleet, and a little further up river on the west bank is the Royal Engineers (RE) base and yacht club, just north of Whitewall Creek. From time to time the Royal School of Military Engineering carries out high speed boat operations in Chatham Reach – at speeds well in excess of the normal permitted limit.

Upnor Port Guide – Local tel code 01634	
Medway Yacht Club	Tel: 718399; www.medwayyc.com.
Water	From clubhouse.
Stores	Shop in village nearby (open Sundays).
Fuel	From club.
Chandler	Pirates Cave, Frindsbury, Tel: 295233.
Transport	Bus services to Rochester and Chatham.
Yacht clubs	Upnor Sailing Club, Tel: 718043; Medway Yacht Club (see Tel number above); Wilsonian Sailing Club.

Looking down Chatham and Upnor Reaches towards Cockham Woods. Chatham Dockyard and the Maritime Marina can be seen, with St Mary's Island beyond the dock basins

Chatham Reach near the church and the Command House

CHATHAM

Chatham Maritime Marina is located on the east side of the river in Chatham Dockyard No 1 Basin. The entrance is about halfway between Upnor Castle and the Royal Engineers base on the west shore. Just beyond the entrance is the conspicuous No 5 Pumphouse building, below which is a long line of moorings in the river.

There is 24-hour lock access with 1.5m over the sill at mean low water springs. A waiting pontoon is situated outside immediately downstream of the lock gates. Opened in 2001, the marina has 300 berths, excellent toilet, shower and laundry facilities, fuel pontoon, boat lifting and hard standing. The Shepherd Neames' Ship and Trades pub is a short walk away, with a convenience store next door. Other than fast food in the nearby factory outlet shopping centre, the only alternative source of supplies is in Rochester High Street some 2½ miles away.

The marina is ideally placed (a 10-minute walk) for visiting the award-winning, 80-acre living museum at the Historic Dockyard Chatham, open daily during the summer. You really should not leave the Medway without experiencing this sizeable slice of maritime history. Allow a whole day as there is so much to discover, including the destroyer HMS *Cavalier* lying in No 2 Dry Dock where Nelson's *Victory* was built, the submarine *Ocelot*, the Victorian naval sloop HMS *Gannet*, and the covered slips, not to mention The Ropery, with its quarter-mile-long rope walk dating back to 1618, where rope is still made commercially.

Shoreside at Chatham Maritime Marina

Chatham Port Guide – Local tel code 01634

Chatham Maritime Marina

	Tel: 899200; Fax 899201; email: chatham@mdlmarinas.co.uk.
VHF	Ch 80.
Lock access	24 hour (draught 1.5m or less).
Water and electricity	On pontoons.
Fuel	Diesel and petrol.
Facilities	Toilets, showers, laundry.
Repairs	20 ton crane.
Stores	Shop nearby.
Food and drink	Bar meals at Ship & Trades pub nearby, Tel: 895200; restaurants in Rochester.
Historic Dockyard	Tel: 823807; www.chdt.org.uk.

Continuing upriver beyond the Maritime Marina, Chatham Reach is dominated by the enormous structures of the covered slips on the Dockyard side. Some of these date back to 1838 when the original 17th century slipways were covered. After the dry docks and Thunderbolt Pier, where there are some Victory Marine pontoon berths downstream, the impressive Anchor Wharf storehouses come into view on the waterfront at the southern end of the Dockyard complex.

On the opposite, west side of Chatham Reach, towards Chatham Ness, are industrial quays where aggregate dredgers operate by day and night.

ROCHESTER

Once past the church and the Command House nestling in the trees, the river starts to swing around Chatham Ness in a north-westerly direction into Limehouse Reach, Rochester. The former commercial wharves on both sides of this reach have been completely redeveloped right up to Rochester Bridge.

It was possible to use Sun Pier to get ashore until it was deemed unsafe and closed in 2008. Whether the planned new-look riverside development will retain access for those of us who still wish to visit Rochester and the nearby Sainsburys by water remains to be seen.

Bridge Reach is no longer as busy with barges, tugs, cranes and sundry craft as it used to be. The Strood canal dock area, and most of Rochester, is undergoing drastic urban renewal as part of the ambitious regeneration scheme for the Medway. As a result the face of the waterfront is changing rapidly – the Radio Caroline ship was gone but the derelict Foxtrot-class

Chatham and Rochester are steeped in maritime history

diesel electric Russian submarine was still moored near Strood Pier in 2008.

The clearance under Rochester road and rail bridge is approximately 20ft (6m) at high water springs. There is not much depth of water at low water springs, but the best arch to use is on the starboard side going up river. In the upper Medway, with shallow draught and lowered mast, it is possible to reach Maidstone and Tonbridge via eight locks, the first of which is Allington.

The Medway looking up Chatham Reach where the river swings west into Limehouse Reach. The bridge at Rochester can be seen in the distance

Faversham Creek looking
downstream below Iron Wharf

Chapter sixteen
The Swale

Tides	Harty Ferry – HW Dover +1.25. Range: springs 5.3m; neaps 3.2m
Charts	Admiralty 2571, 2572, SC5606; Imray 2100 series; OS map 178
Waypoints	**Whitstable Street Buoy 51°23'.86N 01°01'.60E**
	Pollard Spit Buoy 51°22'.98N 00°58'.56E

Medway Yachting Association
     www.medwayya.co.uk

Many editions ago it was pointed out that the Swale is not a river and could more correctly be described as a ria – meaning a submerged valley. Whatever we call it, it divides the Isle of Sheppey from the mainland of Kent, is seventeen miles in length and follows a tortuous course in a general east-west direction.

In ancient days it was the usual route for craft bound for London from the Channel, and it still provides an inside passage between the Medway and the North Kent shore off Whitstable.

The opposing tidal streams meet somewhere near the mouth of Milton Creek. A good time to start through the Swale from west to east is an hour or so after low water at Sheerness.

The West Swale is entered from the Medway between the vast container/car park south of Sheerness, once an area of mudflats known as the Lappel, and the extensive Queenborough Spit, the end of which is marked by an east cardinal pillar buoy (BYB Q (3) 10s).

The facilities at Queenborough have already been described in the Medway chapter on page 163, since this anchorage is often thought of as being part of that river rather than the Swale.

LODEN HOPE

Above Queenborough, see chart on page 161, the river turns north-west through Loden Hope. Drying mud flats fill the whole of the bight from Queenborough

The Kingsferry road bridge spanning the Swale. The railway bridge beyond is lifted for the two yachts to pass through

hard to the jetty on the north-east face of Long Point. A drying horse (shoal) in mid-stream almost opposite the jetty is marked by a green conical buoy but, if the north side is taken, Long Point should be rounded in mid-channel with due regard to mud flats off the north shore. A series of three lit beacons (first two QWG and third QWRG) on the mainland shore are used by large coastal freighters to navigate this narrow channel around Long Point.

As the river turns south along Horse Reach the best water is towards the west side of mid-channel, leaving the red can Long Point buoy (Fl R 3s) to port.

About a mile after Long Point (in Horse Reach) two prominent cable notice-boards will be seen on north-east bank. Abreast of these there is a small horse (shoal) practically in mid-channel. This is marked by two red can buoys and should be passed on its south-west side about one-third of the river width off the Kent shore.

There are two beacons to assist large vessels through Horse Reach. The first is on Ferry Marshes on the south bank (QG) and the second is located on the north bank near the new road bridge (Dir VQ (4) R 5s) and bears 098°.

From Horse Reach, the new (2006) Kingsferry road bridge is seen spanning the river ahead, with the older, lifting railway bridge dwarfed beyond it. Although here the river is narrow and carries quite large ships,

small craft can usually find temporary anchorage on the south-west shore just by the bridges. There is a narrow pontoon which reaches to near the water's edge at low water on this shore immediately adjacent to the new bridge, with a locked gate at the landward end. A similar pontoon on the same bank, just beyond the railway bridge, is used by the Kings Ferry Boat Club whose members keep dinghies on the hard and small fishing boats on drying moorings.

The south buttress of the road bridge shows Iso G 3s and the north buttress Iso R 3s.

The British Rail bridge will open to allow vessels with fixed masts to pass on request, provided that railway traffic permits. In practice this means that from Monday to Saturday the bridge is able to open at 20 minutes past the hour and 10 minutes to the hour. On Sundays it is able to open on the hour.

It is advisable to call up the bridge-keeper on VHF Ch 10 in good time to give him your ETA, and then call again when you are about 10 minutes away. Yachtsmen can no longer rely on the traditional bucket in the rigging or sound signals. If you cannot get a reply, call *Medway VTS* on VHF Ch 74 and they will try to contact the bridge by telephone.

When the bridge is lifted more than three times in two hours, the motors overheat, which means that if you arrive for an opening and it has already been lifted on

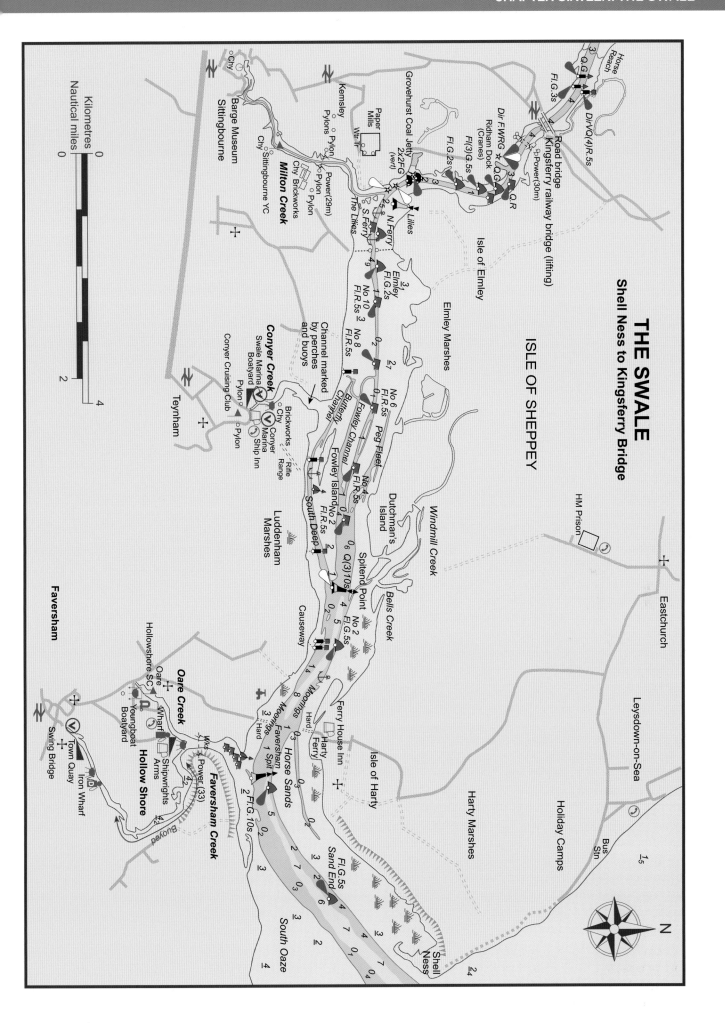

THE SWALE
Shell Ness to Kingsferry Bridge

ISLE OF SHEPPEY

the last three published opening times, you may have to wait at least an hour for the motors to cool down.

Traffic lights are displayed on the south buttress of the railway bridge, near the bridge-keeper's cabin. When both green and red lights are flashing, the bridge is being lifted. When a fixed green light is shown, it has been fully raised. A flashing red light signifies that the span is being lowered, so yachts must keep clear. A flashing yellow light indicates that the bridge is not working and craft should keep clear. If no lights at all are shown, the bridge is down.

The height clearance with the span raised is 27m at low water springs. The width between the bascules is also 27m. Tidal streams run strongly: from three to four knots on the first of the flood and the first of the ebb.

A Dir GWR sector light, on the west bank near Ridham Dock, is there to lead ships through the bridges, on a line of 148°M. The sector lights are very bright and you are advised not to stare directly at the beam at close range.

Just beyond the bridge on the south-west shore is Ridham Dock. It originally served the large Bowaters paper mills at Kemsley and Sittingbourne to which it was connected in the 1920s by a light railway. As well as timber, scrap metal, aggregates and building materials come and go here since the closure of the paper mills. The dock is usually occupied by sizeable freighters for which a look-out should be kept around high water when they may leave via the bridge.

Two port- and two starboard-hand light buoys have been established in Ferry and Clay Reaches between Ridham Dock and Grovehurst Coal Jetty, where the channel is no more than half a cable wide at low water.

A little over half a mile further east is the nominal point at which the two tidal streams meet (see page 184). The river then turns to the east past the entrance to Milton Creek, which may be considered the end of the western half of the Swale.

MILTON CREEK

It is possible, with a shoal draught and a rising tide, to navigate Milton Creek as far as the centre of Sittingbourne. The local Sittingbourne Yacht Club has recently improved the withies by attaching to them orange (port-hand) or green (starboard-hand) floats, which are visible at half tide. The yacht club is based just downstream of the town centre, at Murston Wharf on the east side of the creek, where drying pontoons have been installed. The upper reaches of the creek itself are under threat from a planned low level fixed bridge carrying the Sittingbourne Relief Road which, if built, would be too low for craft with masts to pass under, and would cut off the clubhouse. The club and other local organisations are campaigning (2008) to keep the creek open for yachts and barges.

When Sittingbourne paper mill opened in 1867,

sailing barges brought its timber supply, via the Swale, up Milton Creek; the barges also brought lime and sand for the local cement and brick works and took away the finished product. In *Spritsail Barges of Thames and Medway*, Edgar March describes how '...there was an enormous barge traffic on Milton Creek, sailing to and from the Kentish brickfields, and many a well-known barge was launched into its tidal waters. Fifty years ago it was no uncommon sight to see as many as forty laden barges leave on one tide; today (1948) the creek is practically deserted, wharfs grass grown, barge yards derelict, sheds falling to pieces and hulks rotting away.' Over 500 barges were produced from yards along Milton Creek in its heyday.

The Dolphin Sailing Barge Museum Trust was established in the 1970s at an old bargeyard near the head of Milton Creek in Sittingbourne. The museum provides an insight into the industrial and maritime history of North Kent and also has facilities for barge repair and restoration. The museum is open on weekends and bank holidays from Easter to the end of October from 1100-1700. A website link is via www.thamesbarge.org.uk.

EAST SWALE

In *Swin, Swale and Swatchway* (1892), H Lewis Jones describes the East Swale thus: 'Our Swale adventures are all rather tinged with mud, for on another memorable occasion we tried to turn up from Whitstable to Queenborough on the first of the flood, and found it rather tedious, as we were continually in advance of the water, and had to wait for it upon most of the spits and horses; but though tedious, it was eminently instructive.'

The approach from seaward commences between the Columbine (G Con Fl G 5s) and Whitstable Street (R Can Fl R 5s) buoys about 2½ miles north of Whitstable town, but from this distance the precise entrance to the Swale is not easily recognised. A course of 235°M passing along the south-east edge of the Columbine Shoal, leaving the Columbine Spit buoy (G Con Fl G 10s) to starboard, will lead to the next visible marks in about a mile.

The Pollard Spit light buoy (QR) should be left to port and the Ham Gat buoy (G Con Fl G 2s) to starboard. The Pollard Spit extends north from Whitstable Flats, an area of sand and mud to the east of Whitstable.

From a point midway between Ham Gat and Pollard Spit buoys, a course of 220°M leads into the river, passing Shell Ness to starboard about a quarter of a mile off. Cottages and coastguard buildings are conspicuous above its light-coloured shell shingle beach and, in conditions of poor visibility, Shell Ness is a useful check on distance from the next mark – the Sand End buoy (G Con Fl G 5s), about a mile away on the same course.

Whitstable Flats and the Swale entrance are an oyster

fishery area and care should be taken not to anchor or ground on the oyster beds.

Once inside the river entrance the tides set fairly, but at the entrance they are affected to some extent by the main Thames Estuary streams. Hence there is a tendency for vessels entering on the flood to be set over towards the Columbine, while leaving on the ebb the set is towards Pollard Spit.

Throughout this long entrance the width of the channel is between two and three cables up to the Sand End buoy, after which the channel narrows.

Next there is a pair of buoys off the entrance to Faversham Creek. The green conical (Fl G 10s) to starboard marks the south side of the Horse Shoal, while the other unlit north cardinal buoy is on the end of the spit extending from the north-west bank of the creek entrance.

HARTY FERRY

Immediately to the west is Harty Ferry, the most popular anchorage in the Swale, where there will often be a barge or two brought up. A hard on the north shore provides access to the Ferry House Inn where food is served all day at weekends, making it a favourite destination for local yachtsmen.

It is said that the inn may have begun as a trading post servicing a Roman garrison on Sheppey, with supplies from Faversham on the mainland. About a mile away from the pub, which only recently was put on mains electricity, is the 900 year old church of St Thomas the Apostle, still lit by oil lamps and candles in this remote corner of Sheppey known as the Isle of Harty.

The last ferry service here closed in 1941 – the remains of the winding mechanism from a cable-drawn ferry dating from 1657 can still be seen.

The East Swale showing Faversham Creek, the Horse Sands, Isle of Sheppey, and Whitstable Bay

A favoured berth (except during strong easterlies) is under the north shore near the hard, but beware the fierce current on the early ebb, particularly at night. This can be a dangerous anchorage with strong winds from the east.

There are few facilities available to the boats moored at Harty Ferry, although there is an emergency telephone near the top of the ferry hard on the south bank. Nearby is the Oare Marshes Nature Reserve run by Kent Wildlife Trust. For other services and stores the nearest places are Oare (1 mile) or Faversham (2 miles).

West from Harty, a green conical buoy No 1 half a mile ahead should not be approached too closely, as in south-westerly winds it wanders over the mud.

From here the channel shoals and becomes narrower. Ahead to port will be seen the higher parts of Fowley Island, a long shoal parallel to the Kent shore marked by an east cardinal buoy (Q (3) 10s), behind which lies South Deep. This east cardinal Fowley Spit buoy is not too easy to pick out, but the spit is extensive and shoals steeply to the south, so a careful watch must be kept on the depth.

The main channel, which soon narrows to little more than half a cable, leaves Fowley to port and lies approximately midway between the north edge of Fowley and the Sheppey shore. Passing Fowley Island, the guides are five lit port-hand buoys and then, further west, two green conicals, Elmley and North Ferry, which indicate the best water. The channel is, however, so narrow that a fair wind is essential anywhere near low water.

At Elmley Ferry, two posts mark the hards where James II boarded a boat in 1688 and fled the country. The hards extend well offshore beyond the posts and that off the south shore has some stakes embedded in it. The best water lies a trifle to north of a line midway between the posts. The ferry no longer functions, but the remains of the Ferry House can be seen on the south bank.

ANCHORAGE

Just west of Elmley Ferry, on the mainland side, there is space to anchor, out of the fairway, in about 3m of water.

From here, the river swings round towards the north between the green conical North Ferry and the red can South Ferry buoys, passing a patch of saltings that largely masks the entrance to Milton Creek. The best water will be found more or less in a direct line toward Grovehurst coal jetty, which shows two fixed green lights at night. The entrance to Milton Creek is opposite the Lilies buoy (black and yellow south cardinal with black topmark).

Past Milton Creek, the banks of the river are closer together, and the good water now occupies about a third of the available river width. Although there are few marks to assist, it is fairly easy to negotiate this part

of the river as there is appreciably greater depth than in the eastern end.

Remember that the direction of buoyage and marking changes at Milton Creek.

THE EAST SWALE CREEKS
FAVERSHAM CREEK

Faversham Creek branches off to the south of the Swale just east of Harty Ferry and is marked at its entrance with a north cardinal (BY) buoy, to be left to starboard when entering. Sometimes there is also a port-hand buoy or beacon at the entrance to keep boats off the mud on the east side of the channel.

The creek itself pursues a winding course for about 3½ miles up to the town of Faversham, and at low water was thought by H Lewis Jones to be '…a poor place – a wide ditch, with steep sides and any amount of mud, but very little water.' He spent the night with '…the boat lying in mud of a rank sort, suggesting ague and quinine bitters.' But as so often is the case, 'in the morning the scene had changed. It was high water, and the creek was bankful, and soon a tug came puffing along with a schooner in tow, then some barges and a fishing smack or two…'

For the first half mile towards the junction with Oare Creek (to starboard) the channel is fairly wide and marked with first a pair of port and starboard buoys followed by three more red cans. A very useful chartlet of Faversham Creek can be downloaded from the Faversham town website www.faversham.org.

In behind the seawall at Hollowshore is the Shipwright's Arms, an ancient pub with character, much frequented by those connected with barges, smacks and wooden craft. The pub is famous for its real ales, all from Kentish breweries, and holds an annual beer festival, usually on the late spring bank holiday weekend. The adjacent Hollowshore Boatyard is always interesting because of the old gaffers that congregate there. The services at the yard are those that relate to repairs and maintenance: a slip, a crane and a dock.

Alongside at Iron Wharf in Faversham Creek

Hollowshore and the Shipwright's Arms showing Oare Creek (left) where it joins Faversham Creek

For many years the headquarters of the Hollowshore Cruising Club was in a small shed alongside the large yard shed. However, in 2008 they were forced to find new premises at Oare.

Landing is possible near the inn and boatyard at Hollowshore from about four hours before to four hours after high water. Shallow draught boats can lie afloat throughout a neap tide off the inn.

Above the junction, Faversham Creek narrows and dries right out. Shoal-draught craft with power can make the trip up to Faversham, starting at about four hours flood. Local advice is to follow the curve of the creek between buoys rather than head from buoy to buoy. The creek is occasionally used by barges up to the town wharfs, but there is no longer any commercial traffic.

The creek is fairly well marked with buoys and beacons up to the last port-hand buoy, just before the sewage works on the south side. The channel is then in the centre of the creek up to the Iron Wharf Boatyard on the south shore, where the best water is about 6ft out from their dry dock. The largely DIY yard was set up nearly 30 years ago by Alan Reekie, master of the barge Ironsides, and Peter Dodds, owner and master of the barge Mirosa, and there are good services here. The yard will provide a tug or a pilot if required, and if you plan to go up to the town, you will certainly need local knowledge. Nearby is the Iron Wharf Yacht

Club, a small but comfortable club with an outdoor barbecue which visiting yachtsmen are welcome to use. Traditional boatbuilder, Alan Staley, has a shed and slipway slightly further upriver near the maltings building. Staley is the founder of the Dallimore Association and has been responsible for restoring several of this East Coast designer's wooden boats, all originally built between 1903 and 1953.

A little further upstream on the south shore is Standard Quay, on the outskirts of Faversham, where moorings are for traditional boats, most of which are barges. Here, just as at Hollowshore, there are interesting craft to be seen alongside or in the floating lighter/dry docks. In 2008, Cambria, the last barge to trade under sail, was in dry dock at Standard Quay, undergoing a complete restoration and refit. On the quayside, The Monks' Granary, currently housing a garden centre, is one of the oldest surviving warehouses in Britain. On the opposite shore is a waterside housing development.

About half a mile on, the creek reaches the Town Quay in the fine market town of Faversham, which boasts 500 listed buildings, presided over by the unusual 'crown' spire of the parish church. Once the centre of the nation's explosives industry, Faversham is home to Britain's oldest brewery, Shepherd and Neame, where you will find a visitor centre, shop and brewery tours. The Albion, on the west bank just below

Faversham Creek Port Guide
Local tel code 01795

Pilot and/or tug	Ironwharf Boatyard Tel: 536296; VHF Ch 08, callsign *IronWharf*.
Moorings	Drying.
Water	At yard.
Fuel	Diesel from Ironwharf Boatyard.
Gas	From garden centre at Standard Quay.
Repairs	15 ton crane, shipwrights and engineers (sailmaker and electrician if required).
Chandlery	Small one at Iron Wharf.
Facilities	Toilets, showers and launderette at Iron Wharf.
Stores	Two supermarkets, other shops and banks in Faversham; market Tuesdays, Fridays and Saturdays; Early closing on Thursdays.
Food and drink	Iron Wharf Yacht Club, Tel: 530352, has outdoor barbecue; The Anchor, Standard Quay Tel: 536471; The Albion, Upper Brents Tel: 591411; other pubs and restaurants in Faversham.

the little swing bridge, and The Anchor, near Standard Quay, are handy places for yachtsmen to sample the Kentish ale, or try one of the many other pubs and restaurants in the town.

Access to berths on the Front Brents jetty on the west bank or at the Town Quay on the east side is restricted to about 1½ hours either side of high water, unless you dry out. As even at high water springs there is very little water, the best way to visit the town may be to walk in from Iron Wharf via Standard Quay (about 10 minutes).

According to H Lewis Jones in *Swin, Swale and*

The Albion pub at Upper Brents, Faversham

Spitway (1892) 'In olden days the people of Faversham do not seem to have been very loyal to the Crown for they dug up the coffin of King Stephen for the sake of the lead, throwing the King's body into their creek; and probably they did the same for Queen Matilda. Also, when King James the Second was about to fly the country, they seized his vessel, as it lay in the East Swale. The story is related that the Faversham sailors observing a vessel of about 30 tons lying at Shellness to take in ballast, resolved to go and board her; accordingly they went in the evening with three smacks and about forty men, and in the cabin of it they seized three persons of quality. From them they took 300 guineas and two gold medals, and brought them all three to the shore beyond Ore – one of the three persons of quality was the King.'

OARE CREEK

From Hollowshore it is about a mile to the village of Oare, which can be reached around high water by boats requiring up to 2m of water via a creek marked by withies. There are stages with boats moored to them practically all the way along the south-east bank of Oare Creek, while at the head of the creek drying pontoons have been constructed to form a small marina within a few yards of the road to Faversham. As well as repair and haul-out facilities for craft up to 30ft, Youngboats has a well-stocked chandlery and provides diesel and gas. The site is also home to the new clubhouse and bar of Hollowshore Cruising Club. Access is around 1½ hours either side high water.

Alternatively, it is a pleasant half hour walk from

Oare and Hollowshore Port Guide
Local tel code 01795

Hollowshore Services	Tel: 532317.
Youngboats (Oare)	Tel: 536176; www.youngboats.co.uk.
Water	From yards at Oare and Hollowshore.
Stores	From shop at Oare.
Chandlery	Youngboats, Tel: 536176.
Fuel	Diesel from both yards, gas from Youngboats.
Repairs	Yards at Oare and Hollow Shore. Slipways. Crane up to 5 tons at Hollowshore and 8 tons at Oare.
Transport	Bus from Oare to Faversham.
Yacht clubs	Hollowshore Cruising Club, at Youngboats, Oare, Honorary Secretary Tel: 793606; www.hollowshorecc.co.uk.
Food and drink	Shipwright's Arms, Hollowshore, Tel: 590088. Ferry House Inn, Harty, Tel: 510214.

the landing at Hollowshore along the creekside up to Oare village, with its two pubs, The Castle and the Three Mariners.

CONYER CREEK

There are two ways into Conyer Creek from the South Deep inside Fowley Island. Conyer Cruising Club provides some useful written directions for both routes and has photographs of the entrance at low water on its website.

There are two waiting buoys laid by Swale Marina in the South Deep at the east end of Fowley Island and these, together with a further pair owned by Blackden Moorings, can be used by visitors for an overnight stay provided they are booked beforehand.

Coming from the east (Harty Ferry), the east cardinal buoy at the end of Fowley Spit is left to starboard, before following the lines of moorings up the South Deep to the red port-hand buoy at the west end of Fowley Island. To port is another smaller red can leading to a series of starboard-hand buoys up to the entrance of Conyer Creek. Leave the north cardinal mark (a post with two traffic cones as a topmark) close to starboard and then follow the next sequence of starboard-hand marks (buoys and withies) that lead close to the sea wall near the old Butterfly Wharf. Note

that a little upstream of this wharf the hulks of two barges have collapsed down the side of the creek bank, with some wreckage protruding. Thereafter, pairs of withies with triangular or disc topmarks will lead you, if there is enough water, round the outside of the bends and up to Conyer village.

The second way into Conyer Creek is via a tortuous gulley known as the Butterfly channel. Shoal draught craft approaching from the west (Queenborough) can, starting from No 8 buoy in the main channel, turn south-east and sound across the spit off the western end of Fowley Island into the deeper water of South Deep about 100m away from the sea-wall. Once in the deeper water take a more easterly course towards the red can port-hand buoy at the west end of Fowley Island and then proceed as above.

There are two marinas at Conyer, both of which offer berths alongside drying pontoons, so are only suitable for shoal draught craft.

Conyer Creek Marina is the first to be reached, on the port-hand side just beyond a group of houseboats. The drying pontoons are situated alongside houses which are part of a waterside development on the quay, where Conyer Marine boatyard was previously located. Ted Spears welcomes visiting yachtsmen and groups from clubs – in summer, barbecue facilities are available

Conyer Creek showing the two routes in from the Swale at the top of the picture

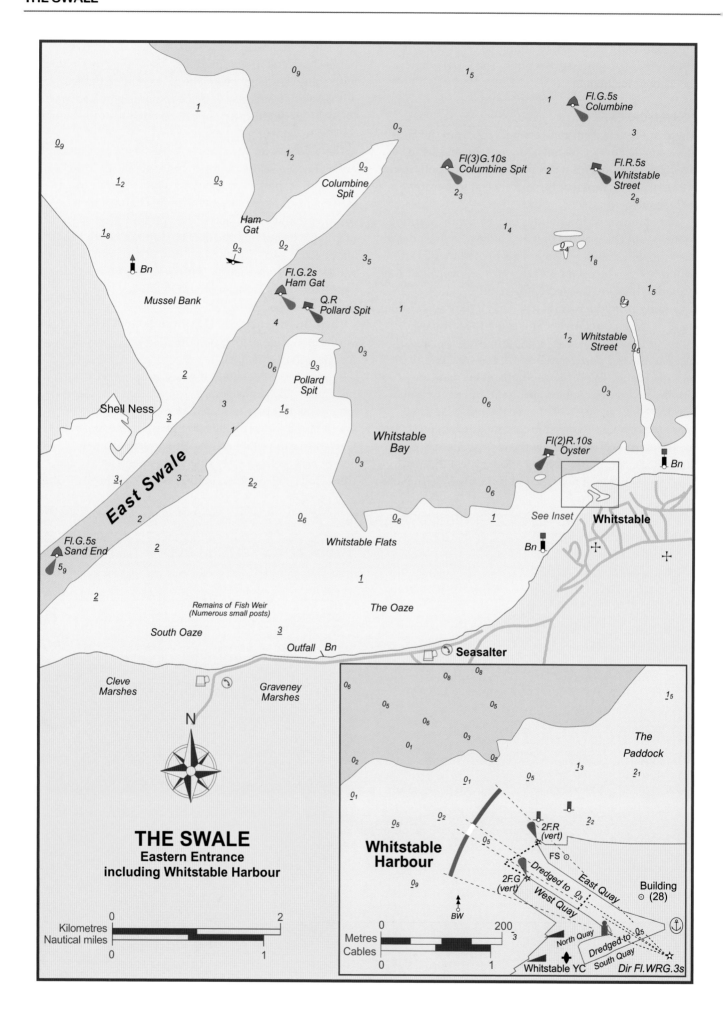

THE SWALE
Eastern Entrance
including Whitstable Harbour

Kilometres
Nautical miles

**Whitstable
Harbour**

Conyer Port Guide – Local tel code 01795

Conyer Creek Marina	Tel: 521384; Mob: 07971 641129.
Swale Marina	Tel: 521562; Fax: 520788; www.swalemarina.co.uk.
Blackden Moorings	Tel: 521725.
Water and electricity	At both marinas.
Facilities	Toilets and showers at both marinas.
Stores	Teynham, 1½ miles away.
Repairs	Swale Marina: travel hoist, 30 ton crane, slipway up to 30 tons, scrubbing posts by arrangement.
Sailmaker	Wilkinson Sails at Swale Marina, Tel: 521503.
Chandlery	Basic fittings at Swale Marina.
Transport	Bus service to Teynham and Sittingbourne. Trains to London, Dover and Ramsgate from Teynham or Sittingbourne.
Yacht clubs	Conyer Cruising Club at Swale Marina Tel: 521562; www.conyercc.org.uk.
Food and drink	Barbecue facilities by prior arrangement at both marinas; Ship Inn, Conyer, food Tuesday to Sunday, Tel: 520778.

– and he will advise on access up the creek.

Further up the creek, past the Ship Inn and the houseboats in The Dock (Blackden Moorings), are the pontoon mud berths of Swale Marina, formerly Jarman's Boatyard. This is at the head of the creek, which dries out completely, but the serviced pontoons can be accessed by most boats for about one hour either side of high water. Visitors' berths are available and club groups can be accommodated by arrangement. Facilities on the site include hoist, crane, slipway, repair workshop, spray centre and sail loft, and a barbecue is available for parties. The Conyer Cruising Club has its new (2008) clubhouse near the marina office.

WINDMILL CREEK
Windmill Creek runs off to the north about one mile west of Harty Ferry. The spit off its western side is marked with a post. It formerly cut some miles inland, but it has now been blocked and is of little interest except to wildfowlers.

WHITSTABLE HARBOUR
This small harbour lies two or three miles east of the entrance to the East Swale. It is controlled by Canterbury Council and is used regularly by small freighters working from commercial aggregate and timber quays. The local fishing fleet also operates out of the harbour, where there is a flourishing quayside fish market.

Whitstable offers emergency shelter to yachtsmen who are prevented from making the Thames or Medway during a westerly or south-westerly blow. However, berthing for yachts is temporary and at the discretion of the harbour master. Moreover, the harbour is busy, dirty and drying, and therefore would only be recommended as a last resort.

The narrow entrance to Whitstable can be reached

The local fishing fleet operates out of Whitstable Harbour where there is a busy quayside fishmarket

In prime position on the seafront, Whitstable Yacht Club caters mainly for dinghies and catamaran sailors

at about Fowley, or even as far west as Elmley on very high tides. At HW Sheerness, it is slack throughout the Swale, and for the first hour after high water the whole body of water moves eastward when, at about Long Point, the westerly stream reverses direction and ebbs back into the Medway. Meanwhile the remainder of the water carries on moving to the east. As the ebb continues, the point of separation of the stream also moves eastwards, until ultimately the separation occurs near Fowley.

As a result of this there is an east-going stream for about nine hours every tide at Elmley, while at Kingsferry Bridge the tide sets to the east for eight hours. By the time Harty is reached, the duration of east and west-going streams is about six hours each, but it is sometimes useful to know that on the north side of the West Swale there is a west-going eddy for as much as an hour before the ebb stops flowing eastward on the south side of the river.

The early ebb is strong, until the banks are uncovered, approaching three or four knots at Kingsferry.

In the East Swale, tides are considerably affected by prevailing winds, with easterlies causing the higher levels.

only over the shoal water that extends for more than a mile offshore. The best approach, not before half flood, is from a position about a mile west of the Whitstable Street red can buoy (Fl R 2s) on a course of 170°M. This is held until within half a mile of the harbour entrance by which time, if it is dark, the Whitstable Oyster buoy (R Can Fl (2) R 10s) will be seen on the starboard bow, while continuing on the same course brings you to within the green sector of a flashing light on the West Quay dolphin just off the harbour entrance.

This dolphin and a conspicuous tall granary building provide useful daylight marks. The light on the dolphin has WR and G sectors and flashes every five seconds. The white sector serves shoal draught boats approaching from the west, while the red sector is to keep craft off the shoal called Whitstable Street. At the head of the harbour is a leading light, Fl WRG 3s, the white sector bearing 127°M into the entrance. The traffic signals on the north-east arm of West Quay show fixed white for harbour open and fixed red for harbour closed.

Whitstable is famous for shellfish, particularly oysters, and hence you will find plenty of seafood restaurants within walking distance of the harbour. Whitstable Yacht Club occupies a prime position on the seafront and, like many sailing clubs along the North Kent shore, caters mainly for catamaran and dinghy sailors. There are, however, some drying moorings along the shore used by shoal draught cruising yachts.

SWALE TIDES

Tidal streams in the Swale are peculiar because of the two outlets to the sea. At LW Sheerness, it is slack water almost throughout the Swale. As the flood commences, it naturally enters from both ends, the streams meeting

Whitstable Port Guide – Local tel code 01227

Harbour master	Tel: 274086; Fax: 265442; email:harbour@whitstable.telme.com.
VHF	Channels 16, 12 or 09, callsign *Whitstable Harbour Radio*; from 0830-1700 (Monday to Friday) or any day from three hours before and two hours after high water (tidal information is available).
Water	Alongside at harbour and at yacht club.
Stores	Shops in town. Early closing on Wednesdays.
Chandlery	Whitstable Marine, The Seawall, Tel: 262525/274168.
Fuel	Garages nearby.
Transport	Train service to London (Victoria).
Customs Office	Tel: 01304 224151 (24hr).
Yacht club	Whitstable Yacht Club (Tel: 272942) can sometimes offer a mooring.
Food and drink	Restaurant and bar at yacht club; pubs and restaurants in town.

The North Foreland looking
north to Margate Road

Chapter seventeen
Cross Estuary Routes

There is a story by Archie White in which an old West Mersea barge skipper tells a young fellow with his first command how he can sneak through the Rays'n, past the Ridge Buoy (or rather where it used to be) over the top of the Whitaker Spit and out into the Swin off Shoebury; thereby reaching the London River well ahead of all the other barges that had been storm-bound with him in the Blackwater.

It is a good story and probably true, because it certainly is possible to cut many corners by using the swatchways (on a rising tide) in the Thames Estuary. However, the loss of some crucial navigational marks, in particular the South-West Sunk beacon which disappeared beneath the waves recently, means that there are not as many relatively safe options as in the past. The Princes Channel, Black Deep and Fisherman's Gat are all regularly used by large commercial vessels and the Port of London Authority (PLA) does advise

recreational craft to avoid them if possible.

Neither the North nor South Edinburgh Channels is buoyed, although they should be navigable with caution.

Foulger's Gat, the swatch through the Long Sand into the Black Deep, which yachtsmen are advised to use in preference to Fisherman's Gat, has been reported in recent years to have a number of depths less than charted at its northern end near the Black Deep No 6.

For these reasons you should be aware that the routes described below are merely suggested passages and should be used with caution, especially the unmarked minor swatchways.

PRECAUTIONS

Before any yachtsman sets out to cross the shoal-infested mouth of the Thames, he or she must give careful consideration to a number of things

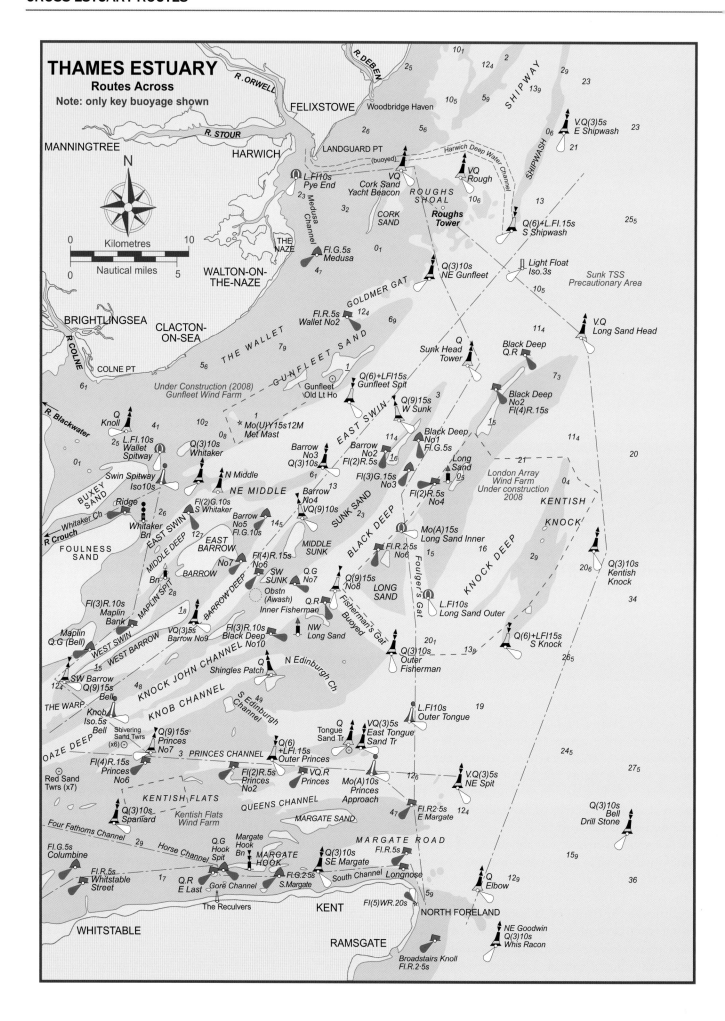

THAMES ESTUARY
Routes Across
Note: only key buoyage shown

MANNINGTREE

R. ORWELL

R. STOUR

FELIXSTOWE

R. DEBEN

Woodbridge Haven

HARWICH

LANDGUARD PT
(buoyed)

Harwich Deep Water Channel

SHIPWAY

V.Q(3)5s
E Shipwash

L.Fl10s
Pye End

VQ
Cork Sand
Yacht Beacon

VQ
Rough

SHIPWASH

THE NAZE

Medusa Channel

CORK SAND

ROUGHS SHOAL

Roughs Tower

Q(6)+L.Fl.15s
S Shipwash

WALTON-ON-THE-NAZE

Fl.G.5s
Medusa

Q(3)10s
NE Gunfleet

Light Float
Iso.3s

Sunk TSS
Precautionary Area

BRIGHTLINGSEA

CLACTON-ON-SEA

GOLDMER GAT

Fl.R.5s
Wallet No2

Sunk Head Tower

Q

V.Q
Long Sand Head

COLNE PT

R. COLNE

THE WALLET

GUNFLEET SAND

Black Deep
Q.R

R. Blackwater

Under Construction (2008)
Gunfleet Wind Farm

Gunfleet
Old Lt Ho

Q(6)+LFl15s
Gunfleet Spit

Black Deep
No2
Fl(4)R.15s

Q
Knoll

Mo(U)Y15s12M
Met Mast

EAST SWIN

Q(9)15s
W Sunk

Black Deep
No1
Fl.G.5s

L.Fl.10s
Wallet Spitway

Q(3)10s
Whitaker

Barrow
No3
Q(3)10s

Barrow
No2
Fl(2)R.5s

Long Sand

London Array
Wind Farm
Under construction
2008

KENTISH KNOCK

Swin Spitway
Iso10s

N Middle

NE MIDDLE

Barrow
No4
VQ(9)10s

Fl(3)G.15s
No3

Fl(2)R.5s
No4

BUXEY SAND

Ridge

Fl(2)G.10s
S Whitaker

Barrow
No5
Fl.G.10s

SUNK SAND

BLACK DEEP

Mo(A)15s
Long Sand Inner

V.Q
Long Sand Head

Whitaker Bn

EAST SWIN

EAST BARROW

MIDDLE SUNK

Fl.R.2.5s
No6

KNOCK DEEP

Q(3)10s
Kentish Knock

R Crouch

MIDDLE DEEP

Bn

BARROW

Fl(4)R.15s
No6

Q.G
No7

Q(9)15s
No8

Foulger's Gat

FOULNESS SAND

MAPLIN SPIT

No7

SW SUNK

Obstn
(Awash)
Inner Fisherman

Q.R

LONG SAND

L.Fl10s
Long Sand Outer

Fl(3)R.10s
Maplin Bank

BARROW DEEP

Fisherman's Buoyed

Fisherman's Gat

Q(6)+LFl15s
S Knock

Maplin
Q.G (Bell)

WEST SWIN

VQ(3)5s
Barrow No9

Fl(3)R.10s
Black Deep
No10

NW
Long Sand

WEST BARROW

Q(3)10s
Outer Fisherman

SW Barrow
Q(9)15s
Bell

KNOCK JOHN CHANNEL

Shingles Patch

N Edinburgh Ch

THE WARP

Knob
Iso.5s
Bell

KNOB CHANNEL

S Edinburgh Channel

L.Fl10s
Outer Tongue

OAZE DEEP

Shivering Sand Twrs
(x6)

Q(9)15s
Princes No7

Tongue Sand Tr

Q

VQ(3)5s
East Tongue
Sand Tr

PRINCES CHANNEL

Q(6)
+LFl.15s
Outer Princes

Red Sand
Twrs (x7)

Fl(4)R.15s
Princes
No6

Fl(2)R.5s
Princes No2

VQ.R
Princes

Mo(A)10s
Princes
Approach

V.Q(3)5s
NE Spit

Q(3)10s
Bell
Drill Stone

KENTISH FLATS

QUEENS CHANNEL

Fl.R2.5s
E Margate

Q(3)10s
Spaniard

Kentish Flats
Wind Farm

MARGATE SAND

MARGATE ROAD

Four Fathoms Channel

Margate
Hook Bn

Fl.R.5s

Fl.G.5s
Columbine

Horse Channel

Q.G Hook
Spit

MARGATE
HOOK

Q(3)10s
SE Margate

Longnose

Q
Elbow

Fl.R.5s
Whitstable
Street

Q.R
E Last

Gore Channel

Fl.G.2.5s
S.Margate

South Channel

NORTH FORELAND

The Reculvers

KENT

Fl(5)WR.20s

WHITSTABLE

RAMSGATE

Broadstairs Knoll
Fl.R.2.5s

NE Goodwin
Q(3)10s
Whis Racon

Charts should be corrected with the latest Notice to Mariners

that may not have seemed important during short distance cruising between adjacent rivers within sight of land. These are:

1. Corrected Compass. If visibility should close in when halfway across, a reliable compass will be essential, used in conjunction with your GPS and other navigational software.

2. Corrected Charts. A copy of this book, even if it is the latest edition, is in no way adequate for crossing the Thames Estuary. Admiralty chart No 1183 will be necessary and must be corrected up to date. Admiralty Leisure Folios 5606 *Thames Estuary South* and 5607 *Thames Estuary North* are also useful, but 1183 is essential because it shows the overall picture.

It should always be remembered that during the several years that often elapse between surveys of a particular area carried out by the PLA Hydrographic Department, significant changes can take place, particularly in the very swatchways that are of special interest to yachtsmen. For this reason, it is advisable to check for any last minute Notices to Mariners, which is nowadays very easy to do electronically. And of course, a reliable echo-sounder will be indispensable.

3. Tidal information. Work out and understand what the tide will be doing at all important points along the route – not only at the time you hope to be there, but also for later times in case you are delayed. For this purpose the tidal diagrams included on pages 8 and 9 will be useful, although the larger scale *Tidal Stream Atlas* (No 249) published by the Admiralty will be even better. Remember that depths will vary according to direction and strength of wind and barometric pressure – tidal predictions are just that.

4. Waypoints. Prepare a list of all waypoints that might prove useful. They should also be plotted on the chart to ensure that they constitute a safe route and have been correctly entered into the GPS or other navigational software.

WEATHER FORECAST

Routine forecasts are available from coastguard Met broadcasts on VHF radio. For on demand forecasts Wiley Nautical offers both a mobile and desktop program. These include forecasts for inshore, offshore and mainland locations. Forecasts are updated four times daily, cover up to seven days ahead, with a detailed break down for each three hour period.

It's good to eventually see this quality of graphical forecasts available cheaply to sailors on the go.

Get it on your mobile: Text 'WEATHER WILEY' to 60030 or visit www.wileynautical.com/weather. Your first three forecasts are free, future requests will be charged to you through your normal mobile bill. Latest rates and discounts are shown on the above website. Usual network operator charges for SMS text messages and downloads apply.

Get it on your computer: Visit www.wileynautical. com/weather. All forecasts are provided free of charge through the desktop application.

EMERGENCY EQUIPMENT

Ensure the adequacy of emergency equipment, including: VHF, flares/smoke signals, life-jackets, liferaft/dinghy.

CONDITIONS IN THE ESTUARY

Since the southbound passage across the estuary will generally be made during the south-west going flood tide, it must be realised that when the wind is from the south-west, as it so often is, then a short and very steep sea gets up in anything more than a moderate breeze.

For many of us, the first time we find ourselves in command of a yacht out of sight of land is when we set out from one or other of the Essex or Suffolk rivers and proceed seaward beyond the Spitway and the Whitaker Bell buoy or round the North-East Gunfleet. The distance across the Thames Estuary between say Clacton and the North Foreland is about 25 miles, so we should not be surprised that it feels different out there amidst the shoals, especially when the buoys don't come up as soon as we would like!

THE SUNK VTS GYRATORY SYSTEM

In 2007 a big ship roundabout centred on the Sunk came into operation. This traffic separation scheme for ships over 300 tons is centred well offshore, to the north-east of the Long Sand Head. There are about a dozen new buoys in the area and some existing buoys have been moved. The ships will turn in an anti-clockwise direction. Yachtsmen most likely to be affected will probably be those on passage to and from Ostend and the Belgian coast, but any yacht in the area should maintain a good look-out, monitor VHF Ch 14, and cross at right angles to the traffic in the designated lanes.

WIND FARMS

The conspicuous 30 turbines on the Kentish Flats offshore wind farm, in the estuary off the North Kent coast between the west end of the Princes Channel and the Whitstable Street buoy, have been operating since 2006.

In 2008, construction of 250 wind turbines began for the huge London Array wind farm on the Long Sand and the Kentish Knock Sand. The latter, when completed, would have surrounded Foulgers Gat, but following objections from the RYA and the PLA the number of turbines has been reduced and there will not now be so many to the south-west of the Gat.

Work on the proposed 30-turbine offshore wind farm at the south-west end of the Gunfleet Sand started in 2008.

SOUTH-WEST SUNK BEACON

Like the neighbouring Little Sunk Beacon, the South-West Sunk Beacon finally crumbled into the sea during the early years of the 21st century and has been designated an Obstn (Awash). There are no plans to reinstate the beacon so there is now no sure way of crossing the Sunk Sand from Barrow Deep to Black Deep. This means that the suggested routes (detailed in earlier editions of this book) for the Swin Spitway or Whitaker Buoy to the North Foreland can no longer be safely recommended.

THE BLACK DEEP/FISHERMAN'S GAT PRECAUTIONARY AREA

Fisherman's Gat is the designated commercial channel and is used extensively by large commercial ships to and from the Black Deep. Recreational craft are advised to avoid this area and also the Princes Channel.

HARWICH OR SUFFOLK RIVERS TO NORTH FORELAND

Those wishing to cross the Estuary from Harwich or the Suffolk rivers can leave Harwich via the Cork Sand north cardinal beacon (VQ), keeping south of the shipping lane. Head on a south-south-easterly course, passing the North-East Gunfleet east cardinal buoy (Q (3)10s) to starboard, to the Sunk Head Tower north cardinal buoy (Q Whis) and alter course to the south-west on entering the Black Deep. Thereafter proceed about seven miles, leaving the Black Deep via Foulger's Gat, before heading to the Outer Tongue buoy (L Fl 10s Whis).

Foulger's Gat, which should be used in preference to the busy Fisherman's Gat, is marked at each end by safe water marks. These buoys are similar in design to the Woodbridge Haven buoy and it has been reported that they are not easy to identify, particularly if you are going north when they can be confused with bigger buoys in the Black Deep.

It should be noted that Foulger's Gat has been reported to have a number of depths less than charted at its northern end near the Black Deep No 6 buoy.

The channel is entered via the safe water mark Long Sand Inner (Mo A 15s), about one mile to the north-east of Black Deep No 6 (R Can Fl R 2.5s). A southerly (°M) course for about three miles will take you through to the safe water mark Long Sand Outer (L Fl 10s), at the Knock Deep end of the Gat. From here, shape a slightly more westerly course for the Outer Tongue, and thence East Margate (R Can Fl R 2.5s) and the Foreland.

An alternative, which is a few miles longer but navigationally more simple, would be to take the 'outside route' heading further offshore from the

The conspicuous turbines of the Kentish Flats wind farm

Bound south through the Swin Spitway

North-East Gunfleet buoy to the Long Sand Head north cardinal (VQ) buoy – taking care to avoid the shipping in the busy Sunk Precautionary Area. A southerly course from the Long Sand Head will lead to the Kentish Knock east cardinal (Q (3) 10s) buoy. Then head in a south-south-westerly direction to the North Foreland and the north cardinal Elbow buoy (Q).

THE TIDE
Southbound
In order to make the most of a passage on a rising tide it will be necessary to leave just before low water. The aim is to get towards the Sunk or thereabouts just as the flood starts running south-westerly and reach the Foulger's Gat (or Kentish Knock if going the 'outside' route), followed by the Foreland, before the north-going stream starts about an hour before HW Dover.

Northbound
When crossing the Estuary for the first time from Dover or Ramsgate, it will be best to stem the last of the south-going tide up the North Foreland so as to get the benefit of the flood through the Foulger's Gat and across the Estuary. Those bound for Harwich or the Suffolk rivers can carry the ebb north.

SWIN SPITWAY OR SOUTH WHITAKER BUOY TO NORTH FORELAND
From South Whitaker green conical (Fl 2 G) head up the East Swin or Middle Deep to pass between the red can Maplin Bank (Fl (3) R 10s) and the green conical

Maplin Edge (Fl G 2.5s). Leave the recently changed to green conical Maplin buoy (QG Bell) to starboard and continue up the West Swin, passing the red can West Swin buoy (QR) to port. At the west cardinal South-West Barrow buoy (Q (9) 15s Bell) alter course to the south-east, leaving the Knob safe water mark (Iso 5s) to port, heading across to the Shivering Sand Tower and the entrance to the Princes Channel (see below).

An alternative option, after the South-West Barrow, might be to use the South Edinburgh channel which, although not buoyed, is navigable with caution. Thence the Tongue Sand Tower, Princes' approach buoys and the East Margate.

PRINCES CHANNEL
The Princes Channel (which is heavily used by commercial ships) commences between the red can Princes No 6 (Fl (4) R 15s) and the west cardinal Princes No 7 (Q (9) 15s Bell) buoys and continues in an easterly direction past the green conical Princes No 1 (QG 10s) for about five miles to the Outer Princes south cardinal buoy.

At its narrowest point, abreast the red can Princes No 2 buoy (Fl (2) R 5s), the deep water is almost a mile wide. From this position, an easterly (magnetic) course will lead past the Princes No 1 green conical buoy (QG), to the Outer Princes south cardinal (VQ (6) + L Fl 10s) buoy, by which time the north and east cardinal Tongue Sand Tower buoys should be in sight, with the red and white Princes Approach safe water mark (Mo (A) 10s) pretty well straight ahead.

The Thames barge skippers were well acquainted with the swatchways of the Estuary

Hook Spit (QG) buoys, marking the narrow swatch over the western end of the Margate Hook Sand. Because of rocky patches off the Reculvers, do not approach the shore closer than two miles or proceed eastwards until these two buoys have been found. The twin rectangular towers of the Reculvers will help in locating the buoys.

Once through the swatch, shape a course of 110°M to leave the Margate Hook Beacon (south cardinal topmark) and the conical green South Margate (Fl G 2.5s) at least a quarter of a mile to the north. From the South Margate buoy an easterly (magnetic) course will lead to the South-East Margate east cardinal buoy (Q (3) 10s) a little more than two miles away.

When these buoys are close abeam, a course can be laid – about 150°M – to clear the Foreland after leaving the red can East Margate buoy (Fl (2) R 2.5s) about half a mile to starboard.

THAMES, MEDWAY OR SWALE TO NORTH FORELAND

There are various routes that can be taken in a west–east direction along the north coast of Kent, but craft from the Thames, the Medway or the Swale are advised by the PLA to use the Four Fathom, Horse and Gore Channels. The use of the well-buoyed Princes Channel further offshore is discouraged because of its use by large commercial vessels.

The historic 'overland' route from Thames to North Foreland departs from the Medway Channel, near Nos 4 or 6 buoys, on a course to the green conical Spile buoy (Fl G 2.5s), whence via the Four Fathom and then the Horse Channel to the East Last and Hook Spit buoys at the entrance to the Gore Channel off Reculver, with its twin-towers – all that remain of a monastery and mediaeval church.

The leg from the Spile to the Gore Channel is not very well marked but off Whitstable to the north of the Spaniard east cardinal buoy (Q (3) 10s) are the conspicuous turbines of the Kentish Flats wind farm.

GORE CHANNEL

This route is closer inshore and rather more difficult because of the many drying shoals off the Kent coast between Herne Bay and Margate.

Starting from the red can Whitstable Street buoy (Fl R 2s), a course of 95°M will lead (after about six miles) to the red can East Last (QR) and green conical

The passage can then be continued to round the Longnose red can buoy, which is about a mile offshore. There is a lit red can (Fl R 5s) about half a mile north of the unlit Longnose.

THE ORIGINAL OVERLAND ROUTE BEHIND THE ISLES OF THANET AND GRAIN

In his book *The First of the Tide* Maurice Griffiths explains how in the days of the Roman occupation of Reculver, the fortifications there '…marked the entrance to an important waterway, a river which then meandered through the Kentish countryside into the Stour by Sandwich, making the north eastern segment of land, Thanet, a true island. Sandwich was then an important seaport on the coast … The small vessels of the day were able to enter Pegwell Bay and work their way into the Thames by this handy inland route, and thereby cut off the long haul round the turbulent North Foreland with its strong and unpredictable tides.'

Now, of course, this river has long since silted up but it was part of the original 'overland' route. The additional part of the short cut was by way of the East and West Swale, across the Medway and inside the Isle of Grain via what is now Colemouth Creek, coming out into the London River by way of Yantlet Creek.

As Maurice Griffiths observed 'A well-manned Roman galley could make this passage on the young flood tide from the Regulbium (Reculver) settlement up to the ford at Londinium (near the present Blackfriars), and be back again with the next ebb the same day.'

The Inner Harbour at Ramsgate has a continental feel

Chapter eighteen
Ramsgate

Tides	HW Dover +0030. Range: springs 6m; neaps 3.2m
Charts	Admiralty 323, 1827, 1828, SC5605, SC5606; Stanfords 9; Imray C1, C8, C30, 2100 series; OS map 179
Waypoints	**Longnose Buoy 51°24'.15N 01°26'.08E**
	No 5 Channel Buoy 51°19'.56N 01°25'.91E
	NE Goodwin Buoy 51°20'.31N 01°34'.16E
	Gull Buoy 51°19'.57N 01°31'.30E
	North Quern Buoy 51°19'.41N 01°26'.11E
	Brake Buoy 51°16'.98N 01°28'.19E

Ramsgate is a strategic 'junction' for yachtsmen from both the UK and Europe. As Charles Pears remarked in *Yachting on the Sunshine Coast*: 'For yachts proceeding down Channel from either the Thames or the East Coast ports, Ramsgate is the first and most convenient harbour.'

In those days (1932) the J-Class 'big yachts' were still taking part in an annual regatta circuit which included Ramsgate '...a week of racing well within sight of the visitors, who crowd upon the jetties to

see the gay sight of the many spick and span craft all a-glitter with polished brass and varnish, gaily painted topsides and sunlit canvas.' Ramsgate Week is still an important event in the Royal Temple Yacht Club calendar, with competitors coming from nearby France, Belgium and Holland to race in the waters off the harbour as they have done since the club was founded in 1857.

Plans to build a harbour at Ramsgate were formed

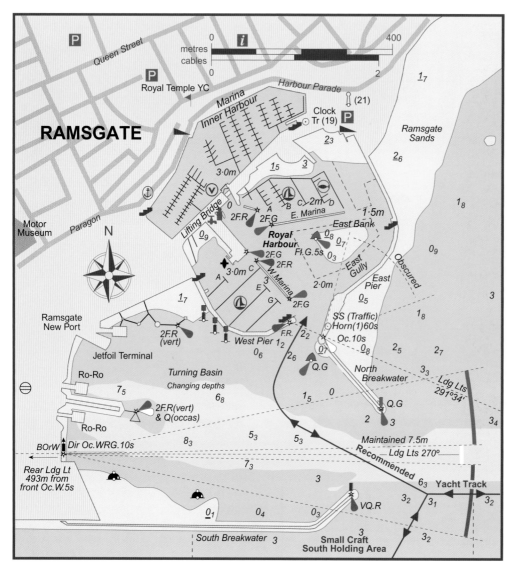

inshore of the buoy and less than two metres below the surface.

Once round the Foreland there are no further problems and a passage half a mile offshore past Broadstairs is quite safe.

As you approach Ramsgate's main beach, which starts with an outfall marked by a dolphin (Fl R 2.5s), beware of the shingle Dike Bank between the dolphin and the East Pier, particularly at low water. A course from the dolphin to a position north of the dredged channel between buoy No 5, a south cardinal (Q 6 + L Fl 15s), and buoy No 3, a green conical (Fl G 2.5s), will be sufficient to clear the bank and bring you to the recommended yacht track crossing point.

Cross the buoyed channel to join the recommended yacht track between the port-hand buoy No 4 (QR) and the north cardinal North Quern buoy (Q).

From Holland, Belgium and Northern France
Approaching from Holland and Belgium you should aim to pick up the North-East Goodwin east cardinal buoy (Q (3) 10s) and then the green conical Goodwin Knoll buoy (Fl (2) G 5s). If coming from France (Dunkerque and Calais) north about the Goodwins, aim for the Goodwin Knoll buoy. From the Goodwin Knoll you then head for the Gull east cardinal buoy (VQ (3) 5s), followed by the Ramsgate Approach (RA) south cardinal buoy (Q (6) +L Fl 15s), and then the East Brake port-hand buoy. These three buoys can be safely left either to port or starboard, but by now you should pick up the leading lights to the harbour entrance (270°T) and then the start of the dredged channel at buoys No 1 and 2. The recommended yacht track is on the south side of the dredged channel, leaving the port-hand channel buoys to starboard.

From Calais, Boulogne or the South Coast
From Calais, south about the Goodwins, you will need to aim for the South-West Goodwin south cardinal buoy

in the early 1700s after a naval squadron that had been sheltering between the coast and The Goodwin Sands was destroyed by The Great Storm. By the end of that century the harbour was completed and in 1821 King George IV sailed from Ramsgate, in preference to Dover, on a visit to Hanover. To show his appreciation of the hospitality he received, the King bestowed Royal status on the harbour.

APPROACHES TO RAMSGATE
From the Thames Estuary
Whether your approach has been the inshore route, via the Four Fathom Channel and Gore Channel, between the Hook Spit green conical buoy (QG) and East Last red can buoy (QR) and inside the Margate Sands, or the outer route via the Princes Channel, care should be taken from the North Foreland onwards.

While there is often plenty of water inshore of the unlit Longnose red can buoy, it is advisable for anyone unfamiliar with the area to leave the Longnose buoy to starboard when rounding the North Foreland as the Longnose Spit extends quite a long way out, and at low water springs there are some very nasty rocks not far

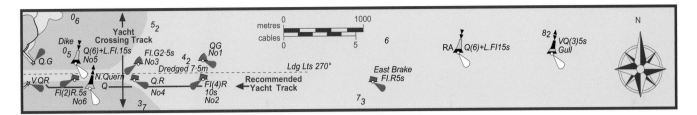

(Q (6) +L Fl 15s). Be aware that the South Goodwin Light Vessel, which was half a mile south of the South-West Goodwin buoy, has been removed.

From Boulogne you should aim to leave the shipping lanes somewhere between the Varne Light Vessel and the South-West Goodwin buoy.

From the English South Coast you need to be at least two miles off Dover Harbour, otherwise you are required to call on VHF for permission to pass the harbour entrances.

Once inside the Goodwin Sands and past Dover, head for the Deal Bank red can buoy (QR). From here, you then have two options:

Option One: you could continue inside the Brake Sands, using the Ramsgate Channel, making sure you leave the B2 green conical buoy (Fl (2) G 5s) to starboard. At high water, once round the B2 buoy, a course direct to the harbour entrance, making sure you leave the west cardinal West Quern buoy (Q (9) 15s) to starboard, is

quite safe. At low water, a course to the yellow racing mark, the Stonar (51°19′.13N 01°24′.50E), would ensure you miss the shoal water of Cross Ledge. This option would be fine for any boat up to 2.5m draught, anything over that and a passage at low water springs.

Option Two: (much safer for boats with a draught of 2.5-3m): from the port-hand Deal Bank buoy (Q Fl R) use the Gull Stream, between the Downs red can buoy (Fl (2) R 5s) and the Goodwin Fork south cardinal buoy (Q (6) + L Fl 15s); then head from the South Brake red can buoy (Fl (3) R 10s) to the West Goodwin green conical buoy (Fl G 5s).

From the South Brake it is possible to lay a course direct to the North Quern north cardinal buoy (Q), but again, for deep draught boats, a low water springs approach should be avoided. A safer option in this case would be to continue down the Gull Stream to the Brake port-hand buoy (Fl (4) R 15s) before turning in to the North Quern.

Ramsgate Harbour looking north showing the turning basin and Ro-Ro terminal

A Canadian yacht entering the Royal Harbour

ENTERING THE HARBOUR

The recommended yacht track is to the south of the buoyed channel with a crossing point (for those approaching from, or bound to, the north) west of the No 3 and No 4 dredged channel buoys. There is a small craft holding area to the south of the southern breakwater if you cannot enter the harbour straight away.

The tide sets across the harbour entrance in a north-easterly/south-westerly direction; the north-going tide runs from about 1½ hours before high water to four hours after high water.

There is a busy Ro-Ro terminal in Ramsgate New Port, which means frequent movements of large vessels and ferries. Ramsgate Port Control must be contacted on VHF Ch 14 before you approach or leave the harbour.

Vessel movements in and out of the Royal Harbour and the approach channel are controlled by signal lights on the East Pier. Three vertical red lights mean that a vessel may not enter or leave. Three vertical green lights mean a vessel may enter or leave. A flashing orange light means a large ship movement is in progress and no other vessel may enter the Turning Basin or leave the Royal Harbour.

Those approaching under sail should bear in mind that it is very much frowned on to enter the Turning Basin under sail, therefore sails should be dropped in good time before entering.

Once in the Turning Basin, cross to starboard without delay and enter the Royal Harbour, keeping close to the West Pier to avoid the shoal patch extending from the East Pier. When you are inside the piers, call *Ramsgate Marina* on VHF Ch 80 for berthing directions.

The West Marina, immediately to port inside the West Pier, is used by berth holders and visiting yachts. The entrance to the Inner Marina is via a flap-gate and lifting bridge, directly ahead; and the East Marina, mainly used by commercial fishing boats, is to starboard of the Inner Marina entrance. There is access to the Inner Marina for about two hours either side of high water; a red and yellow flag by day and a single green light by night indicate that the gate is open. A fuel barge is situated at the end of the Commercial Quay below the RNLI station.

The sand bank that had built up from the East Pier across the entrance was dredged in early 2008. A suction dredger will be brought in on a regular basis to keep a minimum of 3m depth within the Royal Harbour.

The Royal Temple Yacht Club hosts a great many visiting foreign yachts and all visiting yachtsmen are made welcome at its clubhouse overlooking the Royal Harbour. Because of its very good mainline rail connections to London via the Medway Towns, to Ashford International via Canterbury and Dover, Ramsgate is an excellent place to either leave a boat or to change crews.

Once ashore you will find that Ramsgate, with its continental-looking harboursides, promenades and crescents, is steeped in both maritime and military history. The Sailors' Church and Mission at the corner of the Military Road was built in 1878 by a local vicar who wished to provide spiritual guidance and physical help to the crews of the Ramsgate fleet of sailing smacks. The young apprentices, or Smack Boys as they were known, led particularly hard lives and there were rooms for them above the church as well as, a few years later, in the Home for Smack Boys next door. 'Many rescued from shipwreck were cared for' – mostly from the Goodwins. The church today houses a small collection of ship models and paintings and is open for 'Coffee, Rest and Prayer' Monday to Friday from 1015 to 1600 in the summer.

Behind the church is Jacob's Ladder, at one time the only way down to the West Pier, before the Military Road was built. The premises with brick arches underneath Royal Parade would originally have housed workshops and stores – there is a sailmakers and a chandlers there now, along with the Ship Shape Café.

The Dunkirk Little Ships assembled in Ramsgate before crossing to the beaches on the Operation Dynamo rescue mission – one of the craft used in the evacuation is in the Inner Marina.

The West Marina to the left, the gate to the Inner Marina on the right

The impressive building of the Clock Tower on the harbour quayside is home to a Maritime Museum and is the site of the Ramsgate Meridian from which the town's own particular Mean Time, ahead of Greenwich, was calculated.

When it comes to drinking or eating out, there is a plethora of places to choose from on the waterfront nearby or in town. The Ramsgate Harbour Lights Fish Company, in the Port Control building at the end of the East Pier, serves fresh local seafood at very reasonable prices, with spectacular views thrown in. The Royal Temple Yacht Club has a bar with a terrace and a first floor dining room with a splendid view over the harbour.

Ramsgate Port Guide – Local tel code 01843

Ramsgate Port Control	VHF Ch 14 callsign *Ramsgate Port Control*, Tel: 572112.
Ramsgate Royal Harbour Marina	VHF Ch 80 (in the harbour) callsign *Ramsgate Marina*; Marina Office Tel: 572110; Harbour Office Tel: 572100; www.portoframsgate.co.uk.
Facilities	Water and electricity. Amenity block contains free showers, and toilets as well as a coin-operated launderette.
Fuel	Diesel and petrol from fuel barge (0730-1900) at end of quay between East and West Marinas. Gas from chandlery.
Chandlery	Bosun's Locker, Military Road Tel: 597158.
Repairs	Slipways in Inner Marina and near East Marina, 40 ton boathoist.
Sailmaker	The Sail Loft, Tel: 851665; www.northropsails.
Stores	Waitrose, Boots, other supermarkets and shops within walking distance; weekly market on Fridays.
Food and drink	Wine bars, restaurants, pubs, hotels, fish and chips nearby; Ramsgate Harbour Lights, Tel: 592224; RTYC bar and dining room.
Yacht clubs	Royal Temple Yacht Club, Westcliff Mansions Tel: 591766; www.rtyc.com.
Pets	No animals may be kept on board, animals are not permitted to enter from abroad.
Transport	Good connections by rail to London, Medway Towns, Ashford International via Canterbury, Dover; coach service; car and passenger ferry to Ostend.

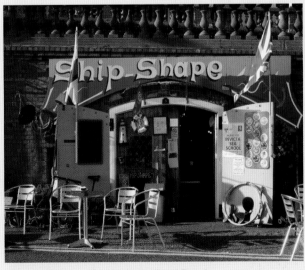

The Ship Shape café beneath the Royal Parade

The Ramsgate Maritime Museum is housed in the Clock House on the harbourside

Iwunda at anchor off Mistley Quay with the family rowing ashore, circa 1955

Chapter nineteen
Fifty years of *East Coast Rivers*

Soon after the Second World War Jack Coote, who had taught himself to sail on the Norfolk Broads and Regents Park Lake, bought an old Broads boat which he kept at Shepperton on the River Thames. He began venturing down the Thames to Holehaven, Leigh-on-Sea, the Medway and the Swale, but the Broads boat was nowhere near seaworthy enough for the tidal reaches, let alone any longer cruises. Jack's next boat, a leaky, wooden 11-ton centreboarder, was built at Southend-on-Sea in 1929 and had been kept for many years on the foreshore at Westcliff-on-Sea.

For the next decade or so the Coote family (Jack's wife Ellen and daughters Janet and Judy) spent almost all their weekends and summer holidays exploring the rivers and creeks of the Thames Estuary in the 34ft *Iwunda*. Initially the boat was laid up during the winter on the Thames at Teddington where the family then lived. So the London River became quite familiar as *Iwunda* made the passage up or down the tideway each autumn and spring, to and from Hoo on the

Medway where the mast would be lowered or raised. In January 1953, at the time of the Great Tide, *Iwunda* was wintering at Conyer, on the Swale. The barge alongside which she had been lying was lifted partly onto the quay and damaged, but fortunately no harm came to *Iwunda*.

The Blackwater became Jack's favourite river and for some years *Iwunda* was moored on the Chelmer Canal at Heybridge Basin, near Maldon at the head of the river. Here Jack met the editor of *Yachting Monthly*, Maurice Griffiths, who was also keeping his boat on the canal at that time. Jack had recently written a feature about the River Blackwater for *Yachting Monthly*, so needed little persuasion by Maurice to prepare a new series of articles and sketch charts on the other East Coast rivers, into almost every one of which he had already sailed *Iwunda*. By popular demand this series formed the basis of the Yachtsman's Pilot for the Thames Estuary – *East Coast Rivers* – a cloth-bound book published by *Yachting Monthly* in 1956, price 9/6d. 'The magician of the swatchways'

Jack Coote at the helm of his Broads boat with young daughter Janet, circa 1948

Maurice Griffiths had a lifelong fascination with these rivers and creeks, and he was later to describe Jack's book as 'the East Coast yachtsman's bible.'

The 'bible' was in fact inspired by a previous yachtsman's pilot published by *Yachting Monthly* in 1927 – *Rivers and Creeks of the Thames Estuary* was written by Lieut Commander John Irving RN, who had drawn the sketch charts and the black and white drawings to illustrate the text. Irving's book had in turn been inspired by the original *East Coast Rivers, Charts and Sailing Directions from The Thames to Southwold*, by Lieut SVSC Messum RN, published by the chart agents JD Potter in 1903. It is thought by some that this publication, long since out of print, could have been the 'drab little book' referred to by Erskine Childers in *The Riddle of the Sands.*

Both Irving and Messum were Navy men, well versed in surveying and producing charts and sketches for Admiralty sailing directions, which is essentially what their two books were. The post-war *East Coast Rivers* differed from the start in that the text was illustrated with photographs as well as sketch charts. Much more information about shoreside facilities and local maritime history was included in subsequent editions, and as a result the book has evolved into its present day form of a cruising companion rather than a pilot guide.

The original black and white sketch charts for *East Coast Rivers* were hand drawn by Jack, who had trained as a commercial artist before going into the photographic industry. He made great use of

2½ inch OS maps for the detail at the top of those creeks that stretched a long way inland, beyond the reach of Admiralty surveys. For many subsequent editions – including the changeovers from feet and fathoms to metric soundings and to IALA buoyage – Jack made all the necessary chart corrections and alterations himself. This painstaking work was really a labour of love and all done in his spare time, his day job being a full-time one with Ilford Films.

The problems of keeping the book up-to-date began the moment the first edition was published. Jack wrote in the preface to the second edition that 'changes have been taking place recently all over the East Coast, such as the removal of the time-honoured Chapman pile lighthouse and the wartime Nore Towers, the building of the new atomic power station at Bradwell and the dispersal of all the naval units and personnel from Harwich Harbour and the Medway…' In the preface to the third edition in 1961 he explained 'It is impossible to keep all the information absolutely up to date in a book of this kind – if only because of the time that must elapse between completion of new drawings and revised text and their subsequent reproduction in book form… I have been greatly helped by many readers of the earlier editions who have informed me of changes in their local waters…'

After it was stated in the first edition that 'there are no facilities or supplies at East Mersea', the indignant owner of the East Mersea Stores wrote to *Yachting Monthly* saying 'we have groceries, fruit, Esso mixture petrol, paraffin – and are open till 8pm daily and all day Sundays. If you would correct the information I should be obliged.'

Being involved in the research for the book in the early 1950s was a great adventure for my sister Judy and me, especially on our summer holiday cruises to Pin Mill, Harwich Harbour or Walton Backwaters at a time when we were reading *We Didn't Mean to go to Sea* and *Secret Water*. We were thrilled to see Alma Cottage and the Beach End Buoy in real life and it was easy to imagine the *Goblin* dragging out of Harwich Harbour into the North Sea in the fog with the Walker children alone on board. The photograph of us aboard *Iwunda* aground on the saltings in Horsey Mere (The Red Sea in *Secret Water*) was used in several of the early editions of the book and is an evocative East Coast Rivers image to this day. On the way to Walton Backwaters there would usually be sixpence on offer for the first crew member to spot the Pye End buoy, which even now is notoriously difficult to find.

On the weekends Osea Island was often our destination and, if the tide served, *Iwunda* would be put ashore on the shingly beach just below the old pier, for a scrub or possibly for some running repairs to her perpetually leaking garboard strakes. While the work was being done Judy and I and the ship's dog would

The centreboarder *Blue Shoal* with the family ashore on Pye Sand, circa 1973

emulate the *Swallows and Amazons* and go off map making and exploring the island.

In those days – before lifelines, stanchions, pulpits, radios, echo-sounders or GPS – sailing was a self-reliant affair. Depth was checked by swinging the lead – an unpleasant task – during which your sleeves always got soaked and muddy as you retrieved the dripping line. A black and white marked sounding pole was kept stored in the shrouds for use in the upper reaches of creeks that were, as Hervey Benham put it, 'little more than enlarged drainage ditches' – this pole became *Iwunda*'s trade mark.

Marinas with handy hose pipes on the pontoons had not so far been heard of, therefore it was the norm at most places to take metal water cans ashore with you in the dinghy as plastic water containers had not yet been invented – let alone glassfibre boats. Details of where to anchor, where and when you could get ashore, and the location of water taps (at East End Paglesham, and some other places, there was a pump that had to be primed), stores, petrol and paraffin were noted – this was all essential information to be published in the book. At Pin Mill, for example, we took a small enamel

This photograph of *Iwunda* aground in Walton Backwaters was used in several of the early editions of *East Coast Rivers*

can ashore, as well as a water can, and walked up the hill to the farm where we got milk practically straight from the cow. In the book it was stated 'Milk from nearby Hill Farm'.

Specialist sailing clothing simply did not exist, most of our gear came from Army surplus shops – oilskins were dreadful sticky garments that could stand up by themselves when you took them off. If we wore life jackets at all, they were made of kapok which would probably have hastened drowning rather than delayed it. Possibly because it had always been drummed into us that you should use 'one hand for the ship and one hand for yourself', we survived.

In the 1960s *Iwunda* was replaced by another centreboarder, the canoe-sterned *Blue Shoal* and she too became a familiar sight on the East Coast, featuring on several *Yachting Monthly* front covers. *Blue Shoal* was fitted with an echo-sounder, which meant the days of the sounding pole and lead line were gone, and we did not run aground quite so often. By the 1970s my sister and I were married and had boats and families of our own. So it was not long before Jack's grandchildren were spending their weekends and summer holidays sailing the rivers and creeks of the Thames Estuary, getting muddy and going aground in time-honoured fashion.

Most of the black and white photographs in the first edition were taken by Jack and he continued over the next four decades to take the pictures himself, including

aerial colour photographs shot with the help of his son-in-law Graham, who obtained a pilot's licence in the 1980s. He and Graham did many flights together and a selection of the resulting pictures were also used in *East Coast Rivers from the Air*, published as an adjunct to the book. The aerial photos, then and now, provide a new perspective and sometimes an explanation for the seemingly inexplicable changes of course that have to be made before negotiating an entrance or reaching the head of a river or creek, particularly if the images are taken at low water.

The 14th edition of *East Coast Rivers* was published in 1993, the year that Jack died aged 80. Since then my sister Judy and I have produced revised text and photographs for several further editions – keeping up the family tradition of shoal draught cruising and combining with it the task of updating the book. Battered, salt-stained and heavily annotated copies of *East Coast Rivers* are always to be found in the cockpit and there is usually a camera at the ready.

In his original preface Jack wrote: 'any success the book may have will be largely due to the enthusiastic help that I have received from many kindred spirits who sail the rivers of the Thames Estuary.' He could not have envisaged then that the input from an invaluable network of family, friends and fellow sailors would still be helping to keep *East Coast Rivers* up-to-date and still in print over 50 years later.

A collection of previous *East Coast Rivers*, including a heavily annotated copy of the first edition published in 1956

Tidal Constants

PLACE		Add (+) to or Subtract (−) from times of HW at:	Height relative to Chart Datum (metres)			
			SPRINGS		NEAPS	
		DOVER	MHW	MLW	MHW	MLW
1 Lowestoft		−1.33	2.4	0.5	2.1	1.0
2 Southwold		−1.05	2.4	0.5	2.1	0.9
3 Orford River	Orford Haven (Entrance)	+0.15	3.2	0.4	2.6	1.0
	Orford Quay	+1.00	2.8	0.6	2.3	1.1
4 River Alde	Slaughden Quay (Aldeburgh)	+1.55	2.9	0.6	2.6	1.0
	Snape Bridge	+2.55	2.9	0.8	2.4	0.8
5 River Deben	Woodbridge Haven (Entrance)	+0.25	3.7	0.5	2.9	1.0
	Waldringfield	+1.00	3.6	0.4	3.0	0.9
	Woodbridge	+1.05	4.0	0.4	3.1	0.9
6 Harwich Harbour	Harwich	+0.50	4.0	0.4	3.4	1.1
7 River Orwell	Pin Mill	+1.00	4.1	0.4	3.4	1.1
	Ipswich	+1.15	4.2	0.3	3.4	1.0
8 River Stour	Wrabness	+1.05	4.1	0.4	3.4	1.1
	Mistley	+1.15	4.2	0.3	3.4	1.0
9 Walton Backwaters	Walton-on-the-Naze (Pier)	+0.30	4.2	0.4	3.4	1.1
	Stone Point	+0.40	4.1	0.5	3.3	1.2
10 River Colne	Colne Point	+0.40	5.1	0.4	3.8	1.2
	Brightlingsea	+0.50	5.0	0.4	3.8	1.2
	Wivenhoe	+1.05	4.9	0.3	3.6	−
	Colchester (The Hythe)	+1.15	4.2	−	3.1	−
11 River Blackwater	Bench Head Buoy	+1.20	5.1	0.5	3.8	1.2
	West Mersea (Nass Beacon)	+1.10	5.1	0.5	3.8	1.2
	Tollesbury Mill Creek	+1.20	4.9	−	3.6	−
	Bradwell Quay	+1.10	5.2	0.4	4.2	1.3
	Osea Island	+1.25	5.3	0.4	4.3	1.2
	Heybridge Basin	+1.30	5.0	−	4.1	−
	Maldon	+1.35	2.9	−	2.3	−
12 River Crouch	Whitaker Beacon	+0.50	4.8	0.5	3.9	1.3
	Burnham-on-Crouch	+1.15	5.2	0.2	4.2	1.0
	Fambridge	+1.20	5.3	0.3	4.2	1.1
	Hullbridge	+1.25	5.3	0.3	4.2	1.1
13 River Roach	Paglesham	+1.10	5.2	0.2	4.2	1.0
	Havengore Creek	+1.10	4.2	0.4	3.4	1.1
14 River Thames	Southend Pier	+1.20	5.8	0.5	4.7	1.4
	Holehaven	+1.30	5.9	0.4	4.7	1.4
	Gravesend	+1.45	6.3	0.3	4.7	1.4
	Erith	+2.00	6.6	0.1	4.9	1.2
	Tower Bridge	+2.40	6.8	0.5	5.9	1.3
15 The Medway	Queenborough	+1.35	5.7	0.6	4.8	1.5
	Rochester	+1.50	6.0	0.3	4.9	1.3
16 The Swale	Whitstable	+1.20	5.4	0.5	4.5	1.5
	Harty Ferry	+1.25	5.7	0.6	5.1	1.2
	Milton Creek	+1.35	5.7	0.6	4.8	0.5
17 Ramsgate/Thanet		+0.20	5.2	0.6	4.0	1.4

Glossary

ENGLISH	DUTCH	FRENCH	GERMAN
Abeam	Dwars	Par le travers	Querab
Ahead	Vooruit	En avant	Voraus
Anchorage	Ankerplaats	Mouillage	Ankerplatz
Astern	Achteruit	En arrière	Ruckwarts, achtern
Athwart	Dwars over	Par le travers	Aufwaschen
Bank	Bank	Banc	Bank
Bar	Drempel	Barre	Drempel
Bay	Baai	Baie	Bucht
Beach	Strand	Plage	Strand
Beacon	Baken	Balise	Bake
Bight	Bocht	Anse	Bay
Binoculars	Kijker	Jumelles	Fernglas
Black	Zwart	Noir	Schwarz
Board	Slag	Bordée	Schlage
Boatyard	Jachtwerf	Chantier	Yachtwerft
Breakwater	Golfbreker	Brise-lames	Wellenbrecher
Bridge	Brug	Pont	Brucke
(fixed)	(Vaste brug)	(Pont fixe)	(Feste brucke)
(lifting)	(Beweegbare brug)	(Pont basculant)	(Hubbrucke)
(swing)	(Draaibare brug)	(Pont tournant)	(Drehbrucke)
Buoy	Ton, boei	Bouée	Tonne, Boje
Cable (distance of approx 183m)	Kabellengte	Encablure	Kebellange
Castle	Kasteel, slot	Château	Schloss
Causeway	Straatweg (door het water)	Chaussée	Damm
Channel	Vaarwater	Chenal	Fahrwasser
Chart	Zeekaart	Carte marine	Seekarte
Chart Datum	Reductievlak: kaartpeil	Zero des cartes	*Karennull
Church	Kerk	Eglise	Kirche
Cliff	Steile rots	Falaise	Felsen am Seeufer
Coastguard	Kustwacht	Garde, Côtière	Kustenwache
Conspicuous	Opvallend	Visible, en evidence	Aufflallig
Course	Koers	Cap, route	Kurs
Creek	Kreek	Crique	Kleine Bucht
Customs	Douane	Douane	Zoll
Degree	Graad	Degre	Grad
Depth	Diepte	Profondeur	Tiefe
Diesel oil	Dieselolie	Gas-oil, mazout	Diesel-Kraftstoff
Dolphin	Dukdarf, meerpaal	Duc d'Albe	Dalben, Dukdalben
Draught	Diepgang	Profondeur	Wassertiefe
Dredged	Gebaggerd vaarwater	Chenal dragué	Gebaggerte fahrrinne
Dries	Droogvalland	Assèche	Trockengallend
East	Oost	Est	Ost
Ebb	Eb	Marée descendante	Ebbe
Echo-sounder	Echolood	Echo sondeur	Echolot
Eddy	Draaikolk	Tourbillon	Stromwirbel
Entrance	Ingang, zeegat	Entrée	Einfahrt
Estuary	Mond	Estuair	Flussmundung
Fair tide	Stroom mee or portant	Courant favorable	Mitlaufender Strom
Fairway	Vaargeul	Chenal	Telweg
Ferry	Veer	Bac, ferry	Fahre
Flagstaff	Vlaggestok	Mât	Flaggenmast
Flashing light	Schitterlicht	Feu a éclats	Blinkfeuer
Flood	Vloed	Marée montante	Flut
Ford	Waadbare plaats	Gué	Durchwaten
Foreshore	Droogvallend strand marée basse	Côte découvrant à	Küstenvorland
Foul tide	Tegenstroom or debout	Courant contraire	Gegenstrom
Fuel	Brandstof	Carburant	Kraftstoffe
Green	Groen	Vert	Grun
Groyne	Golfbreker	Brise-lames	Wellenbrecher
Gully	Goot	Goulet	Graben
Gunnery Range	Ballistiek	Artillerie	Artilleriewissenschaft
Gutway	Goot	Goulet	Graben
Handbearing compass	Handpeilkompas	Compas de relevement	Handpeilkompass
Harbour Master	Havenmeester de port	Chef or Capitaine	Hafenkapitan
Hard	Hard	Débarquement	Landung
Headland	Voorgebergte	Promontoire	Vorgebirge
Height, headroom	Doorvaarthoogte	Tirant d'air	Durchfahrtshöhe
High water	Hoogwater	Pleine mer	Hochwasser
Hill	Heuvel	Colline	Hügel
Horizontal stripes	Horizontal gestreept	à bandes horizontales	Waagerecht gestreift

ENGLISH	DUTCH	FRENCH	GERMAN
Horse	Droogte	Basse	Untief
Island	Eiland	Ile	Insel
Jetty	Pier	Jetée	Anlegesteg
Knot	Knoop	Noeud	Knoten
Landing	Ontscheping	Débarquement	Landung
Launderette	Wasserette	Laverie	Waschsalon
Lead	Lood	Plomb de sonde	Lot
Leading Line	Geleidelijn	Alignement	Leitlinie
Lifeboat	Reddingboot	Bateau de sauvetage	Rettungboots
Light Vessel	Lichtschip	Bateau-phare	Feuerschiff
Lighthouse	Lichttoren, vuurtoren	Phare	Leuchtfurm
Lobster	Zeekreeft	Homard	Hummer
Lock	Sluis	Écluse, sas	Schleuse
Low water	Laagwater	Basse mer	Niedrigwasser
Magnetic	Megnetisch	Magnetique	Mißweisend
Marks	Merkteken	Parcour	Bahnmarke
Marsh	Moeras	Marais	Sumpf
Metes	Geleidelijn	Alignement	Leitlinie
Middleground	Middelgronden	Bancs médians	Scheidingstonnen
Mooring	Meerboei	Bouée de corps-mort	Ankerboje
Mud	Modder	Vase/Boue	Schlick, Schlamm
Narrow	Nauw	Etroit	Eng(e)
Navigable	Bevaarbaar	Navigable	Befahrbare
Neaps	Doodtij	Morte eau	Nippitide
Occulting	Onderbroken	Occultations	Unterbrochenes
Offing	Open zee	Le large	Legerwall
Oil	Olie	Huile	Schimierol
Orange	Oranje	Orange	Orange
Oyster	Oester	Huître	Auster
Paraffin	Petroleum	Pétrole	Petroleum
Petrol	Benzine	Essence	Benzin
Perch	Steekbaken	Perches, pieu	Pricken
Pier	Pier	Jetee	Pier
Piles	Palen remmingwerk	Poteaux	Pfahl
Pilot	Loods	Pilot	Lotsen
Pontoon	Ponton	Ponton	Ponton
Port	Bakboord	Babord	Backbord
Post office	Postkantoor	La Poste	Postamt
Quay	Kaai	Quai	Kai
Radio beacon	Radiobaken	Pylone de TSF	Funkmast
Railway	Spoorweg	Chemin de fer	Eisenbahn
Range (of tide)	Verval	Amplitude	Tidenhub
Red	Rood	Rouge	Rot
Repairs	Reparaties	Réparation	Ausbesserung
Riding light	Ankerlicht	Feu de mouillage	Ankerlampe
Rocks	Rotsen	Rochers	Klippen, Felsen
Sailmaker	Zeilmaker	Voilier	Segelmacherei
Saltings	Zouttuin	Marais	Sumpf
Sand	Zand	Sable	Sand
Shelving	Hellen	Incline	Neigung
Shingle (shingly)	Grind,Keisteen	Galets	Grober Kies
Shoal	Droogte	Haut fond	Untiefe
Shops	Winkels	Magasins	Kaufladen
Showers	Douche	Douche	Dusche
Slipway	Sleephelling	Cale de halage	Slipp, Helling
South	Zuid	Sud	Süd
Spit	Landtong	Pointe de terre	Landzunge
Springs (tides)	Springtij	Vive eau, grande marée	Springtide
Staithe	Kade	Quai	Kai
Starboard	Stuurboord	Tribord	Steuerbord
Steep-to	Steil	Côte accore	Steil
Stores	Voorraad	Provisions	Vorrate
Swatchway	Doorgang	Couloir/passage	Passage
Take the ground	Aan de grond	Echoue	Auf grund sitzen
Tanker	Tanker, Tankschip	Bateau citerne	Tanker, Tankschiff
Topmark	Topteken	Voyant	Toppzeichen
Tortuous	Bochtig	Tortueux	Gewunden
Town	Stad	Ville	Stadt
Vertical stripes	Verticaal gestreept	à bandes verticales	Senkrecht gestreift
Village	Dorp	Village	Dorf
Visitor's berth	Aanlegplaats (Bezockers)	Visiteur	Festmacheplatz
Water	Water	l'eau	Wasser
Weather	Weer	du temps	Wetter
West	West	Ouest	West
Wharf	Aanlegplaats	Debarcadere	Werft
Withy	Buigzaam en sterk	Perches, pieux	Pricken
Wreck	Wrak	Épave	Wrack
Yacht Club	Jacht Club, Zeilvereniging	Yacht Club, Club Nautique	Yacht Klub
Yellow	Geel	Jaune	Gelb

Bibliography

Several references have been made to books relating to the rivers and creeks of the Thames Estuary and this is a list of some of those and other books that are worth seeking through a public library if they are out of print.

Arnott, WG	***Suffolk Estuary***, published by Norman Adlard (1950)
	Alde Estuary, Norman Adlard (1952)
	Orwell Estuary, Norman Adlard (1954)
Baring-Gould, S	***Mehalah, A Story of the Salt Marshes***, Smith Elder & Co (1880) and Forbes Robertson (1950)
Benham, Hervey	***Last Stronghold of Sail***, George Harrap (1947)
Francis B Cooke	***Coastwise Cruising from Erith to Lowestoft***, Edward Arnold and Co (1929)
Copping, AE	***Gotty and the Guv'nor***, first published by T Nelson & Sons and then by Terence Dalton (1987)
Cowper, Frank	***Sailing Tours Part 1***, first published 1882 and then by Ashford Press in 1985
Du Port, Andy & Featherstone, Neville	***Reeds Eastern Almanac 2009***, Adlard Coles (2008)
Durham, Dick	***The Last Sailorman***, Terence Dalton (1989)
Emmett A and M	***Blackwater Men***, Seax Books (1982)
Frost, Michael	***Boadicea CK213***, Angus & Robertson (1974)
Griffiths, Maurice	***The First of the Tide***, Conway Maritime Press (1979)
	The Magic of the Swatchways, first published by Edward Arnold (1932) and Adlard Coles (1986)
	Ten Small Yachts, Edward Arnold (1933)
	Swatchways and Little Ships, George Allen & Unwin (1971) and Adlard Coles (1986)
Innes, Hammond	***East Anglia***, Hodder & Stoughton (1986)
Leather, John	***The Salty Shore***, Terence Dalton (1979)
	The Sailor's Coast, Barrie & Jenkins (1979)
Lewis, John	***A Taste for Sailing***, Terence Dalton (1989)
Roberts, Bob	***Coasting Bargemaster***, Edward Arnold (1949) and Terence Dalton (1985)
	A Slice of Suffolk, Terence Dalton (1978)
Ransome, Arthur	***We Didn't Mean to go to Sea***, Jonathan Cape (1937) and then by Penguin Books
	Secret Water, Jonathan Cape (1939) and then by Penguin Books
Seymour, John	***The Companion Guide to East Anglia***, Collins (1970)
Simper, Robert	***The Deben River***, Creekside Publishing (1992)
Tripp, Alker	***Suffolk Sea Borders***, Bodley Head (1926) and Maritime Press (1972)
	Shoalwater and Fairway, Bodley Head (1924) and Maritime Press (1972)
Wentworth Day, J	***Coastal Adventure***, George G Harrap (1949)
White, Archie	***The Tideways and Byways of Essex and Suffolk***, Edward Arnold (1948)
Wyllie, WL and Mrs	***London to the Nore***, A & C Black (1905)

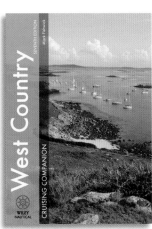
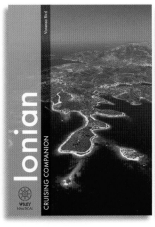

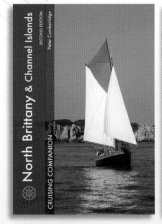
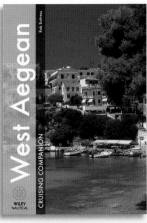
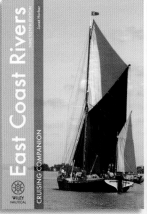